THE CIVIL WAR IN NICARAGUA

THE CIVIL WAR IN NICARAGUA

INSIDE THE SANDINISTAS

Roger Miranda
William Ratliff

Transaction Publishers
New Brunswick (U.S.A.) and London (U.K.)

Library of Congress Catalog Number: 92-1296
ISBN: 1-56000-064-3
Printed in the United States of America

Library of Congress Cataloging-in-Publication Data
Miranda Bengoechea, Roger.
    The civil war in Nicaragua: inside the Sandinistas / Roger Miranda, William Ratliff.
    p. cm.
    Includes index.
    ISBN 1-56000-064-3
    1. Nicaragua—Politics and government—1979- 2. Nicaragua—Foreign relations—1979- 3. Ortega, Daniel. 4. Political leadership—Nicaragua—History—20th century. 5. Frente Sandinista de Liberacion Nacional. I. Ratliff, William E. II. Title.
F1528.M57 1993
972.8505'3—dc20
                                                    92-1296
                                                      CIP

Roger Miranda dedicates this book to his parents, Roberto and Adriana, to his wife, Graciela, and to his children: Adriana Dolores, Roger Adrian, Roberto Adrian, and Jorge Adrian; William Ratliff dedicates it to his wife, Lynn, and to his children: Sharon, Paul, Susan, David, and John. The coauthors also dedicate it to all those who for so long worked, suffered, and even died trying to bring a better life to the Nicaraguan people.

Contents

Preface

Americans discovered Nicaragua on their television sets in 1979, and most didn't understand or like what they found. But they couldn't shake it. For the next decade that tiny country always seemed to be there, a "Vietnam in Central America," in the center of heated controversy over East/West relations, national security, the Reagan Doctrine, human right atrocities, and finally the Iran/Contra scandal. Then in 1990, when a free election was held, the media, politicians, and Americans in general immediately forgot that Nicaragua had ever existed.

Momentarily setting aside historical roots, it all began in July 1979 when a petty right-wing dictator named Anastasio Somoza, long associated with the United States, lost a bloody civil war to a broadly based national uprising led by a Marxist-Leninist guerrilla group called the Sandinista National Liberation Front (FSLN), which had long been associated with Fidel Castro in Cuba. When Somoza fell, the FSLN, which by then had most of the guns in the country, proclaimed itself the vanguard of the people and immediately and deliberately tilted toward the Soviet bloc. Suddenly, hemispheric Cold War tensions, until then associated largely with Cuba, leaped across the Caribbean to the continent, becoming a critical foreign policy issue for U.S. presidents Carter and Reagan and contributing to the rapid deterioration of conditions in Nicaragua and much of Central America.

Americans had a hard time understanding these events and the actors in this intense drama in large part because they knew so little about Nicaraguan society and what made it tick. In particular they had no sense of the nine Sandinista *Comandantes* (commanders), who from July 1979 until early 1990 ran the show from Managua through the FSLN's National Directorate, or of the majority of the Nicaraguan people.

Sandinista government slogans and popular expressions of the decade told a lot about those two layers for anyone who could understand them, and they point to the main themes of our book: (1) how the concentration of "truth" and power in the National Directorate of the FSLN affected the people of Nicaragua and the world and (2) how much the new rulers came to resemble the old dictator they and the vast majority of the Nicaraguan people had just overthrown.

In one slogan—"National Directorate, Command Me!"—the nine co-mandantes tried to legitimize their monopoly on power with the age-old

ploy of saying that the people demanded it. But a colorful expression from
the streets showed how most Nicaraguans came to feel: "The same shit,
only the flies are different" (*la misma mierda, solamente las moscas son
diferente*). That is, for the average Nicaraguan one greedy Somoza had
multiplied to become a crowd of greedy Sandinistas. The ultimate expression of this transformation of the Sandinistas into Somocistas came during
the month before the elected anti-Sandinista government took power in
1990, when with the "piñata" the Sandinista assembly "legalized" the
largest one-stroke property grab in the history of twentieth-century Central
America. In the words of Edén Pastora, the most popular Sandinista of
them all in July 1979, this act of the National Directorate "was more
outrageous than all the political errors they had made in the previous ten
years," and there had been plenty of these. The Directorate, he correctly
concluded, used Leninism and Stalinism to become "scientific
Somocistas."[1]

In this book we will sharpen up the unrefined insights reflected in those
popular slogans and show where they overstated or understated the realities. We will then expand the analysis to show how the Sandinistas
operated, and why, despite an unprecedented opportunity to make things
better, they ultimately betrayed the Nicaraguan people and left the country
and region a lot worse off than they found it.

American politicians, academics, churchmen, and others made tens of
thousands of visits to Nicaragua during the 1980s, but most of these visits
were pilgrimages by True Believers in the Sandinistas generally and in the
nine comandantes specifically. Most of the pilgrims doubtless thought that
backing the Sandinistas was the same as supporting the Nicaraguan people;
very few, as it happened, were observant and/or open-minded enough to
see and understand evidence that contradicted the notions they had taken
with them. Their minds were so closed that they were as surprised as most
of the Sandinistas themselves when the FSLN was overwhelmingly rejected by the Nicaraguan people in the 1990 elections.

But if most activists who visited Nicaragua failed to grasp the interests
of the Nicaraguan people largely because of self-inflicted blindness, a
slightly better case can be made for their ignorance of the top FSLN leaders.
During the 1980s many of their public statements and policies were
contradictory, and the misunderstandings, which were often downright lies,
that came to be "known" about the Sandinistas and their critics were
carefully cultivated by FSLN members and their best friends at home and

abroad. The truth would have been very clear if anyone had had access to the inner-circle thinking and decision making of the National Directorate. But as *New York Times* correspondent Stephen Kinzer put it, that political body led the nation "from behind a curtain no outsider could penetrate."[2]

Until now. This book is unique among all books published on Sandinista Nicaragua because it alone throws that curtain open and gives an account from the inside of how and why decisions were made at the top of the Sandinista government, and what impact they had on Nicaragua, the United States, and world. During 1981 the Nicaraguan coauthor of this book, Major Roger Miranda, was assistant chief of staff of the Sandinista Armed Forces and between January 1982 and the end of 1987 he was chief of staff and top aide to Defense Minister and Comandante Humberto Ortega.

Very few Nicaraguans besides the nine comandantes attended any meetings of the National Directorate or top sessions of the Sandinista People's Army (EPS). Miranda went to Directorate meetings that dealt with military issues—not as an active participant or decisionmaker, but as a resource for Humberto Ortega—and all of the EPS sessions between early 1982 and late 1987, the critical years of the Contra War and U.S.-Soviet tensions over Nicaragua. He is the first to tell, from that high inside perspective, what issues were raised there, how they were debated, how decisions were made and implemented. Unless indicated otherwise, all "inside" information in this book is supplied by the Nicaraguan coauthor.

Here we show how the Sandinistas pursued domestic and international policies that made them lose touch with their people and shed friends and followers at home and abroad, across the political spectrum, a reality they themselves did not fully grasp until 1990. Some of our account largely confirms conclusions other analysts had already reached using historical events and hearsay or scattered evidence available on the comandantes. But much of what we reveal contradicts accepted wisdom and/or covers ground that has never before been even mentioned, much less authoritatively discussed, outside of closed circles at the top of the Sandinista government.

We believe any study focusing on the Sandinista government between 1979 and 1990 must recognize three fundamental components of FSLN thought, the pursuit or playing out of which was reflected in virtually everything that happened during those years. These were the convictions that:

1. The FSLN was the vanguard of the Nicaraguan people and the National Directorate was the vanguard of the vanguard. The nine members of the Directorate were convinced they had or could find all the answers to Nicaragua's problems on their own and that other views, even from within the FSLN, should be tolerated only as long as they coincided with those of the Directorate or until the nine were strong enough to silence them. There were important differences of opinion among members of the National Directorate on tactical matters, but all thought within a debilitatingly narrow strategic perspective. Since the nine believed they alone should rule, and above all others enjoy the perks of leadership, they set up closed institutional structures that would enable them to do so without significant interference.

2. War with the United States was inevitable. Their interpretation of U.S.-Nicaraguan relations during the last century made them militantly anti-American and convinced them that the United States would demand Somoza-like subservience from any successor government. Ironically, being "independent" came to mean active cooperation with the Cuban and other anti-American governments of the Cold War period, an alliance Washington was not prepared to tolerate. Thus the Sandinistas immediately begin building (a) a close dependence on the Soviet bloc, including Cuba, which served as a source of supplies and as a shield against anticipated U.S. opposition to their revolution; (b) the largest army, state security forces, and police apparatus in the history of Central America; (c) support for like-minded guerrillas in the region who, on taking power, would form governments allied to the FSLN rather than to the United States; and (d) a domestic and international propaganda network to project the image of "nationalists beseiged by foreign imperialism" to audiences at home and abroad.

3. Statist economies produce best for the people and nation. This idea was firmly rooted in the mind of FSLN founder Carlos Fonseca Amador as a result of his visit to the Soviet Union in the mid-1950s and, like hatred of the United States, was a belief that tended to pull Nicaragua into the orbit of Cuba and the Soviet bloc. Not incidentally, an anticapitalist statist economy tightened government control over the people generally and made it easier to reward the regime's main supporters, especially at the highest levels, to punish its critics, and to act as an unchallenged vanguard of the vanguard.

Ironically, implementing the policy lines noted in the second category above, though presumably dictated by the inevitability of conflict, was itself what made the conflict with the Americans inevitable. The Carter administration was prepared to live with a statist Nicaragua, even one run by a small clique of nine, so long as human rights violations were minimal or well disguised. For a while, the Reagan administration was even less demanding, but then became moreso. The bottom line was that during the Cold War, no American administration would tolerate another active Soviet ally in the Caribbean Basin—a first in Central America—aiding in the subversion of neighboring countries.

Our analysis will fall into several categories: (1) who the top nine Sandinistas were, with a special emphasis on the Ortegas, how they ruled, and what their relationships were with each other and the Nicaraguan people; (2) how these leaders saw the world through the lenses of militant nationalism and a new Marxism, how they tried to manipulate it through deception, and how this determined their international allies and enemies; (3) the institutions of control in Sandinista Nicaragua—the economy, the Interior ministry and the Army; (4) the Sandinista theory and practice of war and "peace," involving the Contras, neighboring countries and the United States; and (5) what led into and happened to the Sandinista movement after the 1990 election. We end with observations and conclusions on Sandinismo, Nicaragua and the United States.

We would like to give special thanks to several of the many people who inspired and helped us before and during our writing. Roger Miranda specially thanks Ambassador Curtin Winsor, Ann Winsor, and Bert Cherneco; and William Ratliff specifies Roberto Cardenal Chamorro, who died just before the 1990 elections, as well as 31, 11, 8, 13, and 6. We both thank Angelo Codevilla for his invaluable suggestions on the shape of the manuscript, Robert Leiken for many suggestions on the content, Alicia Tompkins for writing early drafts of several chapters, Kelly Wachowicz for conducting some basic research, and the staff of the Hoover Institution Library and Archives. Finally, there are Leigh LaMora, Bill Geimer, and Barbara Abbott of the Jamestown Foundation, who got us together and steadfastly supported our work, and Irving Louis Horowitz of Transaction Publishers, who immediately recognized—as we knew he would—the importance of this story.

ROGER MIRANDA BENGOECHEA
WILLIAM RATLIFF

Notes

1. William Ratliff interview with Edén Pastora, 19 March 1992, in San José, Costa Rica. Ratliff's series of interviews with Pastora, which took place between 16 March and 24 March 1992, are in the Hoover Institution Archives at Stanford University. They will be edited, supplemented with further interviews and published as Pastora's own account of his role in Nicaragua's conflicts.
2. Stephen Kinzer, *Blood of Brothers: Life and War in Nicaragua* (New York: Putnam's Sons, 1991), 172.

Introduction
Victory and Opportunity Lost

In July 1979 a bright new dawn seemed to have come to Nicaragua, after the decades-long night of Somoza dictatorships, just as Sandinista National Liberation Front (FSLN) founder Carlos Fonseca had said it would. The last Somoza fled to Miami on 17 July and two days later the main body of bearded Sandinista troops entered Managua unchallenged by the few remaining members of the former dictator's National Guard. Clad in dirty olive-green uniforms and black berets, the triumphant Sandinistas rode in trucks or marched through streets mobbed with jubilant Nicaraguans, many of whom had fought as indisciplined members of the FSLN in the final battles. The broad front strategy, which had pulled all the national forces who opposed Somoza together in a nation-wide alliance, had finally brought the dynasty down.

The Euphoria of Victory

Managua, the capital of Nicaragua, was in shambles when Somoza fell. It had not been rebuilt after the 1972 earthquake, measuring 6.25 on the Richter scale, that had left much of the city in flames or rubble, thousands dead, and hundreds of thousands homeless. By July 1979, the city had been further devastated by a brutal civil war and was dusty in the scorching summer sun. On all sides Nicaraguans recognized former guardsmen who had become instant Sandinistas by throwing off their uniforms and putting on red and black bandanas, the FSLN colors taken from their revolutionary namesake, Augusto César Sandino, and from their contemporary idol, Fidel Castro. The euphoria was punctuated by gunfire in all directions, even though the enemy had collapsed and fled. It was "guerrilla music," some said, the spontaneous hundred-gun salutes of Nicaraguans heralding a new era. At the sports stadium, named after the departed dictator's father, crowds pulled down an equestrian statue of the dynasty's founder. Nicaragua was free at last.

The streets were packed on that first day and the scene was chaotic. By early afternoon the nine comandantes who were to hold power for the next eleven years had already set up temporary headquarters in the pyramid-shaped Intercontinental Hotel and in the former dictator's messy, abandoned bunker in the hill immediately behind it.[1]

1

Sandinista militants marched into Managua from all directions, wondering if they would be on time for the day's festivities at the rallying point, Somoza's former infantry training school. But when they arrived, many exhausted by months of warfare and the final offensive, they found there was nothing in particular to do: no meeting for the fighters, no formal reunion, only burgeoning confusion and some welcome chance encounters with family and friends.

Although the Sandinista-controlled radio and television stations were broadcasting bulletins, the first order to reach most militants was "Stay off the streets tonight after 7:00 P.M." As it happened, not all the guns heard were being fired in the air by revolutionary enthusiasts. Many guardsmen, scared for their lives, had dropped their automatic weapons with their uniforms in the streets as they fled to churches or Red Cross shelters. In many cases their M-16s and other weapons had been picked up by youngsters, who fired wildly, and not always in the air, or by criminals, who took advantage of the weapons and anarchy to loot private homes and pillage public buildings. Until 1982, when these delinquents were finally disarmed, they were the best armed hoods in Latin America.

The next day the five members of the Junta of National Reconstruction arrived in Managua fresh from their temporary capital in León, Nicaragua's second-largest city, located fifty miles northwest of the capital. The Junta, appointed by the Sandinistas in June as a provisional government in anticipation of Somoza's fall, was dominated by Sandinistas, though this was not widely known at the time, and had no real power in any event.[2]

The longest parade up to that time in the history of the country—stretching several miles—wended its way through the chaotic, ongoing celebrations. It was supposed to introduce the Junta, but the FSLN comandantes were in the vanguard, riding high atop a fire engine, accurately reflecting the real division of power in the new government.

The Junta members were inaugurated at the National Palace on the Plaza of the Republic, now renamed the Plaza of the Revolution, in sight of the polluted waters of Lake Managua. This had been the heart of downtown Managua until the earthquake flattened it. On inauguration day, some hundred thousand people were packed into the plaza, flanked on two sides by the dilapidated palace and the shell of the cathedral left standing after the earthquake. The crowd spread across Bolívar Avenue on the west and into the expanses of overgrown fields and low-lying ruins that had once been a bustling city.

The most popular person present was Edén Pastora, the legendary "Commander Zero," a member of the Tercerista faction of the until recently feuding Sandinista movement. When he appeared, the crowd chanted "Cero, Cero, Cero!" Pastora had directed the occupation of this very National Palace in August 1978 and secured the release of dozens of prisoners from Somoza's jails, among them Tomás Borge, the only surviving founder of the Sandinista movement. The capture of the palace had made the Terceristas, headed by the Ortega brothers, Daniel and Humberto, the foremost organization of opposition to the dictator. Pastora had gone on to be the leader of the Southern Front of the FSLN against Somoza.

In their addresses to the people at the inauguration, the Junta members and comandantes all spoke of unity among Nicaraguans, of getting rid of the personal, ideological, and institutional remnants of Somoza's rule, of the hard tasks lying ahead in rebuilding a new nation. Drawings of three heroes of the revolution stood behind the speakers: Fonseca; Sandino, who had fought against the United States in the early 1930s; and Pedro Joaquín Chamorro, the popular, anti-Somoza editor of the daily paper *La Prensa*, whose assassination in January 1978 galvanized opposition to Somoza across the Nicaraguan political spectrum.

Who's In Charge Here?

Daniel Ortega, with a scraggly black beard and long hair, was the only comandante who was also a member of the Junta. A leader of the dominant Tercerista tendency, he proclaimed to the crowd that "the Junta puts itself at your orders. It is you who will decide our future." The short, bespectacled Borge, who walked with a slight limp attributed to his years in prison, assured the crowd, "You can be certain we will never betray the revolution."

In order to win broad domestic and critical international support in the war against Somoza, the Sandinistas had adopted a broad front strategy devised by Humberto Ortega and other Terceristas. It proclaimed support for largely centrist objectives—a mixed economy, political pluralism and international nonalignment—as well as the open incorporation of a wide cross section of the country's people into the government. Thus, prior to the July 1979 victory, and for some months thereafter, the National Directorate directed much attention to social democrat Pastora and to "bourgeois" leaders like Alfonso Robelo, Violeta Chamorro, and Arturo Cruz, who were given prominent but non-policy-making positions in the new government. "These people are temporary allies," Daniel Ortega remarked in private, "and must be treated with respect as long as they are of use to us. There is no question that they are enemies in the end." As the Pastoras, Chamorros, Robelos, and Cruzes realized that they were figureheads and future enemies, and could never have a significant moderating influence while operating from within, they dropped out and joined different branches of the opposition.

One of the first challenges the Sandinistas faced was becoming public leaders. Like guerrillas from China to Cuba, they had spent years in the mountains, in jails, or in exile, living privately or in small groups without major public responsibilities, often fighting among themselves. Now the situation suddenly had changed and they had to change too. When Somoza fled and the guard collapsed, the nine comandantes had to wash their faces, cut their hair, and jump into new positions as government officials, as public men who could work together. "I'm beginning to feel like a prisoner," Humberto Ortega remarked privately. "I liked the clandestine life better, when we didn't have bodyguards following us around all the time."

When Tomás Borge outlined the Sandinistas' objectives at a public rally immediately after Somoza's fall, he sounded more like a populist declaring a war on underdevelopment than a Marxist-Leninist revolutionary.

> Yes, the war against the National Guard was difficult and bloody, but now a new war begins, a war against backwardness, poverty, ignorance, immorality, destruction. This war will be more difficult and prolonged than the first one. Solutions to problems will require sacrifices, but we are sure the Nicaraguan people are ready for the sacrifices.[3]

But within the new government, the hegemony of the Ortegas, which had emerged within the FSLN after August 1978, was consolidated and assumed extraordinary importance, for it was during this early period that the comandantes set the real direction of the revolution, and thus of the country, for the years ahead. This direction was proclaimed in some detail just two months after Somoza fell in two secret "72-hour" meetings that outlined Sandinista domestic and international policies for the 1980s. These meetings produced the "Analysis of the Situation and Tasks of the

Sandinista People's Revolution," the so-called *72-Hour Document*, a statement of the revolution's objectives, strategy, and tactics prepared by the nine comandantes. The document detailed what the Sandinistas considered an inevitable confrontation with the United States, which would necessitate the consolidation of Sandinista domestic power with the backing of a large and heavily-armed Sandinista People's Army (EPS) in international alliance with Cuba and the Soviet bloc. This orientation brought military and other ties to guerrillas in El Salvador and other countries and the launching of an arms race in Central America. It also brought a domestic civil war as peasants and then other Nicaraguans realized the vanguard of the FSLN intended to make all the nation's decisions with little regard for what the people themselves considered their interests.

Thus the revolution that had brought such hope to the Nicaraguan people was almost immediately directed toward more confrontation, as if the bloodshed of the civil war had not been more than enough to cleanse the nation of an often tragically violent heritage. At the very beginning the comandantes betrayed the country and the anti-Somoza revolution and led the Nicaraguan people into another civil war, this time one that need not have been.

Notes

1. The nine comandantes—three from each of the three mid-1970s factions of the Sandinista movement—were, from the Tercerista or Insurrectional Tendency, Humberto Ortega, Daniel Ortega, and Víctor Tirado; from the Proletarian Tendency, Jaime Wheelock, Carlos Núñez, and Luis Carrión; and from the Prolonged Popular War Tendency, Tomás Borge, Henry Ruiz, and Bayardo Arce.
2. The members of the first Junta were Violeta Chamorro, who was elected president of Nicaragua in 1990, Alfonso Robelo, and three Sandinistas: Daniel Ortega, Sergio Ramírez, and Moisés Hassan.
3. Tomás Borge quoted by Alan Riding, "Managua Welcomes Rebel Government," *New York Times*, 21 July 1979.

PART I
Inside the FSLN

1

Mystique Succumbs to Power

When and How It All Got Started

It is no wonder that students of Sandinismo often are confused about when the FSLN was founded—in 1960, 1961 or 1962—for the founding date and many other historical matters were never agreed on within the National Directorate itself. The most commonly cited year is 1961; Tomás Borge has written that the process of founding the FSLN was initiated before 1960, began to define itself in 1961, the year of its official founding, and was consolidated in 1962.[1]

What were those early beginnings? They were diverse and included the participation of: (1) several members of Nicaragua's orthodox pro-Soviet communist party, the Nicaraguan Socialist party (PSN), in top leadership roles; (2) the Nicaraguan Patriotic Youth (JPN), in its planning stages from early 1958 but formally founded in January 1960, which 25 years later the Sandinista party paper *Barricada* called the ideological and organizational "precursor of the FSLN"; (3) the Frente Revolucionario Sandino, led by the brothers Alejandro and Harold Martínez, who first thought of using the name of Sandino to emphasize the nationalistic character of the anti-Somoza struggle; and (4) the Movimiento Nueva Nicaragua, founded in 1961 by Carlos Fonseca.[2] The New Nicaragua Movement, which had to be re-cast because in the context of the emerging Sino-Soviet dispute it seemed too closely patterned on Mao Ze-dong's New China, was nonetheless, in Borge's words, "the fundamental antecedent of the FSLN."[3]

The spark that set off the Sandinista movement was struck in Cuba in January 1959 when Fidel Castro's guerrilla forces, with broad national support, sent dictator Fulgencio Batista packing off to the United States. FSLN indebtedness to Castro began then and was critically important ever after; it is denied only when the Sandinistas are trying to mislead

9

gullible foreigners. Fonseca himself wrote that "with the victory of the Cuban Revolution, the Nicaraguan spirit of rebellion recovered [the] resplendence" it had lost after the death of Sandino and his followers in the early 1930s. Castro's was the example the few young Turks of the PSN needed to strike out on their own, as Borge recalled it twenty years later:

> The victory of the armed struggle in Cuba, more than a joy, was the drawing back of innumerable curtains, a flash of light that exposed the simple and boring dogmas of the time. . . . For us, Fidel was the resurrection of Sandino, the answer to our reservations, the justification of the dreams of heresies of a few hours before. The victory of the armed struggle in Cuba stirred the enthusiasm of the Nicaraguan people and stimulated the struggle against the tyranny.[4]

That is, the "simple and boring dogmas" of the old Marxists in the PSN were thrown aside and replaced by the more militant "new Marxism" discussed below. For a couple of years after Fidel's victory, some in the PSN still cooperated with the Sandinistas, but later they were on their own. And they were few in number until the late 1970s when the Terceristas figured out how to build a front that would unite the nation.

Borge writes that the FSLN was born "as a political front to unify forces . . . that opposed the dictatorship." It had some success in doing so when it incorporated the likes of social democrat Edén Pastora, though from the beginning Fonseca and other Marxist-Leninist leaders restricted participation. One early problem among the Leninists was what to call the group, specifically whether to bring Sandino's legacy prominently into their name. Fonseca wanted Sandino's name in, but Noël Guerrero— "who in practice was our chief" in 1962, writes Borge—opposed the use of Sandino and was a problem for other FSLN founders in other respects as well.[5] According to Borge, "Sandinista" was not added to the name until 1963, after Fonseca had established his hegemony in the FSLN. What does "Sandinista" add? Víctor Tirado, one of the earliest members of the new movement, quite rightly says it is simply "equivalent to nationalist."[6]

Founding Mystique and Early Disputes

Once the Sandinistas were founded, a rigid process for the selection of cadres was begun in cooperation with the FSLN's Revolutionary Student Front (FER). New recruits were carefully trained. When Roger

Miranda joined the FSLN in Granada in 1969, for example, he and his fellow recruits devoted many hours to studying Sandino's thinking; the history of Nicaragua, with an emphasis on U.S. interventions; and the Somoza dictatorship; as well as the history and objectives of the FSLN. They began by reading Georges Politzer's *Elemental Principles of Historical Materialism*, Marx' *Communist Manifesto*, Che Guevara's *Diary*, Fidel Castro's *History Will Absolve Me*, and later Mao's *Little Red Book*, which became the militants' pocket *Bible*. Ideally, militants were expected to conform to a revolutionary mystique that stressed humility, modesty, honesty, and discipline, the latter in members' personal conduct, devotion to revolutionary duty, and submission to the dictates of the National Directorate. Militants were expected to make such sacrifices as were necessary in the line of duty, including giving up their lives if necessary. In the end, they were supposed to understand that being a Sandinista was a responsibility and not a privilege, that however "petty bourgeois" their origins might have been, they were now "proletarians," devoting their lives to "the people" of Nicaragua and the rest of the exploited world.[7]

Even rigid entrance standards did not keep the Sandinistas from making some mistakes, from choosing people who in one way or the other betrayed or "disgraced" the movement. For example, there were betrayals. When found out, militants who wasted or robbed money from the movement were strongly disciplined, even executed, among them Narcizo Zepeda. A different sort of betrayal was tied to Augusto Montealegre. In 1970, when returning from a training session given by the Palestine Liberation Organization, Montealegre evidently voluntarily told Somoza's security forces much about the FSLN's Managua underground. National Guard strikes against the movement both weakened the organization and sowed confusion and uncertainty in its ranks. In the wake of this betrayal, which was not traced to Montealegre personally until many years later, the FSLN became paranoid and over-suspicious. In reality, the Sandinista movement evidently was riddled with spies, for after Somoza's fall, National Guard intelligence files showed that the dictator knew the whereabouts and actions of virtually every Sandinista leader most of the time. Edin Pastora speculates that Somoza didn't round them all up because in a way the FSLN served his interests: it justified the continuation of U.S. military and other aid to his government and Guard.[8]

Perhaps the most notorious example of disciplining a member was of Borge himself in 1964 for his amorous relations with the wife of another member. According to an internal communiqué that conveys the moral temper of the movement at that time, Borge's actions were "guided by petty-bourgeois attitudes that are totally contrary to the revolutionary mystique." Because of Borge's prominence in the movement, his disciplining became a strong example to others, for as FSLN hero Germán Pomares noted just before his death in battle in 1979: "Comrade Tomás is one of the most focused cadres in the organization, his only problem is his need to always have a woman tied to the end of his bed."

Another sexually related matter became a scandal within the movement. Although most of the comandantes were womanizers, before and after taking power, major showdowns like the one over Borge were avoided by keeping affairs relatively quiet. But one matter that was not kept at all quiet, and caused increasing tensions during the 1980s, was lesbianism. The most persistent lesbian was Comandante Dora Maria Téllez, the model female guerrilla during the anti-Somoza war and later a member of the Sandinista Assembly who for a while held ministerial office. Téllez led a group of ten to fifteen militant lesbians who became a serious irritant in the eyes of the Directorate. The last straw was Téllez' affair with Ligia Elizondo, a Vice Minister of Planning under Henry Ruiz and wife of Roberto Gutiérrez, then chairman of the Central Bank. This one broke up a revolutionary family and the Directorate concluded it had to act even though it felt inhibited because it was a government that had supposedly "liberated" Nicaraguans from the "vices of capitalism." On 12 December 1986 Daniel Ortega spoke to the Sandinista Assembly in these words: "We want you to know that we are not going to punish those who are lesbians. But be aware that the National Directorate will not appoint lesbians to public office." This undoubtedly was one reason the National Directorate rejected her strong candidacy for membership in the Directorate at the Sandinista congress in 1991.

Strategic and tactical differences over how to achieve power, usually present in some degree, escalated to such a point during the 1970s that they were in reality not so much internal disputes as outright conflicts between rival movements, on occasion resulting in the conscious exclusion of one member or another from the FSLN by one faction or another that considered itself the only legitimate bearer of the movement's name. The fighting among the three branches of Sandinismo became so bitter that unity was reestablished only under pressure in a series of meetings with Cuban leaders, culminating in an agreement signed in Havana in March 1979 with Fidel Castro's approval. In the end, all Sandinista factions recognized that the Cuban leader—who had himself actively promoted factionalism among Marxist-Leninist parties all over Latin America during the 1960s—had finally drawn the bottom line correctly: unified the Sandinistas might seize and exercise power despite domestic and international challenges and threats; disunited they were bound to fail.[9]

Getting Started in Power

There has been much speculation about how many Sandinistas there were on 19 July 1979. The standard estimate is that there were about five thousand, which is essentially correct if one counts both those who had fulfilled all criteria for membership—the *militants*—and those who joined the movement during the final offensive against Somoza. Bayardo Arce was quite specific in a 1987 interview when he said that in July 1979 there were fewer than one hundred fifty cadres with more than five years membership; fewer than five hundred who had joined before 1977; and some fourteen hundred who had joined the FSLN by the time of the 1978 urban insurrection, the final criterion for membership.[10] Distinguished militants were called Guerrilla Comandantes while the nine members of the National Directorate were called Comandantes of the Revolution. In this book "comandante" is used to designate the latter unless the other meaning is clearly noted.

After taking power, the nine top comandantes faced the problems, responsibilities, and temptations of any leaders who suddenly find themselves transformed from political challengers to unchallenged political rulers. During the 1980s, FSLN leaders and top cadres responded to their new posts and opportunities in two different ways.

1. As a group, they held together quite well. Edén Pastora delineates four reasons he thinks this was so: 1) ideological identity, or the conviction that the basic Marxist-Leninist objectives of one were the objectives of all; 2) the perception of a common enemy in the United States and its Nicaraguan and regional allies, against which they needed to work in unity; 3) the belief that if they fought among themselves, none would

survive; and 4) the presence of the Great Comandante, Fidel Castro, who would act as the ultimate arbiter when necessary.

In terms of policy-making, though there were many differences of opinion, as described throughout this volume, a single line usually was settled on in the National Directorate and followed thereafter. Indeed, the critical underlying problem was not the disagreements within the Directorate but precisely the degree of basic unity of opinion: the existence of a single worldview that did not leave room for alternate interpretations and policies that could have taken Nicaragua down a very different and more constructive path. From the beginning, and in many respects increasingly, this tunnel vision of the National Directorate separated the movement from the majority of the Nicaraguan people, neighboring countries, and the United States.

2. Individually, many Sandinistas abandoned the revolutionary mystique and succumbed to the strong personal temptations that come with great political and economic power. This was one of the developments that most repelled Edén Pastora—as well as the majority of the Nicaraguan people—and finally drove him to conclude that the Sandinista leaders had never been driven as much by the desire to achieve social justice for all Nicaraguans as by envy of the Somozas and a determination to hold total power so as to enjoy everything that power put in their grasp.[11]

Plotting the Future

The first major meeting of the FSLN membership after victory occurred in September 1979 and produced the *72-Hour Document*. The meeting of FSLN militants on 21–23 September both pointed out the basic direction of policies for the next decade and demonstrated clearly that the National Directorate was going to rule by fiat. Everything that occurred in the militants' meeting had been carefully planned on 18–20 September, during closed-door sessions of the nine comandantes. At the time, most militants had little objection to this delegation of power in the short term, for they believed their leaders, with more experience, knew what they were doing. Before long, however, many militants began to resent being totally excluded from decisionmaking, even in the Sandinista Assembly, which was set up to be consultative.

The three-day session for cadres, which got into many details deliberately left out of the printed document, was held at what had been Somoza's infantry school in Managua, later named the Carlos Agüero School. Sessions were conducted in the school's modern, North American-style auditorium which was about 150 feet long and 60 feet wide. The comandantes were up front, while the militants sat in the comfortable, attractive rows of seats that only two months before had been used by Somoza's elite guard. Militants were required to remain at the school day and night for the full three days, for discussions, meals and sleep, some said because it soon became obvious that the speeches were going to be so tedious that few who went home would have returned.

Daniel Ortega, on the raised podium, read the *72-Hour Document* aloud in a monotone, talking in fits and starts, for he was a painfully boring speaker in the early days.[12] He commented on some aspects of the document as he went along, setting the stage for discussions held in nine working groups, each led by one of the comandantes, during the afternoon and the following day. According to Ortega, the seventy-two hour session was to (1) redefine Sandinista strategy in general now that Somoza had been overthrown, (2) overcome the internal divisions among leaders and followers, and (3) identify priorities for the years ahead. The priorities were (1) national defense, specifically the development of the military and internal security forces to defend the revolution against domestic and international enemies; (2) consolidation of the government and development of the national economy; and (3) making the Sandinista Front a party.

After the seventy-two-hour meetings, the FSLN militants knew where the movement and country would be going under Directorate leadership. Decisions and policy implementation would pass down from the nine comandantes through the militants who had attended the September meeting, the ministries headed by the comandantes and other top Sandinistas, the mass organizations, the base organizations, and the FSLN dominated media, most importantly the party paper *Barricada*. When several copies of the *72-Hour Document* were somehow "liberated" and non-Sandinista Nicaraguans and others learned what was in store for them, most of the outsiders did not like what they saw.

Notes

1. Tomás Borge, *La paciente impaciencia* (Managua: Editorial Vanguardia, 1989), 183–84. Among the conflicting published claims on founding dates are statements that the FSLN dates from 1960–1961, Humberto Ortega, *50 años de la lucha sandinista* (Managua: Ministry of Interior, nd), 116; July 1961, Tomás Borge, "Carlos, el amanecer," 107; 1961, Carlos Fonseca, "Cronología de la resistencia sandinista," in Carlos Fonseca, *Obras: Viva Sandino* (Managua: Editorial Nueva Nicaragua, 1985), 2: 166; and 1962, Carlos Fonseca, "Con la revolución siempre," in A. Sandino & C. Fonseca, *Nicaragua: la estrategia de la victoria* (Mexico City: Editorial Nuestro Tiempo, 1980), 134, where Fonseca writes "in 1962 the Sandinista Front was born."

2. Tomás Borge, "Carlos, el amanecer ya no es una tentación," *Casa de las Américas*, Havana, May-June 1979, 105; *Barricada*, 11 January 1985; Borge, *La paciente impaciencia*, 165, 170; Ratliff interview with Edén Pastora, 16 March 1992.

3. See Estatutos del Movimiento Nueva Nicaragua," in Borge, *La paciente impaciencia*, 176–78; and Ratliff interview with Pastora, 16 March 1992.

4. Borge, "Carlos, El Amanecer," 107. Also, see Carlos Fonseca, interviews and articles in Fonseca, *Obras: Bajo la Bandera del Sandinismo* (Managua: Editorial Nueva Nicaragua, 1981), 1: 338, 359.

5. On the intention to unify anti-Somoza forces, see Borge, *La paciente impaciencia*, 184. Many later Sandinista officials and supporters have read Guerrero out of the history of the movement: the acceptable founders are Fonseca, Borge and Silvio Mayorga. On Guerrero's role, see Borge, *La paciente impaciencia*, 193 and passm.; Borge, "Carlos, el amanecer," 108; and Donald Hodges, *Intellectual Foundations of the Nicaraguan Revolution* (Austin: University of Texas Press, 1986), 165–66.

6. See Borge, *La paciente impaciencia*, 183–84; Borge, "Carlos, el amanecer," 109, 110, and Hodges, *Intellectual Foundations*, 165–66, 191.

7. The critical aspects in "the life and development of the vanguard" were spelled out in the FSLN's 1977 *Nicaragua: On the General Political/Military Platform of Struggle of the Sandinista Front for National Liberation* (Oakland, CA: Resistance Publications, 1978[?]), 23, written largely by Humberto Ortega. These included: selective recruitment; constant political and ideological formation; constant tactical and technical preparation; revolutionary discipline; cultivation of such qualities as combative militancy, honor, firmness, revolutionary authority, attitudes and experience; opposition to personalism; and support for unity and collective leadership.

8. Ratliff interview with Edén Pastora, 20 March 1992.

9. Some of the already documented disputes are covered in David Nolan, *The Ideology of the Sandinistas and the Nicaraguan Revolution* (Miami: University of Miami Press, 1984), 33–104; and Hodges, *Intellectual Foundations*, 197–255. On Castro's earlier policies, see William Ratliff, *Castroism and Communism in Latin America* (Washington: AEI, 1976), esp. chaps. 2, 5, and 6. Also, Ratliff interview with Edén Pastora, 20 March 1992.

10. Arce interview in *Excelsior*, Mexico City, 25 June 1987, cited by Michael Radu, "Nicaragua," in Richard Staar, ed., *1988 Yearbook on International Communist Affairs* (Stanford, CA: Hoover Institution Press, 1988), 99.

11. Ratliff interview with Pastora, 19 March 1992.

12. For the text of the document see, FSLN National Directorate, "Analysis of the Situation and Tasks of the Sandinista People's Revolution" (*72-Hour Document*),

in Mark Falcoff and Robert Royal, eds., *The Continuing Crisis: U.S. Policy in Central America and the Caribbean* (Lanham, MD,: Ethics and Public Policy Center, 1987), 493-517.

2

The Vanguard of the Vanguard

The National Directorate consisted of the nine Comandantes of the Revolution who held almost absolute power and, in the words of the Stephen Kinzer of *The New York Times*, as a group directed the nation "from behind a curtain no outsider could penetrate."[1] And as so often happens when power is concentrated in this way, the comandantes themselves found it increasingly difficult to see and hear back through the curtain and lost touch with the interests of the Nicaraguan people. The Directorate quickly became the center of arrogance, intolerance, and repression of all who disagreed with the comandantes' collective will. It cultivated within the government the "either/or," "for us or against us," mentality that had characterized the FSLN from the beginning but had been papered over during the late 1970s.

The Sandinistas created a dictatorial, antidemocratic system in Nicaragua, yet within itself the Directorate was an essentially democratic organization. Each member was free to express his ideas and disagreements without fear. This is not to say that each comandante had equal influence within the Directorate, which certainly was not the case, but that each could speak his mind and, when the votes were taken, each had only one vote. As a general rule, decisions were made by consensus, after serious discussions, with compromises made on all sides. When issues were not susceptible to compromise—the choice of a presidential candidate or the choice between supporting a guerrilla war in El Salvador or in Guatemala—the minority accepted the preference of the majority.

Cutting the Cake

One of Humberto Ortega's favorite recollections about Fidel Castro, which he retold on every possible occasion, related to the Cuban leader's advice on the distribution of major offices and responsibilities in the

Sandinista government. A few days after the revolution, Fidel met with the Ortega brothers and others in Havana. At one point he drew the two aside and offered this simple yet critical advice: "Be very careful in cutting up the cake." Humberto answered, "Don't worry, we are sharing the cake because that is the only way to control the whole thing." Fidel knew that the Ortegas understood.

The major offices were passed out to the nine comandantes, who collectively made up the National Directorate, with each comandante getting his sphere of influence. But only three men, who never changed, dominated the government and nation: Daniel Ortega, Humberto Ortega, and Tomás Borge. Of these three, the Ortegas held the top positions and they alone could not have been easily replaced had something happened to them. On several occasions, Humberto remarked, "If Daniel or I were to die, refilling our posts could cause a fight within the National Directorate. If Tomás were to die, Luis [Carrión] would take his place. The others are irrelevant." This didn't mean that the others' work was unimportant, however, for the others often played important roles, prominent among them Jaime Wheelock as minister of agriculture and Bayardo Arce as head of the Directorate of International Relations (DRI). Lower-level Sandinistas, especially the more social-democratically inclined like Edén Pastora, usually found themselves shifted around or in secondary or even ceremonial positions. One Sandinista of social-democratic tendencies who was highly placed was Army Chief-of-Staff Joaquín Cuadra. Individual comandantes were assigned to serve as conduits to individual Nicaraguans or foreigners. For example, Tomás Borge was the link to U.S. Ambassador Harry Bergold, Humberto Ortega to Manuel Noriega, and Jaime Wheelock to Violeta Chamorro.

On 15 September 1980 the National Directorate announced the institutional framework for its absolute domination of the party, government, and nation. The critical institutional arms of the Directorate were:

1. The Executive Commission, consisting of Bayardo Arce, Daniel Ortega, and Jaime Wheelock, that is to say one member from each of the three FSLN factions of the late 1970s. (As the Contra War expanded, Defense Minister Ortega and Interior Minister Borge were added.) The commission generally met once a week and was charged with drawing up the agenda for Directorate meetings and with guaranteeing and controlling the implementation of the Directorate's decisions. The com-

mission could make independent decisions so long as they fell within the guidelines set by the full Directorate.

While this body helped concentrate control of the FSLN in the National Directorate, for some years it was a center of conflict among Directorate members themselves. Bayardo Arce was coordinator of the commission until August 1985, when Daniel Ortega, who had been elected president of the country in late 1984, maneuvered himself into the position. One particular problem area between the two was foreign affairs. For a long time it was unclear whether that was Arce's realm or, especially after his inauguration as president in January 1985, the president's and Foreign Minister Miguel D'Escoto's. Foreign ambassadors couldn't figure it out, and many simply made two reports, one for Arce's DRI and one for the Foreign Ministry. As Daniel consolidated his leadership in party and government, power moved increasingly into his hands, though the regular process remained to reach decisions on international affairs first in the Directorate.

2. The Military Commission, which was responsible for matters related to military defense and national order. It was coordinated by Humberto Ortega, with Borge, Carrión, and various chiefs of the EPS and MINT.

3. The State Commission, responsible for the affairs of government, coordinated by Daniel Ortega, with members Ruiz and Wheelock.

4. The National Secretariat to oversee the professional structures of the FSLN, including the Department of Organization and Masses (DORMA), the Department of International Relations, and the Sandinista Labor Union (CST). Its comandantes were Víctor Tirado and Carlos Núñez, who had taken control of the Department of Propaganda and Political Education (DEPEP).

5. The Committee for Departmental Direction (CDD), which represented FSLN authority in each of the 16 departments (states) of the country.

6. The Sandinista Assembly, defined as a consultative organ of the Directorate and made up of the most important Sandinista militants.

This reorganization fixed power in the hands of the Directorate and from this point on it was impossible to separate the state, the army, and the mass organizations from the top FSLN leadership. For example, one day Humberto Ortega would meet with the most important chiefs of the EPS and give directions as minister of defense and the next day he would appear as a member of Directorate to approve political programs for EPS officials that would guarantee their loyalty to the FSLN, educate them in the principles of Marxism-Leninism, or direct them on what the EPS budget would pay FSLN cadres. It created a labyrinth in which all the passages were interconnected, but with only one entrance and one exit—the National Directorate of the FSLN.

This reorganization not only gave the Directorate power in the country as a whole but formalized antidemocratic operations within the FSLN itself. While the FSLN was operating as a guerrilla force, cadres understood that decisionmaking had to be centralized. But when the Sandinistas became the rulers, many cadres increasingly pressed for lessening the concentration of power. The Sandinista Assembly was really little more than an effort to pacify or shut up those below the nine comandantes who wanted to be heard. From the beginning the Assembly had only a consultative role, but very soon assemblymen realized that they were not really even being consulted. They were simply called into session to be told what the Directorate had decided before announcements appeared in the newspaper. Thus Assembly members complained that sessions were boring and *pro forma*. Talking with an American researcher in 1989, Moisés Hassan said the Assembly was "simply a rubber stamp, a circus." [2]

Elitist Democracy within the Dictatorship

The National Directorate typically met once a week, unless an emergency required more. All nine comandantes attended; there were no excuses for absence except being out of the country or seriously ill. A very few other high officials were present on special assignments, sitting in a row behind the comandantes. Major Roger Miranda attended those sessions dealing with military affairs, for example, and on Humberto Ortega's behalf read the minutes of all meetings and extracted from them those matters of particular interest to the military. These visitors said nothing unless addressed by one of the comandantes. A moderator was elected to conduct the sessions at the beginning of each meeting; usually the duty was rotated among the comandantes. The meetings always began at 8:00 A.M. on Friday and continued until all work was completed, usually between 2 P.M. and 4 P.M. Drinks and sandwiches were provided so that no interruptions were needed or allowed, unless some extraordinary incident occurred. Long meetings became a problem because attention drifted and comandantes began to walk around, eat more, and talk among themselves.

When the comandantes arrived, there usually was joking and small-talk. The session began with a period of "Criticism and Self-criticism," a practice considered particularly important in the formation of Sandinista militancy. The Ortegas were often criticized for arriving late for Directorate meetings, which some considered an affectation and assertion of power adopted from Castro; over the years they improved somewhat. Arce was criticized for scandalous personal behavior, Borge for seeking undue publicity. Other examples are described below. The most serious "punishments," however, were verbal admonitions.

Each comandante was free to participate as much or as little as he wished. In fact, the most active were Daniel, Arce, Borge, Wheelock, and Carrión. Humberto would avoid joining in as long as he could, but participate vigorously when driven to do so; he preferred to speak late in the discussion so that he could take the others' remarks into consideration and judge the correlation of forces. Ruiz and Núñez said little; Tirado was the most absentminded of all. A simple majority—five votes—was needed to carry a motion and voting was done by a show of hands.

The discussions of issues were wide-ranging and often heated. Just the same, the votes on most strategic matters, such as the candidacy for national elections, had been settled in advance. The directorate never seriously considered holding an election in the early 1980s for several reasons. First, they rejected the idea of a "bourgeois" style election on principle. Second, there was the problem of choosing the FSLN candidate. Edén Pastora would have been the obvious choice immediately after Somoza's fall for he was by far the most popular of the Sandinista leaders. But Pastora was totally unacceptable as a candidate for the same reasons he had been excluded from the National Directorate in the first place: he was an uncontrollable social democrat. Thus the Directorate would have had to choose a candidate from among the nine, and the Ortegas knew that during the early years it would have been hard to deny the candidacy to Borge. By the time 1984 came around and the Directorate decided it had to hold an election for strategic reasons, the Ortegas had consolidated their positions. They held a series of private meetings before the Directorate session scheduled to nominate a candidate and lined up support for Daniel from the Proletarian tendency—Wheelock, Núñez, and

Carrión. In the end, Daniel got eight in support of his candidacy, with one abstention—Borge. It was decided that Borge should announce Daniel's candidacy, so as to remove rumors that he had opposed the decision. This was one of the most difficult and humiliating times in Borge's life, but as a highly disciplined Sandinista he played his part. In intimate circles, Humberto commented: "Do you know when Tomás will be president of this country? Never!"

Personalities and Power Struggles

In reality, though the seventy-two hour meeting presented a unified political line to the militants, the sessions had by no means completely achieved the objective of overcoming the deep differences within the leadership, nor could they realistically have been expected to do so. And with so much power concentrated in the hands of so few people over the years, and such serious domestic and international problems to be dealt with, differing views and personalities continued to weigh heavily within the leadership of the movement.

Here Tomás Borge was in many respects the pivotal figure, for while he was popular with the rank and file—though not nearly as popular at first as Edén Pastora, who after July 1979 never approached the influence of the top nine within the government—he was on bad terms with Humberto Ortega and Jaime Wheelock, who led the Proletarian tendency. It was not just that these men did not like each other, it was also that Borge, who as a cofounder of the movement and a powerful orator, had a head start toward being the dominant leader in the new government, the FSLN candidate for Nicaraguan president. The Ortegas were deeply concerned during the early years by Borge's popular following and ability to communicate publicly, which in the beginning neither of them could do at all well. Indeed, the Ortegas did not communicate well in relation to most of the other comandantes who, as public speakers, could be rated as follows, from the best to the worst: Borge, Wheelock, Arce, Núñez, Ruiz, Carrión, Daniel Ortega, Tirado, Humberto Ortega.

The Ortegas, who controlled the dominant Tercerista faction of the FSLN, had the top leadership positions, including the presidency, in mind for themselves and their friends. The Terceristas were soon joined by the Proletarians, who didn't like or trust Borge either, in a common cause to restrict Tomás's power. The latter soon realized he was a distant third in the power structure: the Ortegas not only had the two most important positions, there were two of them from the same faction in those positions.

The feud between Humberto Ortega and Borge was in part related to differences in strategic perspectives, as is discussed elsewhere in this book and by some other analysts. But problems of power and personality were equally important and also predated the 1979 victory. These played a key role year after year during the 1980s in the formation of alliances and policies. Almost anything that happened could be occasion for conflict between Borge and Humberto, and their personal differences developed into conflicts between the ministries they headed, Interior and Defense. Sometimes they were even reflected in such petty ways as Humberto's refusing to attend social functions in a foreign embassy if Borge was expected to be there.

Long before July 1979 Borge had become a legend in the Sandinista movement, not just because he was its only surviving founder but because of the hardships and tortures he had endured in the struggle against Somoza. Borge had no use for Humberto, who had spent most of the Somoza period abroad. Borge often described Humberto as "a petty-bourgeois opportunist who only knows how to talk about revolution in foreign cafes" and as "an errand boy for Carlos Fonseca." Humberto wasn't much kinder to Borge, whom he called "a vainglorious dwarf who thinks that revolutionary merit comes only at the point of a pistol." Borge thought much better of Daniel Ortega because the latter had taken part in more armed actions and spent many years in Somoza's jails. Thus Daniel sometimes was able to serve as an intermediary between his brother and Borge.

Despite their commanding positions, the Ortegas were seriously concerned about having Borge as minister of the interior, a very important position they could not deny him. They and others were concerned about Borge's being head of MINT because there he was in charge of the following forces.

- The General Directorate of State Security (DGSE) forces, which were not only the foundation of Borge's power but central to the survival of the entire regime. Borge put the DGSE under Lenín Cerna, who left the Terceristas to join Borge in the GPP Tendency but spent the critical years of the war in Mexico. What Tomás didn't know was that after Somoza fell, and Cerna recognized that the Ortegas had greater power, the chief of DGSE reported everything Borge said and did to the Ortegas. "Whenever Lenín calls me,"

Humberto told Miranda, "get ahold of me immediately, no matter what I am doing or what time it is." But Humberto kept Cerna's cooperation in perspective, commenting one day on the nature of the power struggle between Borge and the brothers:

> This is a silent, clandestine war in which the one who wins will be the one who has the most recent information on what his adversary is thinking and doing, and in this context Lenín is important for us. But never think, Miranda, that Lenín supports us because he is loyal to us. He knows we have the reins of power in this country. Lenín is faithful only to power. He would sell his own mother for power.

• Personal security forces for all the comandantes. Humberto was especially paranoid about his security. When Indira Gandhi was assassinated by one of her guards, Humberto remarked, "Now you understand, Miranda, why I am so much against having Tomás in charge of my personal security; body guards are like your wife, you have to take care of them yourself." Borge's beefs in the personal security field were of a different nature: he was angry that the security for Humberto and his family included eighteen vehicles and nearly 350 soldiers and officials, that is to say about half of the total security forces available to the nine comandantes.

• The elite special Pablo Ubeda Troops (TPU), originally a division of MINT under Borge, consisted of approximately four to five hundred elite troops superbly trained in commando and antiterrorist operations by Vietnamese instructors. The TPU were fiercely loyal to Borge and caused great anxiety among the other comandantes, who feared that Borge might use them to capture or slaughter his critics—as Salvadoran guerrilla leaders sometimes did—"resolving" internal differences on Borge's behalf with lightening attacks before the EPS could get itself together to respond. Humberto tried to create his own special troops, but his never came up to the standard of the TPU. In the mid-1980s, by devious maneuvers within the National Directorate, described below, the TPU was moved from MINT into the EPS, where its loyalty to Borge and its uniqueness were dissipated.

From early on there were tensions between Borge and Humberto Ortega over another military force, the Frontier Guard Troops (TGF), which were originally and remained under Humberto's control. Borge argued that since they were performing duties aimed at enhancing the work of customs and migration, they should be in the Interior Ministry, as these forces were in the Soviet bloc countries. The TGF was also active in early stages of the Contra War. Humberto strongly opposed Borge's play to have the TGF put under his command, however, and he spoke to Jaime Wheelock in 1981 to line up support for his stand in the Directorate:

Look, Jaime, I am worried that besides the State Security, the police and the TPU, Tomás is now trying to get the TGF. This is too much hardware under his control. You know as well as anyone that our internal differences are not all resolved and that if the situation becomes much more complicated again, Tomás would not hesitate to turn these arms against us.

With Wheelock's support in the Directorate, the TGF remained under Ortega's control.

Another important cause of tension within the Directorate was the conflict between the Ortegas and the rest of the comandantes, led by Bayardo Arce, over who controlled the EPS, Humberto personally or Humberto as a representative of the National Directorate. The Ortegas tried in every way to control the EPS and have the complete loyalty, in particular of its principal chiefs, to Humberto personally, while the Directorate sought to draw its loyalty to the FSLN's top leadership body as a whole. In the sessions of the National Directorate, Arce argued, "The only way we can guarantee that the EPS doesn't become an institution above the power of the National Directorate is to have its structures at all levels subordinate to the FSLN more than to its respective military commands."

In pursuit of this limitation on Humberto's authority, the National Directorate reserved the following authority to itself:

1. to approve the EPS budget and the number of young people who could be incorporated by the draft;

2. to approve the promotion of officers above the rank of major;

3. to approve military incursions into Honduras and Costa Rica;

4. to approve delivery of arms to any guerrilla movement;

5. to approve appointments of the principal officers of the EPS—chief and subchief of general staff, chiefs of military districts, air force, marines, navy, and rearguard, and members of the general staff—on the basis of recommendations made by Humberto;

6. to award the Carlos Fonseca Order to any member of the EPS;

7. to approve any request for arms Humberto made to friendly countries.

Humberto's authority was absolute with respect to the following matters:

1. military promotions up to and including the grade of major;

2. troop movements that did not cross national borders in the course of a war;

3. awarding medals created by the EPS;

4. approving assignments to holders of positions not considered principal officers.

Further, Humberto had to appear before the National Directorate to defend or ask for increases in his budget. Joaquín Cuadra would explain the military aspects of the war, after which Humberto would give a political perspective on the situation and then, invariably, ask for more money. Ortega often had trouble convincing the Directorate that the EPS needed more human or financial resources. For example, in mid-1985 he came up with the thesis of the "strategic defeat of the Contras." Arce commented:

> I don't understand how Humberto can tell us that the Contras are defeated strategically and at the same time ask us for more personnel and more money, which we don't have and would have to take from other social and economic projects. What kind of a strategic defeat is this? I don't get it.

It was a tough question for Humberto to answer, particularly since he knew his colleagues thought the war had gone on far too long with no end in sight. Humberto's answer was less that of a military strategist than of a politician who knew how to manipulate his listeners in the language of the street.

> When I speak of the strategic defeat of the Contras, I don't mean that they will be finished off tomorrow. What I mean to say is they have lost the strategic initiative and though it is going to take a long time to get a military victory, that victory is nonetheless guaranteed. Look, it's like in the boxing ring, when the adversary shows signs of tiring and weakness we concentrate more of our energies on him to beat him into the mat. In this sense, the EPS has to concentrate more men and resources to accelerate the process of strategic defeat of the Contras.

The watchword of 1985 was "the strategic defeat of the counterrevolution," of 1986 was "accelerating the strategic defeat of the counterrevolution," and of 1987 was "deepening the strategic defeat of the counterrevolution." Predictably, this line of argument became increasingly less convincing as time passed.

Voting Blocs and Influence

There were three "sure votes" for the Ortegas in the bosom of the Directorate: the Ortegas themselves and Tirado. The "allied votes" were those of Wheelock, Carrión, and Núñez, members of the Proletarian Tendency that had clashed more with the Prolonged War tendency of Borge than with the Ortegas; indeed, the Ortegas had openly defended Wheelock against attacks by Borge and Arce. The three "opposition votes" of Borge, Arce, and Ruiz were the least cohesive, for Arce could flip from support for Borge one week to support for the Ortegas the next.

Immediately after Somoza's fall, before the drafting of the *72-Hour Document*, the Tercerista Tendency, headed by the Ortegas, formed an alliance with the Proletarian Tendency. This fairly solid majority of six, dominated by the Ortegas, played the leading role in passing out political and military positions and in making decisions on the direction and consolidation of the revolution. The Prolonged Popular War Tendency of Borge, Ruiz, and Arce—to which Fonseca had belonged before his death in 1976—had two choices: break with the other comandantes or get what they could and go along with majority decisions. They chose the latter course, in accordance with Fidel Castro's recommendation, the discipline of the revolutionary mystique and their recognition that even if it was not ideal, it was necessary to assure the dominant role of the Directorate in the country and perhaps their very survival. By and large, this general division of forces and discipline held up as long as the Sandinistas were in power.

This alignment of loyalties and division of influence and spoils can be accounted for on three grounds: ideology, power, and personalities. Ideologically, the comandantes fell into two general categories, the orthodox and the pragmatic. In general the more orthodox Prolonged Popular War and Proletarian tendencies tried to twist Nicaraguan conditions around to fit into their versions of Marxism-Leninism, though the former were more dogmatic than the latter. The leaders of the Tercerista Tendency were more pragmatic in their evaluations of Nicaraguan realities, and prepared to be more flexible in their alliances and policies. The spirit of the pragmatist approach was well conveyed in Humberto Ortega's 1981 statement that "to be a good Marxist you have to be a good Sandinista, and to be a good Sandinista you have to be a good Marxist." This was more than a play on words for it implied the flexibility that enabled the Terceristas to develop the broad front that defeated Somoza and dominated the Directorate.

The Proletarians were less inclined than the Prolonged War Faction to think in terms of the mountains and could adapt better ideologically to the new government in the city. They also realized that by coming up with the winning strategy, and thus the confidence of most Nicaraguans, in addition to Castro and his international friends, the Ortegas would wield the knife when cutting up the cake of power.

The comandantes could be broken down in another way as well: the "históricos," as Humberto Ortega called them, and the rest. The históricos were those who were in the historical directorate dating back before 1977: Tomás Borge, Víctor Tirado, Daniel Ortega, Humberto Ortega, and Henry Ruiz. In 1982 the pecking order was formally set by date of entry in the movement, beginning with the five históricos, in the above order, followed by Jaime Wheelock, Bayardo Arce, Carlos Núñez, and Luis Carrión. The most disputed member was Wheelock, who had joined the FSLN before Arce but whose stature was weakened by a perceived "ideological vacillation" and the fact that he alone among the comandantes had once taken asylum in a foreign embassy. Wheelock was placed above Arce because he had the support of the Ortegas, a favor he never forgot.

Thus in Humberto's judgment, Wheelock, Arce, Núñez, and Carrión were members of the Directorate by accident. That is, if the divisions of the mid-1970s had not occurred, Wheelock, Núñez, and Carrión would not have been members of the Directorate. In mid-1987 Humberto once became so infuriated with Arce that in a meeting of the Directorate he shouted, "You're only here by accident, if Pedro Aráuz [a member of the historic Directorate] hadn't been killed you wouldn't be sitting here with us" and the two almost came to blows. Daniel insisted that Humberto write an apology, and the latter wrote a letter which said: "Brother, remember that we are humans with defects as well as assets and we are all subject to committing errors. . . . As a revolutionary brother I ask you to forgive me for what happened today. You know I have always recognized your revolutionary merits and your leadership qualities." When Roger Miranda personally delivered the letter, Arce said, "Yes, Miranda, and what does Humberto want now?" "Only to be sure you received the letter," Miranda said. Arce opened the letter and read it. "Tell him I received it," he said bluntly, and left.

The first grand alliance of the Ortegas and the Proletarians was in March 1980 when Carrión was transferred from under commander-in-chief of the EPS to vice-minister of the Interior, that is from the number two man for Humberto to the number two man under Borge. The presence of Carrión in the EPS drove Humberto crazy because though the former was a military subordinate he was a political equal and thus in a sense seemed to challenge him in the military hierarchy. Humberto went to Wheelock and playing on the latter's long-standing feud with Borge, convinced him that Carrión should be watching Borge in Interior. "Look, Jaime, you and I know we don't have to worry about me, but we do need to worry about Tomás." Borge opposed moving Carrión to Interior, but the majority voted to do so anyway for two reasons: to limit Borge's power within the ministry and, more specifically, to have Carrión oversee the state security, the most powerful structure within the ministry.

Sitting in on Sessions of the Directorate

In order to give a better "feel" for these Directorate sessions, the issues raised, and how the discussions were carried out, portions of several meetings will be reproduced here, though some of the substantive issues raised are also analyzed in other chapters.

• During the 1980–83 period, there were heated debates within the Directorate to define a military strategy to thwart the anticipated U.S. invasion. The two main positions were represented by Borge, on the one hand, and the Ortegas, on the other.

Borge, influenced by his conception of prolonged people's war and the Vietnam experience, argued that the EPS simply could not confront the far superior technology and armaments of the Americans. This Yankee superiority had to be compensated for by the EPS's capacity to maneuver, to keep from being an easy target, to be able to retreat to the mountains and begin a prolonged war of resistance if necessary, as Sandino had done, a strategy Arce once threw in the face of U.S. diplomat Thomas Enders. Borge argued, "It is suicide to openly fight the Gringos because they have all the military power to destroy us in the kinds of encounters Humberto is planning. We must retreat to the mountains to take advantage of the conditions of the land. In the mountains we will be invincible. The mountains will be the graveyard of the Gringo invaders."

Humberto saw Borge's position as a mechanical application of what had happened in the time of Sandino and in Vietnam, experiences that had nothing to do with the concrete conditions of the Sandinista Revolution threatened by U.S. imperialism. He argued that in time of war, Nicaragua would be so blockaded that it would be impossible to supply a prolonged war, and what is more, to retreat to the mountains was to admit defeat.

The decisive battles against the invading forces will be in the cities on the Pacific, not in the mountains. With the support of the Soviet Union and Cuba we are developing a type of army capable of defeating an invasion. When we go to the mountains, it is because the war is lost and we have lost power, and from that moment we again become a guerrilla movement which in time will be eliminated. Our strongest social base is in the cities of the Pacific, not in the mountains. Finally, it is technically impossible to take the tanks, cannons and planes the Soviets are giving us into the mountains. We must make every city a common graveyard for thousands of imperialist invaders.

In private, Humberto worried that the doctrine he presented to the Directorate was full of holes, but he thought it superior to Borge's and it was the one approved by the Cubans and Soviets. The doctrine was revised to Humberto's greater satisfaction in the mid-1980s, as explained below.

• The comandantes decided in the beginning that they should support guerrilla wars abroad, but they could not immediately agree on which guerrillas to support first and just what the guerrilla forces should receive. The question of "who?" quickly narrowed down to the guerrillas in Guatemala or those in El Salvador. Bayardo Arce and Henry Ruiz leaned toward Guatemala and led in expressions of doubt about whether the Salvadorans could survive, much less triumph. "The Salvadorans don't have it yet," Arce argued, "so we shouldn't throw in first with them. No real experience, no unity, bad geographical conditions for a protracted war against the Salvadoran army."

But Daniel Ortega, pacing back and forth, made the argument that finally carried the day.

Conditions are more favorable in El Salvador than anywhere else. If we and the Cubans get them to work together, train them and supply them, the army will be caught by surprise. Geographical limitations will be compensated for by population density, and the population will be a good source of guerrilla recruits. Further, geographical characteristics and proximity of the common borders between Nicaragua, Honduras and El Salvador will facilitate the flow of military supplies.

Arce was put in charge of operations in support of guerrilla groups abroad in line with the Directorate's decision to assist guerrillas in the following priority: El Salvador, Guatemala, Costa Rica, Honduras, and then other countries in the hemisphere.

• The Ortegas were the most pragmatic and creative members of the Directorate, using any matter to preserve their power, at the expense of ideology whenever necessary. Examples of this range from an incident relating to psychological warfare to a greater willingness to negotiate with the United States. For example, in 1983–84 it was common to burn American flags at FSLN-led demonstrations in Managua. The Ortegas proposed that effigies of Ronald Reagan be burned instead. Humberto said, "When we burn the flag of the United States, we burn the patriotic symbol of the gringos. When this is seen on television in North American homes it can cause resentment in citizens who oppose Reagan's policy against Nicaragua but don't like to see their flag stomped on and burned. On the other hand, if we burn a figure representing Reagan, many Americans will even support what we are doing." The Directorate unanimously voted for the change and the flag burning stopped.

• Another instance of maneuvering within the National Directorate occurred at the end of 1984 and showed how the Ortegas could seize an incident of bad judgement on Borge's part and turn it to their advantage. The Ortegas were deeply concerned during the early 1980s by Borge's command of the elite Tropas Pablo Ubeda, as noted above, fearing that their rival might at some point use these forces to strike suddenly against National Directorate rivals to seize power for himself. By early 1984 Humberto was scheming how to get the TPU out of the MINT and into the EPS, but since Arce, Ruiz, and Carrión, in addition to Borge, were openly against such a move, he did not take it to the National Directorate until the opportunity burst upon him on 5 November of that year.

In October-November 1984 some hundred TPU troops disguised as Contras, under the command of Enrique Schmidt, recruited about forty disaffected peasants while secretly hunting Contras in the Bijagua region of central Nicaragua. Meanwhile, an undercover agent of State Security led a Contra force of about fifty and its commander, Pedro Torres, called Ciclón, into a minefield in the Bijagua area. When the Contras realized they had been tricked and were surrounded by enemy troops they opened fire, but were quickly shot down or killed by mines laid by the more numerous TPU forces. Among the Sandinistas, Schmidt was the only casualty, killed instantly by a shot through the heart, according to the medical report. The Sandinista paper *Barricada* said that the TPU had annihilated a "Somocista task force" of 76 and that Schmidt had died heroically "after the enemy had been virtually annihilated."[3]

Who was Enrique Schmidt? An official in MINT who at that time was Minister of Communications in Daniel Ortega's government. Borge had put him in charge of this TPU mission without Ortega's authorization. Why? The matter was raised at a meeting of the National Directorate.

Never before had Borge been in a tighter spot. In effect, he was sitting in the chair of the accused. Borge usually conducted himself in Directorate sessions with a firm voice and tone of utmost security, as if he were reaffirming that he was the sole survivor of the FSLN's founders. But this time his head was either lowered or his eyes glanced above everyone's heads. He spoke defensively, haltingly, with an insecure tone, choosing his statements and words very carefully. He had wanted to try Schmidt out, he said, before transferring him permanently from Communications to serve as chief of the TPU. Finally he asked the Directorate to excuse him for what had happened and to give Schmidt both the FSLN's maximum decoration, the Order of Carlos Fonseca, and a promotion to the rank of commander.

The Ortegas had not yet even launched their offensive. Humberto began: "I would like to have the TPU fighting the forces of Toño or Renato [Contra commanders] instead of preparing mine fields. What the TPU has done is act like a dunce." Then Daniel picked up the attack:

> To me it simply looks like Tomás has commanded one of the ministers without my authorization, grabbing my authority. What explanation am I going to give for Enrique's death? If I say I didn't know he was on this mission, I look like I don't control my own ministers, but if I say I did know, everyone's going to ask, are things so bad I now have to send ministers out to conduct military operations? I don't think we can give Schmidt the Carlos Fonseca Order because this would signify approval of what Tomás has done.

In the end, the Directorate strongly admonished Tomás, gave no award or promotion, and assigned only Tomás and Luis Carrión, as minister and vice-minister of MINT, to go to the funeral, with no official representation from the Directorate. Borge put as good a face on the affair as possible, with a quick announcement in *Barricada* on 6 November that Schmidt had been posthumously awarded MINT's own Pedro Aráuz medal, which Borge could do without National Directorate approval.

And the incident had far deeper repercussions, for the TPU was soon moved from MINT to the EPS, where it suffered losses and was demoralized, and was later superseded by Humberto's own elite troops, the PUFE.

* In August 1987, when Daniel Ortega returned from having signed the Esquipulas II peace treaty in Guatemala, the FSLN held a series of emergency sessions to try to convince the Directorate that signing the accords was to the benefit of the revolution. Prior to Ortega's departure for Guatemala, the Directorate had given him permission to act independently, but no one expected he would be signing a treaty. Daniel described the accords as

> one more arm that enables us to eliminate the Contras, even though it will in some degree benefit the internal reactionaries. But there is no doubt it is better for us to take on the imperialists now on political terrain than to continue the war that is wearing us down in terms of human and material resources. It isn't the Contras that are going to defeat us, but our own collapsing economy.

Some in the Directorate weren't buying this line. The debate went on for three days and afterward Daniel went to Cuba to explain it to Fidel Castro. After approval was finalized, the comandantes, joined by Joaquín Cuadra and Roger Miranda, went to lunch and Daniel remarked, loud enough to be overheard by all, "Bayardo had to be on vacation for us to reach these accords." In fact Arce had been on vacation when Daniel got his vote of confidence from the Directorate before leaving for Guatemala. Arce blushed and half laughing responded, "Daniel loves to put me down."

* On 19 October 1987 the nine comandantes and five other top officials met in the elegant César Augusto Silva Convention Center in Managua. Built in colonial style during the Somoza period, the hall became the center of political and social activity for the regime after the Sandinistas took power. The meeting was in the large and ornate Barro Room. The comandantes sat at an L-shaped table, with the other five, including Roger Miranda, seated to their rear. A podium and large lecture board stood in front of the comandantes, and several small tables of food and drink were on the sides.

Both the substance and the format of this meeting were distinctive since the session was more to inform and give approval than discuss. After Daniel's late arrival, the meeting began. Army Chief Joaquín Cuadra spent two hours explaining the technical and military aspects of two plans proposed by the Soviets for the Sandinista military, the first dealing with the anticipated end of the Contra War and the second with massive military expansion between 1990 and 1995.[4] His visual aids included maps and charts tacked to the board behind the podium.

Almost as soon as Cuadra began, Daniel Ortega was back on his feet, pacing, his hands locked behind his back. The meeting had Interior Minister Borge on the spot, though one might not have guessed his interest for he was slouched back in his chair. As always he was taking notes, sometimes poker-faced, sometimes scowling. He in particular was concerned about the proposed expansion of the military for he quite rightly saw it as strengthening the hands of the Ortegas and diminishing the relative power of his ministry.

After Cuadra finished, there was a period of spontaneous, disorganized discussion around and in back of the table. Everyone was asking the same, obvious questions. "Why are the Soviets offering all this?" "What cards do they have under the table?" "How can we afford it?"

Humberto rose, interrupted the chatter, and gave a short commentary on the political implications of the second plan. "The Soviets are thinking in strategic terms," he said. "The size of their offer surprised me as much as it has the rest of you. The Soviets want to make the Sandinista army into the Israelis of Central America." Then it was Daniel's turn. He called on the Directorate to stop speculating as to what the proposal meant and just approve it. "The Soviets don't act impulsively," he concluded, "and they know what they are doing. If they want to put this much support into the Nicaraguan Revolution, we should accept it and expect them to help us through with the ongoing expenses. This may be just the shield against the United States we have long sought from them."

• An example of the kind of event that could lead to an emergency meeting occurred on 12 November 1984. At 9:00 A.M. that morning there was a series of explosions at the military general staff headquarters (EMG) on a rise overlooking Managua. They caused utter confusion and alarm. Immediately, Roger Miranda received a phone call from Humberto Ortega, the general saying he had heard explosions near his house, too, and had alerted his security guard. Then Daniel called to report explosions near his house. Then calls came in from throughout Managua, from Chinandega, from Juigalpa, from Bluefields, from Masaya, from Puerto Cabezas. Explosions everywhere, simultaneously, but evidently no damage. An emergency meeting of the military staff was followed by one of the Directorate.

General Arnaldo Ochoa, then head of the Cuban military mission in Managua, explained what had happened: the "explosions" had been caused by the Americans' supersonic spy SR-71 "Black Bird" overflying Nicaraguan territory, breaking the sound barrier. Ochoa reported that the plane, which had also overflown Cuba the same day, had highly sensitive cameras which could photograph from great distances at high speeds. Why? Just weeks earlier the American government had said it thought MiG-21 fighters were going to be delivered to Nicaragua; several days previously the head of the Soviet mission in Managua had reported that a Soviet ship would indeed deliver arms at the port of Corinto in the second week of December, but that they would be six antiguerrilla MI-25 combat helicopters, the flying tanks so recently deployed with such deadly force in Afghanistan. The concern was heightened by Ochoa's assertion that, based on his experience, the SR-71's presence was almost always associated with invasion plans. But the overflights continued, the helicopters were delivered, and there was no invasion.

Is Daniel Ortega Stupid, or What?

Many people in the United States, whatever they think of U.S. policy toward the Sandinistas, have come to the conclusion that Daniel Ortega is stupid or at least particularly prone to public relations blunders. He presents a bad image: he isn't glib, he seldom smiles, some of the things he does strongly suggest that he is an automaton. Oliver North said he exuded "negative charisma": "When this guy enters the room," North wrote, "it feels like three people just left."[5] It is true that Daniel is an intense individual who often rubs people wrong, though he became much more at ease in public during the course of the 1980s and even smiled a lot and became hip during the 1990 presidential campaign.

The prime exhibit in this case against Ortega's intellect or judgment is the trip he made to the Soviet Union in April-May 1985, immediately after the U.S. Congress voted down a bill to give aid to the Contras. Ortega's trip was the main point supporters of aid to the Contras used to get Congress to reverse its position six weeks later and vote $27 million aid to the resistance. But these events did not demonstrate Ortega's stupidity or bad judgment as much as they did the shallowness of those

Congressmen who changed their votes and the tenor of much talk around Washington and in the media. We will examine this series of events to show how differently a couple of actions—the Congressional votes, the trip to Moscow—can seem when viewed from different perspectives. From Ortega's position—which was that of the National Directorate—these were the issues:

1. In early 1985 the Directorate did not fully understand the role of Congress in the U.S. political system, despite the commentaries of Foreign Minister D'Escoto, who had lived for a long time in the United States. On the basis of developments during the early 1980s, the Directorate was convinced that the Contras had become strong; that they had some of their own sources of supplies; that no matter what Congress did, the Reagan government would continue to support them somehow or other; and that the war would not soon be over. Therefore, the congressional vote in April to give the Contras a paltry $14 million in nonmilitary aid was not considered particularly important.

2. The comandantes considered the congressional vote and other matters noted below in long-term strategic rather than short-term tactical terms. The Directorate looked on the U.S. Congress and Congressmen with mixed concern, amusement, and contempt. The Democrats in Congress were considered unintentional, but also unreliable, allies. Many of them voted as if they hadn't a clue what the real issues were and changed their minds every time some new secondary event occurred; the fact that they changed their votes in June simply confirmed this judgment. The Directorate also concluded that these Americans and others like them were so shallow in their thinking that whenever their support *was* of real importance, they could be buttered up and won over when needed with short-term promises, appeals, gestures, and actions. It would have been foolish in the extreme to believe that playing ball according to the whims of these Congressmen and others like them was as important for the Sandinistas as relations with strategic allies.

3. On the other hand, the alliance with the Soviet bloc was strategic in nature, involving the kind of military and economic cooperation and aid the Sandinistas needed to survive over the long term. As it happened, the second level of the tripartite meetings for the 1986-90 bilateral military protocol had just concluded in April 1985 in Havana. The next level in the protocol routine was the formal signing in Moscow and it was decided that Daniel should demonstrate Sandinista solidarity with the Soviets by

going himself this time, in large part because in March 1985 Mikhail Gorbachev had taken over as secretary general of the CPSU. The National Directorate was determined to make this highest-level contact with Gorbachev as soon as possible both to cement the long-term relationship and because the FSLN needed an immediate increase in economic aid, among the critical items being petroleum.

In this case, and in many others as well, the comandantes—unlike many Congressmen and others—recognized and acted upon the differences between shorter-term tactical and longer-term strategic allies and interests.

Sidestepping and Defying the Directorate

The nine comandantes clearly understood that they should take no actions that might make one member of the National Directorate more equal than the others, that they would always abide by the decisions of the Directorate as a group and never make contacts or alter policy without authorization to do so. But there were many evasions and transgressions, some petty and some of considerable consequence. Humberto went beyond his authority on many occasions, usually with the support of Daniel. For example:

• The Directorate decided in 1984 that no gifts from individual comandantes should be paid for with state funds; if the state paid for a gift, it was to be given by the Directorate as a whole. But Humberto set up his own policy of material incentives for some high officers of the EPS. Requests for the gifts—refrigerators, a Toyota, a Rolex watch, or whatever—were made in Humberto's name and delivered free to the recipient in his name only. (Wearing a Rolex watch, in particular, had become a symbol of distinction within the Sandinista hierarchy, as it was in Cuba. At a meeting with the EPS chief in Managua in 1984, Cuban America Department chief Manuel Piñeiro, acting on behalf of Fidel Castro, gave a Rolex to Salvadoran guerrilla leader Joaquín Villalobos.) While this emphasized who was boss of the EPS, it did not seriously challenge the power of the other comandantes.

• From the beginning of the revolution, the EPS was considered subordinated to the decisions of the entire National Directorate and it was customary to hang a photograph of all of the comandantes in the offices of the various military units. At the beginning of 1987, however, the two

Ortegas replaced the group photos with shots of just themselves and the Directorate criticized the change. Humberto denied he knew anything about it and blamed Col. Hugo Torres for acting on his own authority, while Torres insisted he was only "following orders." When the Directorate ordered the group photos restored, Humberto did so only in those units that were frequently visited by FSLN activists, and not in the others.

• Sometimes decisions were simply arrived at outside of the Directorate meetings, where weight was more easily thrown around, pressure applied, deals struck. For example, as described above, in 1984 the Ortegas worked outside of the formal meetings to line up the votes to nominate Daniel rather than Borge for the FSLN presidential candidate. The Directorate meeting and discussion were mere formalities.

• In late 1987 Salvadoran Communist party chief Shafik Handal met privately with Humberto Ortega and the latter promised to send ground-to-air missiles to the Salvadoran guerrillas, though he was not authorized to do so. The next day the Directorate assembled in the morning. Bayardo Arce entered, having heard the day before about Humberto's promise, and he was obviously furious. His face was lined from a bad night's sleep, and he was both smoking more than normal and chewing his nails worse than usual. He sulked in and sat down at the table, not even greeting Borge, a close friend, who always sat at his left. The meeting didn't begin on time because Daniel came in late.

The nine had hardly settled in their chairs when Arce began:

I have to raise a point that concerns me deeply. Since 1980, on your command, I have been responsible for all relations with the revolutionary movements of Latin America, and especially with the "cousins" [the Salvadoran guerrillas]. But yesterday Handal went to a meeting I knew nothing about and Humberto promised we would send them "arrows" [ground-to-air missiles] right away.

As Bayardo heated up, Daniel frowned and began shaking his head. He obviously was annoyed not only with what Humberto had done but at his brother's failure to even tell him about it in advance. Up to this point Humberto, surprised by this unexpected criticism in front of the Directorate, had kept his eyes riveted on Arce.

But Arce had hardly begun, and as he spoke, Humberto slowly looked down toward the table, effectively admitting his guilt. "What is more," Arce continued,

Humberto said we would begin immediately to train the cousins in how to use the arrows at an air force training school. I won't have anything to do with this kind of shit. If I am responsible for the care of the cousins, Humberto has no business promising anything, and certainly not things we haven't even agreed upon in the Directorate. Humberto is grabbing authority from me and making me look like an asshole with the cousins.

Humberto's only response, laden with characteristic evasion and false humility, was: "Bayardo is right. I had no idea such an informal chat with Handal would cause such repercussions. I will be more careful in the future."

• Jaime Wheelock had been much castigated as the only comandante who had ever sought asylum in a foreign embassy. And yet all the comandantes had plans for just such asylum for their families in the event of a U.S. invasion. Borge was responsible for working out a plan to save those 120 or so people closest to the members of the Directorate, utilizing the Soviet embassy. The Ortegas had their own plan, however, managed by Roger Miranda, because they didn't want to be part of such a large group and because they didn't trust Borge. What is more, they did not like the choice of the Soviet Embassy but preferred a country with a tradition for political exile and yet one on good terms with the United States. They decided on Spain and settled on an empty house next door to the Spanish embassy in Managua, in the luxurious Las Colinas area, where José Maria Alvarado, former minister of communication had lived prior to breaking with the Sandinistas and moving to Costa Rica. At the first sign of a U.S. invasion, the Ortega family would be moved to the empty house and as soon as the invasion was confirmed they would go to the embassy and ask for asylum.

• In 1987 the Ortegas on their own tried to open talks with the United States through a feeler to Panama Defense Forces chief Manuel Noriega and an unprecedented protocol meeting with a new U.S. military attaché in Managua. These efforts, described elsewhere, came to nothing.

• Whereas the comandantes had to agree and move jointly on policy-related issues, they could not agree and did not move anywhere on producing an official history of the Sandinista movement. The events of the 1970s in particular had left many differences of opinion and even hostilities among the comandantes with respect to the roles played by various revolutionaries, dead and alive. But for the first half of the 1980s, Humberto Ortega used the Institute for the Study of Sandinismo (IES), founded shortly after the revolution, to produce his version of the anti-Somoza war and the FSLN.

The Directorate had delegated Humberto to set up the IES within the EPS because the army had sufficient funds to cover its considerable cost. Thus, officially, Humberto was managing the institute on behalf of the Directorate, but he was using it for his own ends. In the early years, only the Ortegas seemed to recognize the importance of the IES's role in recording what had happened in the war against Somoza. The Directorate did not even monitor early publications and thus it did not immediately realize its bias.

Roger Miranda oversaw the institute on Ortega's behalf and the staff consisted of people Humberto was sure would do his bidding, among them his wife, Ligia, Miranda's wife, and assorted friends and relations of the Ortegas. In its archives, the IES held documents that were unknown to most members of the Directorate, including some that Humberto and Daniel wanted to keep secret that reflected the bad relations between the Ortegas and Fonseca during the last year of the latter's life. The bias of the IES publications was evident in *Why they Always Live Among Us*, for example, which was published in 1982. The book seemed to contain the official biographies of the heroes and martyrs of the fighting in Masaya, among them Camilo Ortega, the brother of Humberto and Daniel, who was killed in February 1978. But the volume reflected Humberto's close supervision, and the Ortegas' critics protested that among its many faults it greatly overplayed Camilo Ortega's role as an early strategist for the Tercerista front against Somoza.[6]

In early 1984, having become fully aware of the bias of the IES publications, the Directorate charged the IES with drawing up an outline for an official history of the FSLN, and a very detailed proposal was presented a year and a half later, in the middle of 1985. It provoked prolonged and heated debates within the Directorate at the end of 1985 and finally was rejected because only the Ortegas and Víctor Tirado agreed on the essence of who did what—particularly Tomás Borge—in the revolution. Since on this matter even the alliance with Jaime Wheelock's faction broke down, the whole idea of a history was shelved indefinitely. In early 1986 Bayardo Arce began agitating to have the institute removed from Humberto's control and put under his own as the comandante in charge of party affairs. This was done in mid-1986, though Humberto still retained much influence since the staff, loyal to himself, remained essentially the same.

Notes

1. Kinzer, *Blood of Brothers*, 172.
2. Stephen F. Diamond, "Class and Power in Revolutionary Nicaragua," (PhD diss., University of London, December 1990), 209.
3. "Sub-comandante Schmidt cae en acción heróica," *Barricada*, 6 November 1984.
4. These military plans were revealed by Roger Miranda in late 1987. Humberto Ortega immediately confirmed the substance of Miranda's revelations on 12 December on Managua Domestic Service; see *Foreign Broadcast Information Service, Latin America*, 14 December 1987, 19.
5. Oliver L. North, with William Novak, *Under Fire* (New York: HarperCollins Publishers, 1991), 230.
6. Instituto de Estudio del Sandinismo, *Porque Viven Siempre entre Nosotros* (Managua: Editorial Nueva Nicaragua, 1982), 100-01.

3

Daniel and Humberto Somoza

Daniel and Humberto Ortega were in their early thirties in 1979 when they took over the two most important positions in the Sandinista government. From the beginning of the regime, they were the first two among nine "equals" in the FSLN. One historic irony remarked on by the Nicaraguan people was that two brothers were again in charge of the country, one as president and the other as chief of the military. The brothers in question were, of course, Daniel and Humberto Ortega during the 1980s and the parallel was with Luis and Anastasio (Tacho) Somoza for a while during the Somoza dynasty. Some Nicaraguans lost no time in referring to the Ortega brothers as Luis Ortega and "Tachito" Ortega. Picking up on Marx quoting Hegel to the effect that history repeats itself, first as tragedy and then as farce, it was widely remarked that at least on this Marx and Hegel had been right: the Somozas had been a tragedy and the Ortegas were a farce, though with a terrible dose of tragedy mixed in. A second parallel is that both pairs of brothers became millionaires at the expense of the impoverished Nicaraguan people.

The Ortegas remained the most important FSLN leaders after the inauguration of President Violeta Chamorro in April 1990, though on the surface their relative positions were reversed: whereas Daniel as president during the Sandinista regime held the dominant political office of the 1980s, Humberto was the only comandante to retain a powerful position under the Chamorro government in the early 1990s. In fact, throughout the Sandinista period, Humberto's influence on Daniel often made him the dominant force behind the scenes.

We have much to say about the Ortegas elsewhere in this book, and our objective here is not to repeat those comments but to round them out with more detail. After touching briefly on their pre-1979 careers, we will focus on their lives, characteristics, and activities during the 1980s.

From Kids to Commissars

Daniel was born in 1945 and Humberto two years later, both in La Libertad, Chontales, on the eastern side of Lake Nicaragua. Though they were not founders of the FSLN, both became members early on and were among what Humberto called the "historic" comandantes, those who predated the conflicts of the 1970s. They were born into a poor family and grew up under difficult economic circumstances. Both attended Catholic schools: Daniel graduated from high school and Humberto reached the junior year. Though they were not very good students in classes, they developed substantial "street smarts" that served them well within the Sandinista movement. Humberto believed that almost everything should be decided by fighting, and he was very good at it. In fact, prior to taking power the two brothers were known as "the Ortega knifers" (los puñales Ortega).

The brothers were strongly influenced by the anti-Somoza ideas of their father and while still young became involved in military and/or terrorist activities against the Somoza government and the United States. (After Daniel was elected president in 1984 he said, "the only thing I regret is that my father can't be here.") Daniel became a member of the FSLN in 1963, recruited by Lenín Cerna, and Humberto joined officially in 1965, though both had long been active in youth movements tied to the country's official Communist party, the PSN, or the Sandinistas. Before Daniel was jailed in 1967, he participated in several bank robberies and was a member of the execution squad that killed Gonzalo Lacayo (Gonzalito), a well-known torturer of the Somoza government, on the streets of Managua.

After the Somoza crackdown on the Sandinistas in 1967, while Daniel was spending seven years in prison, Humberto moved around. He passed some time in Cuba for military training and in 1969 tried to spring Carlos Fonseca from a Costa Rican prison. During the abortive jailbreak he was injured in both arms and largely lost the use of the right one. He was jailed with Fonseca in Costa Rica but both were released in October 1970 after a LACSA airliner hijacking led by FSLN member Carlos Agüero, whose commando team included Humberto's future wife, Ligia Trejos. After military training in North Korea, he spent much time in Cuba with Fonseca. While Humberto considered this a chance to get to know the FSLN founder and his thinking better, Borge liked to charge that since

Humberto sometimes served coffee or ran errands for Fonseca, he was simply the latter's personal valet. Daniel was released from prison in 1974 in exchange for a group of prominent officials taken hostage at a party in Managua. Back in Cuba, but without Cuban support, Humberto pulled together the ideology of the Tercerista—or insurrectional—faction of the FSLN, the broad front strategy that brought Somoza down in 1979.

Humberto Ortega is often credited with devising the Tercerista strategy. But Edén Pastora, who was active in the FSLN for many years, thinks Ortega has gotten a lot more credit than he deserves. Pastora says Humberto Ortega's greatest talent during the war against Somoza was in surrounding himself with people who were more capable than himself and then, at least at times, listening to them. These included Herty Lewites, Carlos Coronel and Pastora himself, who for years had urged a more open policy than the FSLN's Marxist-Leninist leaders would accept. As noted above, Borge said the FSLN was formed to pull in all Nicaraguans who opposed the dictator, but it fact Fonseca and the others had closed the door on a broadly based movement. Pastora is undoubtedly correct when he concludes that the FSLN never would have won the war against Somoza at all if Fonseca had lived, since he, the dominant founding leader, was so passionately sectarian. As early as 1970, in a meeting in Mexico with Henry Ruiz, Borge, Arce—the least flexible of Sandinista leaders—and others, Pastora urged the opening of the movement to other sectors. Nothing happened. Several years later, in Costa Rica, Pastora began to organize a broader movement including Ernesto Cardenal, Tito Castillo, Carlos Coronel and Samuel Santos, among others, and tried to get the Frente to open to these people. Later in the decade, when the distinctive Tercerista line was finally promoted by the Ortegas, it was essentially what Pastora and some others had proposed for years. As always, Pastora says, Humberto had compiled the relevant data, processed it and used it to his advantage. Thus in reality, according to Pastora, Tercerismo was the creation of many people, including Carlos Coronel and himself, as compiled and presented by Ortega. On the other hand, Robert Leiken has noted that even the basic Tercerista documents often read like united front statements of the Communist International and reflect a strong grounding in those ideas and documents.[1]

The Ortegas were the most pragmatic of the nine comandantes, and Humberto more so than Daniel. Both began as romantic, ultranationalistic, anti-American Marxists, but as the years passed they became increasingly inclined to use ideology to get and maintain power and privilege. Indeed, Humberto was a sort of Noriega who was prepared to ally himself with anyone if that suited his needs at the moment: he cooperated with Alfonso Robelo and the social democrats to seize power from Somoza, he joined the Soviet bloc to maintain power during the 1980s, and in early 1992 he gave a medal to the U.S. military attaché in Managua as part of his move to make himself acceptable in Washington.

In many respects the two brothers held the same or similar positions on major political issues, but in most other respects Humberto and Daniel were not at all alike. Daniel was somewhat more committed to Marxist ideology and less flexible in his thinking and actions than Humberto and often sought his younger brother's advice. Within the Sandinista movement, Daniel was more disciplined and a better mediator, often effectively rebuilding political fences that Humberto (or others) had knocked down. We have already noted that Daniel often acted as a bridge between his brother and Borge, but there are many other examples of his finding a compromise or getting his way. For example, Ernesto Cardenal, frustrated by the culture-related bullying of Daniel's wife, Rosario Murillo, several times tendered his resignation as cultural minister, but Daniel always convinced him to remain in office. He did the same for many years with Moisés Hassan, the professor and undercover Sandinista whose membership in the 1979 Government Junta tipped the balance in the direction of the FSLN. From the first year, Hassan was a critic of the demise of the revolutionary mystique. He was removed from the Junta in 1981, but he stayed on to serve in ministerial and vice ministerial positions until 1985 when he tendered his resignation from the FSLN. Daniel talked with him at great length to get him to stay, arguing that he should not leave the FSLN during the war, that none of the other parties offered him anything better, and that his critique of the Sandinistas was just and would be acted upon as soon as the war was over. Hassan spent the next four years as Sandinista mayor of Managua. But when the war was as good as over in 1988, and no reforms were made in the FSLN, Hassan resigned again and became an open critic of the regime.[2]

Mirror, Mirror, on the Wall

Humberto, more than Daniel, was always conscious of carrying his image as an infallible Comandante of the Revolution. This meant he expected Nicaraguans to recognize him as their superior and foreigners to give him the recognition he felt was his due. He tried to maintain this elevated image in a variety of ways. For example, he did not drink alcohol unless he was with only a small group of friends. More negatively, he engaged in elaborate maneuverings and petty put-downs of others to assure or inflate his self-esteem. Since he was intensely jealous, he never wanted anyone (except Daniel) equal to or over him, as when he felt Carrión challenged him in the EPS. Also, on the petty level, Humberto thought driving was beneath his dignity. Whereas Daniel liked to drive his own car, Humberto always wanted a chauffeur, and the higher ranking the better, thus to demonstrate that he could order even such an important person as Joaquín Cuadra—not only the second in command of the army but the scion of a big name Nicaraguan family as well—to drive him around.

The defense minister constantly fished for compliments and/or reassurance. After he had given a public speech, for example, he would ask, "How did it go, Miranda?" and Miranda would respond that it was fabulous, extraordinary, or moving when in reality it had been something between tedious and terrible and everybody knew it. When Humberto spoke in public he was repetitive, often stuttered, and sometimes didn't even get his idea across. Before speaking he would practice his talk, even coordinating the gestures, but he forgot it all when he started speaking. Thus he spoke as seldom as possible and, when he couldn't avoid saying something, he tried to be brief.

Humberto could not stand being wrong. When he simply could not escape responsibility, as when he promised ground-to-air missiles to the Salvadoran guerrillas without authorization, he feigned innocence of any intentional wrongdoing. But his favorite tactic was to blame Miranda or someone else. For example, early in 1987, during the discussions by Central American governments of the Arias peace plan, Cuba sent a lieutenant colonel to be its first military attaché in Managua. This was an essentially diplomatic position, complementing the role of the Cuban military mission, which had been active undercover in Nicaragua from 1979 and therefore never had formal diplomatic status. Customarily, the arrival of an attaché would be given media coverage, but Humberto decided that such coverage would be inadvisable while negotiations were going on. So Ortega told Miranda to inform Raúl Castro of this via the then-head of Cuba's military mission in Managua, Brigadier General

Néstor López Cuba. Miranda told López and two days later the latter returned with a curt response from Raúl: "I was surprised by your message. If you don't want our military attaché, we will recall him." Humberto spoke immediately to Daniel and, probably, to some other members of the Directorate, and they decided Humberto's decision should be reversed and the attaché given formal presentation. Humberto told Miranda to apologize to López Cuba saying that he, Miranda, had misunderstood Humberto's original message.

Humberto's ego also created tensions with the Cubans, though when it came to Fidel and Raúl he sometimes gave in. For example, Cuban advisers in Nicaragua always called Humberto "Minister," which he was, and that was what they called Cuban Defense Minister Raúl Castro. But Humberto wanted to be addressed by his military title, "Commander in Chief," which differentiated him from other ministers and even implied that he was "chief" of the nine ruling commanders. In Cuba that title was reserved for Fidel. When calling him "Minister," the Cubans were failing to massage Humberto's ego and showing their inability to adapt to specifically Nicaraguan conditions, which Humberto took as a personal put-down.

An instance of tensions with the Castros occurred just before the thirtieth anniversary of the Cuban Revolutionary Armed Forces (FAR) in November 1986. Humberto was invited to attend and the Cubans said they would give him the award of the thirtieth anniversary in a special ceremony. Humberto felt he should be given some more distinguished and unusual award, but Raúl insisted that the anniversary award would be especially honorific because he, Raúl, was conferring it. Humberto considered not going, or sending Joaquín Cuadra, but he and Daniel decided that that would simply make relations worse and he should accept the humiliation. Humberto remarked to Miranda on how hard it was to deal with Raúl, whom he called "the Chinaman" (el chino). However humiliating it may be, he said, "the poor brothers in the family sometimes have to suffer the whims of the rich ones."

Like Fidel, Humberto and Daniel delighted in demonstrating their importance by making others wait for them, whether at a meeting of the National Directorate or elsewhere. But behind that image he (Humberto) was vacillating, insecure, suspicious, often changing his mind, and not bothered by openly lying when he thought it would serve his personal interests to do so.

Humberto was careful with his physical appearance, indeed downright vain, and it was he who finally got Daniel to scrub up, cut his hair and dress better after their years of fighting against Somoza. Under the influence of Sergio Ramírez and Miguel D'Escoto, Daniel soon began wearing civilian suits at some international meetings, except when Humberto pressured him into wearing the olive green military suits the comandantes had all received as gifts from Fidel Castro. Daniel suddenly became hip in his dressing during the 1990 presidential campaign when he thought a new image would get him more votes. Humberto preferred to stay with the military uniforms most of the time. These suits, Humberto thought, gave him a distinct personality, and he wore his neatly ironed with four gold stars on each shoulder. On occasions when he did not wear his military clothes, Humberto was a careful, often natty dresser with expensive European and North American tastes, wearing leather shoes by Bally, shirts and pants by Pierre Cardin, a Rolex watch, and smoking Marlboros. He would spend long periods of time looking at himself in mirrors to be sure his glasses, his shirt or pants, looked just right.

Socially speaking, Daniel was generally reserved, austere, even glum or hardbitten, lacking in graces and personality. But Humberto was more gregarious, almost always energetic and at least on the surface a confident and secure man. Humberto is a great dancer, for example, at parties excelling especially in cumbias and mambo, while Daniel can hardly dance at all.

Nicknames and the Movies

Nicaraguans have a strong tradition of giving nicknames and after taking power the Ortegas began using private nicknames for most of those they worked or dealt with. Among the members of the National Directorate: Borge was "Maria Elena" because they thought of him as a woman, always whining or bellyaching, especially about Humberto; Arce was "the growler" (*el gruñon*), because of his grumpy personality; Víctor Tirado, a Mexican by birth, was "El Chachalaco," so tagged because of his physical resemblance—a large upper lip—to a comic actor on Mexican television; Luis Carrión was "Buggerman" (*el mocoso*) because he was always picking his nose; Carlos Núñez was "Big Mouth" (*trompudo*) because of his big mouth; Jaime Wheelock was "the farmer" (*el agricultor*) because of his work as head of the Department of Agriculture; and Henry Ruiz was "the humble one" (*el humilde*) because of his relatively simpler life-style. Ruiz's other nicknames among the Sandinistas were "the peasant" (*el Campesino*) or his alias during the war against Somoza, Modesto.

Outside of the National Directorate were Sergio Ramírez, called "Rag Doll" (*la muñecona*) because of his physical appearance, army Chief-of-Staff Joaquín Cuadra, known as Achilles after the Greek warrior who had the one vulnerability, Cuadra's "heel" being his social extraction from a wealthy family, and Lenín Cerna, the head of State Security, who was "the monster" (*el monstruo*) partly because of his tubby appearance but mainly because his behavior in his job was that of a monster. Among the foreigners, besides Raúl Castro, who as we have noted was called "the Chinaman," there were: Fidel Castro, "The Master of the Cheeses" (*el Señor de los Quesos*), because he so loved, served, and talked about cheeses, and Panamanian leader Manuel Antonio Noriega, branded "Crimeface" (*Cara de crimen*) because of his scarred face and criminal activities. Prominent North American officials, including Ronald Reagan, were generally called by their actual names.

Humberto was a street fighter himself and preferred movies that somehow paralleled his life-style. Like most other top Sandinista officials, he preferred violent movies from the United States, such as "Rambo" and "Dirty Harry," though he also was drawn to Mexican films, particularly those of comedian Cantinflas. Humberto did not like Soviet or Cuban films, as he—and other comandantes—had nothing but contempt for most Soviet products in general, which were uniformly of low quality and boring. Each year Humberto was invited to vacation in the Soviet Union, and each year he refused, going instead to Cuba, Mexico, or the Nicaraguan resort of Montelimar, an old Somoza ranch on the Pacific coast.

See Who's Under the Bed

Humberto constantly felt personal and impersonal threats to his well-being. He was always afraid that someone was waiting around the corner to shoot, poison, or otherwise kill him. He was attended during the day by Joaquín Cuadra and Roger Miranda. He worked in what had been the last Somoza's bunker, which he left almost unchanged from the dictator's day. To be sure, he put up portraits of Sandino and Fonseca, and Somoza's bed was replaced by a large conference table and an exhibit of guns. But otherwise it was much the same as Somoza left it. Humberto even used Somoza's desk. When sitting at his desk in Somoza's bunker, although almost no one knew it, Humberto kept a .357 Magnum revolver in his lap to forestall any assassination attempt.

Humberto's house was a fortress with thick walls and several hundred guards who were always around: he played baseball with them, ate with them, and made them virtually part of his family. He kept close watch over their activities by reading their mail, getting them to spy on each other, and so forth. One escort named Vanegas always tried Humberto's food to be sure it was safe to eat, at times joking, "Comandante Ortega eats my leftovers." In 1982 some of Ortega's personal guard went to Puerto Cabezas and participated in the executions of a number of Miskito Indians who had risen up against the government. Humberto approved of this use of his guard because, once having taken part in such executions, it would be more difficult for them later to betray him and they would, at the same time, be less hesitant to kill anyone who threatened their chief's life. On the impersonal level, he was terrified of airplanes and would travel by air only when no other form of transportation was possible. When he did fly he would grasp the arms of the seat so tightly on takeoff and landing that his knuckles would turn white.

Ligia, Rosario, and their Families

Being so different, the Ortegas only visited each other at home on business affairs. They had no joint family or social activities that could be avoided. They did not get together for holidays such as Christmas, each family having its own celebration, nor did one ever turn up at the other's birthday party. But this isolation from each other was not just because of personal differences; it was also because their even more different wives hated each other as much as Humberto hated Tomás.

Daniel's wife, Rosario Murillo, is a bossy, dominating woman who had a strong impact on her husband's work at several levels. She came from a family that could send her to study in Switzerland and England, where she developed a liking for cultural activities, especially writing poetry. She always dressed in flashy, unusual clothes, and her attire and actions often led Humberto to mumble to his closest friends, "That woman is disgracing Daniel."

Some considered Rosario the real power behind Daniel and thought her hand could be seen in his speeches as well as both of their actions. There was no speculation about some of her other powers. She ran many of the cultural affairs of the country through a new organization Daniel created for her, the so-called Sandinista Association of Cultural Workers (Asociación Sandinista de Trabajadores de la Cultura; ASTC). The ASTC was charged with spreading "Sandinista culture," though it was never entirely clear what that culture was. She often rendered the minister of culture, Ernesto Cardenal, a mere figurehead. (An exiled secretary-general of the ministry says he once heard Cardenal raving about Rosario, "That bitch! She's worse than Dinorah," referring to Somoza's mistress.)[3] Humberto's reaction was unequivocal: "What damn use is there having that woman directing cultural activities from that outfit when there is already a ministry of culture!"

On other occasions she called on Daniel to help her manipulate others in the government. One day in 1982, for example, she called Roger Miranda to ask the EPS to loan her a couple of military trucks to carry an artistic group from Managua to Matagalpa. Seeing no reason why trucks intended for troops should be used in this way, Miranda said none were available. A few minutes later Daniel called and in a most amiable tone said, "Miranda, could you do me a little favor and help Rosario out with a couple of trucks for an activity tomorrow in Matagalpa?" "I'll take care of it, comandante," Miranda answered. She got the trucks and whatever else she wanted in the future, so as to keep Daniel from having to call again.

Humberto's wife, Ligia Trejos, known as Marcela, was just the opposite of Rosario, an unassuming woman in her actions and dress, with almost no public profile. A Costa Rican by birth, she was long a member of the FSLN and one of her husband's rescuers from the Costa Rican jail in 1970. After 1979 she worked part-time in the FSLN's research institute but quietly devoted most of her time to raising their three daughters and two sons. (One of the girls was Ligia's, and one of the boys Humberto's, by other partners, the boy living most of the time in Cuba with his natural mother). Ligia proudly admitted, "I live for Humberto and my children." Humberto said, "I do politics while my wife takes care of the children; she does what I can't do, and I do what she can't do. It's a natural division of labor." Comparing Ligia to Rosario, Humberto added: "If I had a wife like Rosario, I would long since have thrown her on the compost heap."

This opinion was long shared by most members of the FSLN. At the first FSLN congress in July 1991, when party members for the first time had a chance to vote on members of the Sandinista Assembly, Rosario was conspicuously and overwhelmingly voted out of office.

Like most of the other comandantes, Humberto was a womanizer, consciously a symbol of machismo who enjoyed having affairs with the wives of friends and subordinates though he was less obvious about it than Borge or Arce. He had some problems with Ligia as a result, and yet in other respects he was a good father with a deep devotion to the well-being of his family. Whenever possible, the two parents avoid travelling together in case there should be an accident and the children be left without parents. In 1987, when his wife needed a serious operation, Humberto took her to Mexico. Raúl Castro in particular was offended by this, during a time of already rocky bilateral relations, since the Cubans made much of their supposed medical advances. But Humberto said, "The Chinaman can eat shit if he thinks my family is going to be dependent on his favors. Besides, I don't have much confidence in the quality of Cuban medicine."

Humberto also had other characteristics that should be noted. Like Somoza, he understood that for many people personal relations, such as the giving of sinecures and other gifts (including money) was more important than ideology. In most cases, he cultivated real loyalty from those who worked with him. He knew how and when to forgive mistakes, to give a person a bonus or another chance, and he remembered those who had done him a favor. He generally avoided precipitate action, tried to listen to all parties in a conflict, and was truly sympathetic in his way toward the needs of the poor.

While usually Humberto was patient, he had impulsive moments as well. On occasion he said or did things during these moments that later caused him no end of trouble. For example, in 1981 he remarked that there were not enough lampposts in Managua to hang all the opposition leaders that needed to be eliminated, a comment for which he was admonished by the Directorate. And at the end of 1989, after the U.S. invasion of Panama, he threatened death to opposition leaders who supported any U.S. action against Nicaragua.

Notes

1. Ratliff interviews with Pastora, 19 March and 20 March 1992. Also, Ratliff phone interview with Robert Leiken (in London) on 10 April 1992.

2. Ratliff interview with Hassan, Palo Alto, CA, 2 May 1991.
3. Xavier Argüello, quoted in Lloyd Grove's largely fawning article, "Rosario's Revolution," *Vanity Fair*, July 1986, p. 63.

4

The New Rich

During their years fighting in the countryside and urban areas, or when living abroad, the Sandinista comandantes repeatedly proclaimed their adherence to ideals of justice, humility and equality. One component of the powerful revolutionary mystique was the routine and at first largely sincere downplaying of material goods, the love of which was regarded as a petite bourgeois weakness. Their chief target of criticism was the Somoza family, but the attack was leveled as well at all who robbed or exploited for personal gain. The condemnations of exploiters continued into the new government, as when Daniel Ortega said on 7 January 1980: "Our revolution has to look with suspicion on all people who refuse to understand that the right to rob, the right to exploit can not exist in this country. . . that against these Pharisees Christ used the right of force and threw them out of the temple with a whip." Almost exactly a decade later, in his concession to Violeta Chamorro, Ortega promised that the Sandinistas would abide by the results of the election and concluded: "We were born poor and will be satisfied to die poor."

But in fact it wasn't like that at all. In this chapter we will tell how the vanguard—we will focus mainly on the two Ortegas, though they were not the only ones who did it—took over luxurious real estate and turned to gracious living immediately after taking power. Even as their chosen policies set the economy in a tailspin, prompted foreign opposition to the regime and precipitated ever greater suffering for the majority of the people, the Sandinistas as individuals and as a movement seized large portions of the nation's remaining wealth and became the new bourgeoisie or even aristocracy. This systematic pillage began in July 1979 with quickly honed skills at fleecing the nation. The systematic and comprehensive pillage peaked between the election and the inauguration in 1990 during the "piñata" land-grab.

The Sandinistas Go Bourgeois

After the overthrow of Somoza, the majority of the Sandinista militants blatantly helped themselves to everything they could get their hands
on. Those comandantes and other top officials who did not so obviously
do so, like Henry Ruiz, were an exception, though even Ruiz raised
questions. For example, the United States ambassador to Mexico during
the early Sandinista years, John Gavin, remembers meeting Ruiz and
noting that he was wearing designer clothes from head to foot, and Edén
Pastora has said he isn't sure whether Ruiz was "humble in his arrogance
or arrogant in his humility."[1] The Sandinistas themselves did not really
grasp the increasing level of resentment toward them, and how isolated
they had become from the Nicaraguan people, until they lost the 1990
elections by a landslide. And this reality was missed by many foreign
visitors and supporters who went to Nicaragua wanting to be impressed
rather than trying to objectively evaluate the policies and actions of the
FSLN, the conditions and preferences of the people, and the good of the
country and its neighbors. Increasingly during the 1980s, the mystique
became a fog of deception the Sandinistas hid behind and their foreign
admirers could not penetrate.

Perks of the New Rich

After July 1979 all sorts of property throughout the country, but
especially in Managua, became war booty, with goods distributed according to power and prestige within the Sandinista movement. An enormous
hoard of riches was left by the Somozas and their closest friends, from
ranches and houses to furniture and electrical appliances. Almost all of
it fell into the hands of high members of the FSLN, especially the nine
comandantes. They did not take it over in their own names, but as
"property of the people" (*area de propiedad del pueblo*), or APP. During
the early years of the revolution, one frequently heard members of the
Directorate and Sandinistas one level below them say, "All this I have is
not mine, it belongs to the people, to the revolution. We didn't fight for
personal reward but for the well being of the people." As time passed,
fewer and fewer Sandinistas expressed the thought this way, particularly
at the top levels of the movement.

After July 1979, it was common to see a group of armed militants arrive at a house and take it over in the name of Comandante So and So. Sometimes several Sandinistas wanted the same prize. At times those who had already taken over a house in the name of a prominent member of the FSLN had to move on if a troop from one of the nine comandantes arrived and demanded occupancy. The real problems arose when groups representing two or more of the nine arrived at the same place; then all held their ground until it was negotiated by the comandantes themselves.

The whole concept of people's property was copied from the Cubans and hard for the ordinary Nicaraguan to understand. In particular it was hard for "the people" to understand that all these riches confiscated from the Somozas were theirs when only certain sectors of the FSLN benefited directly from them. Since all the property that was confiscated was called "property of the people"—houses, factories, luxurious vehicles, land—it wasn't long before ordinary people were passing a number of judgments, saying, "Well, these things may be called the property of the people or whatever you like, but the fact is that someone else is using them for us"; or "If this factory is the people's, then I have a right to take this desk home with me."

The Sandinistas said they were simply confiscating properties of Somoza and his supporters and thus the takeovers didn't cost the people anything. But not all the property taken had been owned by the Somozas or their top associates, and most of what was occupied was subsequently put through large-scale, costly renovation, all of which was charged to the national budget as a "people's expense." Perhaps the most extreme cases were those of Tomás Borge and Humberto Ortega.

Borge first moved into the mansion of General Luna in Los Robles and lived in Roman splendor until the Directorate told him the luxury he had adopted was too conspicuous. Then he moved into the mansion of Luis Manuel Debayle, an uncle of Somoza and a symbol of Somocismo. Pastora among others publicly criticized the extravagance of his life there. So he then moved to a lower-middle-class sector of Managua called Bello Horizonte, trying to give the impression he had not departed from the mystique of years past.[2] There he took over half the barrio and turned several dozen small dwellings into one mansion for himself with a perimeter of guard houses, remodeling everything and topping it off with an Olympic-sized swimming pool. Humberto confronted Borge one day at a meeting of the Directorate, saying "Tomás, the last time I came back from Cuba I saw your swimming pool from the air." And he added, sarcastically, "Don't you think it's a bit large? Everyone who flies in is commenting on it." A little taken aback by the challenge, Borge responded, "Why I don't know. It's the first time I've heard any comment on it," which may have been literally true though the story of the pool was spreading through the upper levels of the FSLN. Humberto himself loved to use the pool story to scoff at the "false populism of Tomás." In any event, shortly after the confrontation with Humberto, Borge turned the pool area into a club that could be used by certain MINT officials. Borge also had other expensive tastes, such as traveling for a while in an armored car, while other officials used Toyotas or Jeeps.

Humberto Ortega took over three houses in the luxurious Santa Maria de los Lagos sector south of Managua on the road to Masaya. He joined them together and remodeled them to his and his wife's tastes at a cost of almost $100,000. The remodeled house included a master bedroom with smoked glass walls looking out on a private garden, large kennels for his dogs, and a baseball field where he played with off-duty guards. He built a high wall around the house, in keeping with the tendency of Managua during the 1980s to become a City of Walls. With a salary of no more than $300 per month, Humberto also had seventeen servants for himself and his family, not counting the security forces.

Daniel Ortega took over the luxurious house of Jaime Morales, an anti-Somoza banker, businessman, and columnist for *La Prensa*, in the El Carmen residential district. By a series of "legal" maneuvers, the house, which with additions became two blocks long, was his throughout the 1980s. Father Miguel D'Escoto, who became Sandinista foreign minister, helped himself to the magnificent estate and fabulous art collection of banker Roberto Incer. Just before the 1990 election, a journalist for the Mexican leftist paper *La Jornada* asked Vice President Sergio Ramírez about allegations of Sandinista corruption. Ramírez responded, "I own nothing. The house I live in is state property, and I will move out when I leave office." But as the journalist then observed,

Ramírez lied. During the two months before the inauguration, the Sandinistas gave themselves over, with a rapacity rarely seen, to transferring thousands of urban and rural properties and hundreds of state enterprises into the hands of fellow party members and all by means of fraudulent sale or outright donation. . . . In order to cover their greed with a false humanitarian veneer, the Sandinistas have also given tens of thousands of impoverished slum dwellers legal title to their pathetic little plots.

The Sandinistas looted the House of Government of desks, chairs, typewriters, computers, television cameras, video cassettes, files, paintings, even bathroom towels. They transferred into their hands state-owned vehicles, including motorcycles, tractors, military trucks and even Mercedes sedans. They took radio transmitters, shops, factories, hotels, restaurants, travel agencies, import-export offices, amusement parks, and huge ranches, everything adding up to more than a million acres. And they then destroyed most of the evidence, from bank files to government documents. The Mexican journalist estimated they stole some $700 million in state property, and the private property they took must have been at least twice that.[3]

Daniel Ortega loudly defended his keeping the Morales house, and in effect the entire Sandinista grab, when he told Extravision TV in Managua: "I have never had my own home, and I believe I have the right to one. . . . Because of the commitment I have with the poor and destitute, I am not going to leave the house." To do so, he concluded, would be like telling the government to expel "thousands of poor people" from their land and houses. But the grab infuriated many Sandinista followers who felt the whole spirit of the movement and years of work had been disgraced, and it humiliated those foreign supporters who retained even a shadow of objectivity. Moisés Hassan called this pilfering of the destitute nation's resources "an incredible raping of the country."[4] When the anti-Sandinista delegates who controlled the legislature after the election raised the "piñata" issue in the summer of 1991, Luis Sanchez Sancho, the leader of the Communist PSN, branded the FSLN Nicaragua's "new landlords, new latifundistas, new oligarchs." He voiced a common attack on the piñata beneficiaries when he wrote, "A person who hangs out in a million-dollar mansion taken by force from its legitimate owners does not have the moral authority to speak for the poor. Nor do those who enriched themselves with other people's things at the cost of the total misery of almost all the Nicaraguan people."[5]

While in office, the comandantes set up foreign bank accounts to stash away money they filched from their ministries, private business deals, and elsewhere. Mario Castillo, known as "Concho," who set up Humberto's accounts, is discussed later. Daniel's "Concho" was Herty Lewites, much of whose fortune came from founding the dollar stores, from restaurants and from the tourism industry which he managed as

Tourism Minister; Borge's was Paul Atha; and Arce's was Samuel Santos.

The nine comandantes—and Sergio Ramírez and René Núñez, who became members of the National Directorate in July 1991—traveled through the city in armed caravans. These caravans automatically took the right of way, ignored traffic signals, and jammed the streets. Fidel Castro traveled this way in Cuba, but he was only one person. To make things worse, in Managua these caravans were moving around all the time at high speeds in a city with very few good streets, causing many accidents. Anyone who tried to pass a caravan was fired upon by private guards concerned that the person passing might be trying to attack the official, first with a warning burst and then shots directly at their car. This security policy was never explained to the population, however, so that over the years many people were machine gunned and never even knew why. When non-Sandinista Nicaraguans were asked about the caravans, a typical response was: "Look, friend, during Somoza's time we didn't have this problem. People seldom encountered a Somoza caravan, but now you run into at least one every day."

One particularly embarrassing experience occurred in early 1982. Alejandro, the chief of the Soviet military mission, and some of his colleagues, were returning from Lagoon Masaya in a Toyota microbus. Unexpectedly, they were sprayed with machine gun fire when their driver tried to pass Humberto Ortega's unmarked caravan. Typically, Humberto's caravan did not stop to see what damage had been done to whom; in this case the shots had immobilized the car by puncturing its radiator and shooting out its tires, but there were no injuries. Early the next day Alejandro arrived at Humberto's office, very concerned and to say the least annoyed. Humberto apologized, saying "I beg your forgiveness, but you know that we are the constant targets of the CIA and can never lower our guard." Alejandro responded, "Comrade Minister, I understand what you are saying, but it had better not happen again." Shortly after this incident, phosphorescent gloves were obtained from Panama so that the manual warning signals could be given and seen at night. Humberto Ortega continued to use a caravan after the 1990 election and in October of that year his guards were accused of fatally shooting a teenager when the latter reportedly tried to pass the general's convoy.[6]

Humberto and the Concho Scam

The Concho scam showed that the conspiracies churning within the lives of the gods of Managua, as Moisés Hassan describes the comandantes, were just as great as those experienced by the gods of Olympus. And it showed how a tricky businessman/gangster who had represented the Alfa Romeo firm during the Somoza period could manipulate Humberto's vanity and put millions of dollars from a destitute country in his own pocket and that of his comandante sponsor. Indeed, Concho-type scams were carried out by the con men of other top officials as well and showed how much top Sandinistas gave in to the temptations of power and self-aggrandizement.

Mario Castillo was on the verge of bankruptcy in mid-1979 when he met Humberto through Joaquín Cuadra and began massaging the comandante's enormous ego. Concho was the only person who openly called Humberto commander-in-chief; privately, he elaborated to Humberto: "In this country there are ministers and ministries, but there can only be one commander-in-chief." Ortega's large ego swelled to hear such things. Concho then convinced Ortega that he should not just carry out today's revolution but put something aside for the future. He urged the creation of an office to centralize foreign purchases—those in dollars—for the EPS that could charge a commission that would go into a personal account for the defense minister. His argument was simple, "Look, chief, business is business and you won't be doing anything illegal. It is perfectly normal to collect commissions for being an intermediary between buyer and seller."

First Humberto and Daniel arranged for the cancellation of Concho's debts. Then Humberto gave Concho about $500,000 no one knew was left over from the contributions of governments and individuals during the war against Somoza. Concho formed a corporation in Panama called Alfa Comercial, registered in the names of Castillo and his wife (surname Sánchez)—the sister of Contra leader Aristides Sánchez—so as to avoid the negative publicity that would come if someone found out Ortega had an account in his own name and deposited the money in it. He was made the chief purchasing agent for EPS deals involving dollars, charging up to 40 percent commissions. Originally, deposits were made in the National Bank of Paris in Panama. Additional funds were siphoned off through the so-called reserves of the Commander-in-Chief.

The money in these accounts supported the high life-styles of Humberto and his extended family, Concho, and his family, and were used to buy the "necessities" of the high life for the top military officers: fancy houses, Betamaxes, Rolex watches, Toyota land cruisers and American appliances—the trademarks of the new elite—which officers could get only from Humberto in the comandante's name.

By 1984 Concho was becoming the subject of much talk in Managua, for it had not gone unnoticed that he had become conspicuously rich during the short time he had been purchasing agent for the EPS. Humberto decided Concho should move to Spain where he could set up an import/export office. But when Concho left, Humberto lost control of him. Concho finally ended up in Miami. He returned about $1 million from the account to Humberto, but kept at least that much for himself, no one being quite sure how much he got since he had the only complete records. Humberto had to start again almost from scratch. From the beginning of 1985 through 1987, his new account (#58946) was tended by Roger Miranda. It was in the National Bank of Paris, this time in Switzerland, in the names of personal aides Ramiro Contreras and Roberto Sánchez. By the end of 1987 it had grown again to nearly $1.5 million.

But Humberto did not forget Concho. In early 1987 the comandante met in his office with the Argentine guerrilla Enrique Gorriarán Merlo. Gorriarán had spent much of the late 1970s and 1980s in Nicaragua, where he was known as Frank or Baldy (*el Pelado*), living in a house in Villa Panama given him by the FSLN National Directorate. As a leader of the People's Revolutionary Army (ERP) guerrilla force in Argentina during the early and mid-1970s, he had picked up considerable experience and a solid reputation as a political assassin; indeed, he had personally led the attack that killed Somoza in Paraguay in September 1980. Humberto told Gorriarán he needed "exemplary punishment" for someone who had stolen several million dollars from the EPS. Gorriarán said "no problem," until he heard that Concho lived in the United States. He asked for a couple of months to investigate and was advanced $10,000 to do so. Six weeks later he sent a message to Humberto via his wife giving extensive detail on Concho, his contacts and his daily activities, but concluded:

General, if you tell us to go ahead with this mission we will do so, but permit me to say that the United States is not Paraguay. The police system there is very tight and any small mistake we might make could have serious repercussions for ourselves and for you. The operation is possible, but the price you have to pay in case of a mistake may be too high. General, think about this and tell me your decision via my wife.

Humberto knew Gorriarán was brave but also prudent, and in a couple of days he decided the price of this "exemplary punishment" was too high and the matter was dropped.

Notes

1. Ratliff interviews with Gavin, in Los Angeles, CA, 1 October 1991, and with Pastora, 19 March 1992.
2. He went to great and often unsuccessful efforts to try to convince some visitors of his stoicism. See, for example, Merie Linda Wolin, "Nicaragua Under the Sandinistas: Borge," *Los Angeles Herald Examiner*, 5 May 1985.
3. See Joaquín Ibarz, "Piñata Theology," originally published in *La Jornada*, 12 May 1991, trans. Timothy Goodman in *Crisis*, September 1991.
4. Quoted in William Ratliff, "Out of Power, Sandinistas Still Act Like Kings, *The Wall Street Journal*, 26 July 1991.
5. Luis Sánchez Sancho, "Sandinistas defienden 'La piñata,'" *El Nicaraguense*, Managua, 14–20 Junio de 1991; Luis Sánchez Sancho, *La Prensa*, 11 June 1991.
6. Jose de Córdoba, "A Political Neophyte and an Ex-Sandinista Run Nicaragua Today," *The Wall Street Journal*, 12 September 1991.

PART II
Sandinista Thinking and Allies

5

Worldview and Ideology

As Somoza government corruption increased dramatically in the wake of the 1972 earthquake, opposition to the dictator spread across almost all social and economic classes in Nicaragua. Disgust with Somoza led to dozens of guerrilla attacks and other efforts by many Nicaraguans to end the dynasty. But within the spectrum of armed and nonarmed opposition to Somoza, the Sandinistas considered themselves unique. And they were, but not entirely for the reasons they thought. They believed their uniqueness lay in the correctness of their worldview and ideology. The FSLN's founders and militants were convinced that they alone had dug deeply into the true national and international roots of Nicaragua's dictatorship and underdevelopment. It followed, they thought, that they alone would be able to lead the long and painful struggles that would bring both an end to the Somozas and then constructive revolutionary change in the future. But in fact their uniqueness lay in the mere *existence* of a militant ideology (whatever its content) that could hold them together for many years as a band of determined fighters even when they were dealt severe blows by Somoza's guard. And while it served them well during the war against Somoza, it also closed their minds to the true, potentially constructive alternatives before them once they were in power.

The Sandinistas always loudly professed a dedication to revolution founded in a passionate nationalism and a carefully cultivated revolutionary mystique. In moments of candor they admitted an adherence to their own version of Marxism-Leninism, which seemed to give them greater intellectual substance and coherence than other opponents of the dictator. For years these convictions and dedications sustained the FSLN through Somoza's repression, even when on several occasions they were reduced to a handful of members, split into warring factions, or torn by power rivalries after taking power in 1979. The convictions of the FSLN leaders were buttressed by the encouragement of thousands of "internationalists," militant foreign supporters of the Sandinistas from the United States, Europe and other Latin American countries. There were often as many as two thousand internationalists in Nicaragua at a time after the revolution, for short to extended periods of time. Moisés Hassan has said that these "anti-imperialist," antibusiness, usually Marxist foreigners had an "incalculable influence," direct and indirect, on the thought and actions of the new government. According to Edén Pastora, these American intellectuals, churchmen and others were often more anti-gringo than the Sandinistas themselves and they had a great impact both in Nicaragua and in shaping views in the United States.[1]

Before and after July 1979, the Sandinista worldview reflected above all else the FSLN's strategic vision of Nicaragua's historical and anticipated future relationship with the United States and the conviction that the "East" and "liberation" would defeat the "West" and "repression" in the Cold War. Nicaraguan foreign and domestic policies—which the Sandinistas always considered intimately related—were determined or at least greatly influenced by their view of the United States and its political and economic systems. Sandinista ideology flowed from and reinforced this worldview.

This perspective led to a four-isms view of Nicaragua and the world and how to deal with both. The four isms were: (1) anti-imperialism, mainly meaning anti-Americanism, and the expectation of inevitable conflict with the United States; (2) proletarian internationalism, or the need for ties to the governments of Cuba and the Soviet bloc, which the Sandinistas were confident would prevail over the gringos in the end; (3) revolutionary internationalism, or support for anti-imperialist revolutionaries around the world, emphasizing after 1979 the Farabundo Martí National Liberation Front (FMLN) guerrillas in El Salvador; and (4) democratic centralism, that is the pursuit of political, economic, and military independence, consolidation, and development through absolute power residing in the National Directorate of the FSLN, the vanguard of the vanguard.

Anti-imperialism/Anti-Americanism

At the core of the Sandinista movement was a militant nationalism born of a particular reading of modern Nicaraguan history. Almost all

Nicaraguans have a strong sense of nationalism that makes them critical, in varying ways and degrees, of U.S. policy toward their country during the twentieth century. The significance of this attitude toward the United States tends to be discounted by North Americans, who have little real sense of history or recent experience with being the underdog in a bilateral or multilateral relationship.

The two essential aspects of U.S. policy that historically drew the most criticism and resentment from Nicaraguans were: (1) U.S. intervention in Nicaragua's internal affairs, even if usually at the request of some Nicaraguan player in a domestic power struggle, sometimes followed by a period of U.S. military presence; and (2) U.S. involvement in the creation of, and then in varying degrees support for, the National Guard and the Somoza family dynasty. Many Nicaraguans believed U.S. policy was guided by the sentiment expressed in the evidently apocryphal comment about Somoza attributed to Franklin Roosevelt: "He may be a sonofabitch, but he's our sonofabitch." Most Nicaraguans—Sandinistas and non-Sandinistas—suffered to some degree under Somoza and the guard, including many who were less hostile toward Washington's real and alleged role in these events and relationships. For the Sandinistas and many other Nicaraguans, the main historical figure around whom criticism of the U.S. had long revolved was Sandino, who had led an uprising that focused in part on anti-imperialism from the late-1920s until he was ambushed and murdered in February 1934 by national guardsmen under the orders of Anastasio Somoza García.

But the degrees of criticism and the spirit of the nationalism itself were very different among Nicaraguans, and the differences were decisive. Most Nicaraguans could be considered "moderates" in their attitudes toward the United States; while some of these looked favorably on the United States, all considered it suicidal to pick a fight with such a gigantic and powerful neighbor. They recognized, sometimes grudgingly, that because of its proximity, size, and strength, the United States was bound to be their main trading partner and a major force influencing their lives. But they believed those influences could be reduced and/or made more constructive than destructive if the proper relationship could be found.[2]

The Sandinista view of the United States, on the other hand, was always much more hostile and, not coincidentally, paralleled that of Fidel Castro in Cuba. It was based on a totally negative reading of U.S. involvement in Nicaragua, past, present, and projected into the future. It

72   The Civil War in Nicaragua

judged the United States, no matter which political party was in power, to be inherently opposed to free and independent political and economic development in Nicaragua or anywhere in the Third World. Since this view saw the United States as an inevitable and mortal adversary of Nicaraguan independence, and thus of the Nicaraguan people, no Sandinista militant thought that after the fall of Somoza in July 1979 the United States would sit by and watch its Central American empire slip away country by country. Thus for the Sandinistas, and their leaders in particular, the only serious questions were when the showdown with the United States would come and what form it would take.

What is more, contrary to the image the Sandinistas often tried to project publicly, the inevitable confrontation was not with Republicans as distinct from Democrats, nor with Ronald Reagan as a "conservative cowboy" in contrast to Jimmy Carter, the champion of human rights. The conflict was with American administrations generally, for to the Sandinistas, the two major parties were not fundamentally different. "The two parties have a common denominator," Daniel Ortega said several times before the Sandinista Assembly, "and that is an imperialist mentality. In the end, Democrats and Republicans are the same; they only differ on how to destroy us. The Democrats may seem more subtle, but don't forget that they have a more bellicose history than the Republicans and have started more wars—Korea, the Dominican Republic, Vietnam."

All Sandinista domestic and international planning after the revolution was focused directly or indirectly on preparing for this eventual show-down. The rationale of Sandinista policies in the 1980s was, if conflict with the United States is inevitable, but independence is worth fighting for, then Nicaragua has to undertake domestic and foreign policies that will make the people as able as possible to defend their interests in this confrontation. One of the great triumphs of Sandinista disinformation was to convince so many outsiders that the Sandinistas were prevented from living in peace with other Nicaraguans, their neighbors, and the United States by the militantly anti-communist, bellicose Ronald Reagan.

The Sandinista attitude toward the United States was conveyed in many private comments and public statements by FSLN founder Carlos Fonseca and others during the nearly two decades between the founding of the movement and its victory in 1979.[3] In the most popular terms, it was expressed in the Sandinista anthem, which calls on the Nicaraguan people to "fight against the Yankee, the enemy of humanity." More substantially, the *72-Hour Document* states that "American imperialism" is "the rabid enemy of all peoples who are struggling to achieve their definitive liberation." At a working group of the seventy-two-hour meeting in September 1979, Luis Carrión developed this theme for FSLN militants:

The new government must place special emphasis on defense. Don't be fooled by Somoza's departure. We are beginning an even more difficult struggle which will involve more direct confrontation with the gringos. In our historical struggle for independence and socialism, this confrontation is inevitable. We must prepare for it.[4]

It was not surprising that when Daniel Ortega's September 1979 speech to the United Nations General Assembly—given just days after the seventy-two-hour meetings—was reprinted in Nicaragua, it was entitled, "Imperialism, Fundamental Enemy of the Sandinista Revolution."[5]

Though the conviction of inevitable confrontation dates back to the beginning of the Sandinista movement, if anything it increased during the course of the struggle against the Somoza dynasty. That is nowhere clearer than in the postrevolutionary (1981) revision of the 1969 historic program of the FSLN. The 1969 program, which presented the FSLN's sketchy view of Nicaragua's history and future under Sandinista leadership, was the first major official statement ever issued by the movement. In it, the FSLN explained the need for a people's patriotic army to defend the revolution "against the inevitable attacks which will be launched by the exploiting classes after they have been overthrown." In the substantially revised 1981 version, the program states that the army "will defend the rights won against the inevitable attack by the reactionary forces of the country *and Yankee imperialism.*"[6]

In early 1982, Borge explained the revolution's *true* primary objective—not the simple "war on poverty" he mentioned in July 1979, which is quoted above—in this way:

When the revolutionary victory occurred, a new phase began, during which there was still a need to unite the broadest Nicaraguan social strata in order to confront the common enemy of all Nicaraguans: U.S imperialism. This means that the new phase, which follows the victory, places the greatest emphasis on the defense of our nationality; on the struggle on behalf of the national sovereignty; on the right of self-determination; and on the need to unite all Nicaraguan patriots to confront a cruel and colossal enemy: Yankee imperialism.[7]

In practical terms, this attitude meant above all that the Sandinistas opposed anything the United States supported and supported almost anything the United States opposed. Two examples make the point. When Iranians took over the American embassy in Teheran, the Nicaraguan delegate to the United Nations, Víctor Hugo Tinoco, stated, "While we do not agree with the Iranian process and methodology that contravenes the laws of diplomacy and international law, we cannot stand in the way of this strong anti-imperialist feeling and the people's repudiation of the United States." Also, when the Soviet Union invaded Afghanistan, Tinoco received strict orders to abstain from supporting a draft resolution calling for the immediate withdrawal of Soviet troops by arguing that the draft resolution was "motivated and inspired by U.S. imperialism."

The New Marxism

Some American friends of the Sandinista revolution, or other commentators who just didn't know any better and/or weren't interested in the evidence, spent much of their time during the 1980s saying the Sandinistas were not Marxists. But many statements since the early 1960s demonstrated that the Sandinistas considered themselves Marxists and much of the open feuding of the 1970s was over which interpretation of Marxism was correct. Even the Central Report of the first FSLN party congress in July 1991 stated: "We defined the FSLN as the vanguard detachment that applies Marxist-Leninist principles in a creative manner."[8] The key words here were not just Marxist-Leninist, but "creative," for the Sandinistas were adherents to a "new Marxism" similar to that espoused by Fidel Castro.

As with Fidel Castro, the Marxism-Leninism of the most important Sandinistas—which would more clinically be called Stalinist Leninism—came in almost all cases *after* the commitment had been made to fight the ruling dictator and the United States. To be sure, the founders and some later members of the FSLN came from the PSN, the country's orthodox communist party, or its youth organization, but these militants had joined the PSN or some later related group because they opposed Somoza and the United States. Thus the Sandinista version of Marxism-Leninism provided an intellectual framework for anti-American views already held.[9]

The nationalistic bent of this hybrid Marxism is reflected in the words of Comandante Víctor Tirado, who called on Nicaraguans to fight with

a single revolutionary ideology, interpreting and transforming society in the land of Sandino, with its principles of sovereignty, independence and national unity; this is the ideology of national liberation in the fight against imperialism, an ideology that springs from the depths of the history and thought of our heroes and martyrs. An ideology that, besides, integrates the experience and thought of the great thinkers of national liberation in Latin America and of humanity: of Bolívar, Sandino, Marx, Lenin, Ho Chi Minh, Mao Tse-tung, Martí, Morazán and all those who fight against imperialism.[10]

This new Marxism gave Sandinismo a kind of coherence, depth, and pizzazz that made it more respectable to old believers and attractive and acceptable to potential recruits. In line with the views of Fidel Castro, it placed more emphasis on revolutionary feeling and attitude than on the intellectual core of Karl Marx's thought, which to most of the Sandinistas had come to mean "bookish" ideology and stale formulas. With this emphasis on action, it also confirmed the need for armed struggle to overthrow Somoza and gave a framework for thinking in terms of continuing conflict even after the FSLN took power.

The inclination toward seeing violence as the road to progress followed the Cuban example and the track of Nicaraguan history and political culture. Throughout the nineteenth and twentieth centuries, political disputes, including most changes in governments between the Liberals (in León) and Conservatives (in Granada) were determined or influenced by warfare or other forms of violence. That violence invariably involved Nicaraguans, among the most famous being Sandino and Somoza, but sometimes also Americans, the latter ranging from the nineteenth-century adventurer William Walker to the twentieth-century Marines.

Tangible Consequences of Worldview

Whereas there is evidence that prior to taking power Fidel Castro was at least as fascinated with Hitler as he was with Marx, the Sandinista comandantes, before they took power, were adherents to their own visions of Marxism.[11] In power, the comandantes' proclaimed adherence to Marxism-Leninism, as part of their openly declared hostility to the United States in the international context of the Cold War, had two important organizational/practical consequences. These were (1) the development of and justification for the Leninist vanguard—the Sandinistas, or more accurately the National Directorate of the FSLN—to set and carry out domestic and international policies of a Stalinist state; and (2) the formation of ties to governments and groups abroad that had similar domestic policies and international interests, particularly those that could provide some of the vital military and economic support the Sandinistas needed to pursue their revolutionary goals. Thus even as the Sandinistas rejected everything that smacked of Somocismo, they established a similar, and in many respects even stronger, governing clique at home and dependency on a different bloc of foreign powers.

Lenin's call at the beginning of the century for a vanguard of professional revolutionaries, and his defense of that vanguard's dictatorial role in the course of seizing power and governing, was just what the comandantes wanted to hear and just the model they sought. While Latin America had a long tradition of iron-fisted rulers, the concept of the vanguard revolutionary party entered in the wake of Lenin and Leninist movements around the world. The Sandinistas as a movement proclaimed that it was their historically chosen, tightly disciplined, armed political force that alone represented the true interests of the Nicaraguan people. Given enough confusion and mistakes by everyone else at home and abroad—and for years these were plenteously forthcoming—the FSLN would be able to seize and hold political power in the country.

But Lenin's impact went further, for it justified the formation of a vanguard of leaders within the "vanguard" party, putting the real power in their hands. Toward the end of their struggle against Somoza, and under pressure from Fidel Castro, the top leaders of the three feuding FSLN factions settled their disputes enough to form the National Directorate, the unchanging vanguard of the vanguard, consisting of three men from each faction. After taking power, the Directorate pressed its authority down through the FSLN, the Sandinista Assembly, the EPS, the police, security forces, and mass organizations in undertaking what the comandantes argued was the transformation of the country in defiance of all domestic and international forces that would thwart their vision of the future. Yuri Povlov, in the 1980s a high-level Soviet foreign ministry official, rejected the notion that the Sandinistas were seriously Marxist, commenting that their ideology was first and foremost a justification for the formation of a vanguard of the vanguard through which they would hold and exercise power. Edén Pastora went a step farther, arguing that in a fundamental sense even the changes were superficial. After the 1990 "piñata," he became convinced that the self-proclaimed Marxist-Leninist comandantes "adopted the communist formula as a way to maintain themselves permanently in power," concluding that "Immediately after taking power, they became Somocistas."[12]

The second consequence of adherence to Marxism-Leninism was of great importance at the very end of the war against Somoza and after the Sandinistas seized power. It allowed the FSLN to step into the Cold War camp of the Soviet Union, to acquire international allies who for years provided the military and economic support the Sandinistas desperately needed to pursue their anti-imperialism but could never have generated on their own. Forming this international alliance meant a self-fulfilling prophecy, however, with respect to the United States, for it guaranteed conflict with Washington. It was not so much that American policymakers during the Carter and first Reagan administrations cared about Sandinista "Marxism" as a domestic ideology in this small Central American country as it was the Sandinista decision to join Cuba and the Soviet bloc, thus causing a shift in the strategic balance in the Cold War in the hemisphere. Just as Cuba had become the first permanent ally of the Soviet Union in the Western Hemisphere, specifically in the Caribbean, and thus truly launched the Cold War in Latin America, so the Sandinistas became the first ruling Soviet ally in Central America, with a new set of strategic consequences. Like some Americans, Soviet leaders also quickly recognized the primacy of the strategic issue—a point confirmed explicitly by Yuri Povlov—rather than the intellectual content of the ideology. And as in the Cuban case, Moscow quickly turned its attention from the old orthodox Communist vanguard party in Nicaragua to the advocates of the "new Marxism," those who actually held political power and were bent on conflict with Washington.[13]

The Sandinista role in the Cold War was discussed on various occasions by Humberto Ortega and other FSLN officials. One such discussion occurred at the end of 1985 when Soviet vice-minister of foreign relations Completov visited Managua. The vice-minister opened the discussion with Ortega with a reference to the heavy economic responsibility the Soviet Union had to Cuba. He expressed his agreement with the National Directorate's decision not to declare itself socialist, thus giving it greater maneuverability in the international sphere in the confrontation with the United States. This also allowed it to make better use of the private sector,

78 TheThe CivilCivil WarWar in NicaraguaNicaragua

which the Soviet Union believed had a role to play in all "socialist" countries. He continued, saying that the Soviet Union was facing an aggressive and warlike imperialism in the Reagan administration, and that the American Star Wars program had forced the Soviet Union to initiate a similar and very costly program of its own. He concluded by reiterating Soviet support for the Sandinista cause and confidence in its ultimate triumph in the confrontation with the United States.

Humberto responded by stating the National Directorate's position on Nicaragua's role in the Cold War:

> The Directorate feels it is playing a very important role in the confrontation between the Soviet Union and the United States. . . . We feel our confrontation with North American imperialism is not isolated but part of a strategy of global confrontation between the Soviet Union and the United States. . . . We too have forced the North Americans to commit resources to financing the mercenary war we are confronting, resources they could otherwise put toward social programs in the United States. In this sense, the Soviet leaders should understand that the economic resources delivered to the Sandinista revolution are part of the resources that should be assigned to the global confrontation with the United States. . . . We realize that the Soviet people and government have made great sacrifices to assist us, but we too are contributing the blood of hundreds of young patriots who are dying on the field of battle to defeat the mercenary army directed and financed by the United States.

Ortega concluded by expressing his confidence that the EPS would win the war against the mercenaries and that the Soviet Union would triumph in its confrontation with North American imperialism.

Notes

1. Ratliff interviews with Moisés Hassan, 2 May 1991, and Edén Pastora, 19 March 1992.
2. Arturo Cruz Sequeira, a former Sandinista official, discusses the more moderate approach in "The Origins of Sandinista Foreign Policy," in ed. Robert Leiken, *Central America: Anatomy of Conflict* (New York: Pergamon Press, 1984), 95–99. Though a social-democrat, Edén Pastora took a harshly critical view when he said that Americans resent a true nationalist more than they do a communist; they don't know how to work with gentlemen, only with servants. Ratliff interview with Pastora, 20 March 1992.
3. For example, see "Programa del Frente Sandinista de Liberación Nacional," *Tricontinental* (Havana), March-April 1970; and the 1977 *General Political/Military Platform*, written mainly by Humberto Ortega.
4. Roger Miranda attended the sessions conducted by Carrión.
5. See Ortega contribution to *La revolución a través de nuestra Dirección Nacional* (Managua: Secretaría Nacional de Propaganda y Educación Política del FSLN, 1980), 45.

6. The original text is found in the Cuban periodical *Tricontinental*, 17 (Marzo-Abril 1970): 61–68, translated in the English edition of *Tricontinental*, same date, same pages; our translation is from the Spanish edition, 67–68. The 1981 version is *Programa Histórico del FSLN* (Managua: Departamento de Propaganda y Educación Política, 1984), quotation from 39, emphasis added. The revised version is translated in *Sandinistas Speak*, ed. Bruce Marcus (New York: Pathfinder, 1982), 13–22.

7. Tomás Borge speech of 1 May 1982 in *The Central American Crisis Reader*, ed. Robert S. Leiken and Barry Rubin (New York, Summit Books, 1987), 231. Also see Daniel Ortega, *El acero de guerra o el olivo de paz* (Managua: Editorial Nueva Nicaragua, 1983), 89; and *Plataforma Electoral del FSLN* (Managua: Casa Nacional de Campana, 1984), 12.

8. *Barricada*, suppl., 20 July 1991, trans. in *Foreign Broadcast Information Service* (Latin America), 24 July 1991, 21.

9. David Nolan explained this mind-set: "Sandinismo was created in the minds of its adherents from a set of intuitive feelings and emotional reactions to the modern Nicaraguan environment. . . . Revolutionary theory, in the form of Marxism-Leninism, was adopted as a means of systematizing their world view and giving it clear definition." *The Ideology of the Sandinistas*, 122–23. Bertram D.Wolfe, one of the world's foremost students of Marxism, has noted that Marx's original writings have been "buried under successive layers of commentary and interpretation, popularization, oversimplification, and specious rationalization to produce [such Marxisms as] Castroism, which, for intellectual purposes, we need not take too seriously yet whose influence on political acts and political passions may be serious indeed." Wolfe, *Marxism: 100 Years in the Life of a Doctrine* (New York: Dial Press, 1964), xv.

10. Víctor Tirado López, "Sobrevivencia y unidad nacional," in Víctor Tirado, *Nicaragua: una nueva democracia en el tercer mundo* (Managua: Vanguardia, 1986), 253–54.

11. On Castro's admiration for and use of Hitler, see Hugh Thomas, *The Revolution on Balance* (Washington: Cuban American National Foundation, 1983), 19; and Georgie Anne Geyer, *Guerrilla Prince: The Untold Story of Fidel Castro* (Boston: Little, Brown and Company, 1991), 41–42, 131–32.

12. Yuri Povlov, former Soviet ambassador to Costa Rica (1982–87), head of the First Latin American Division (1987–89), and then head of the Latin American Department (1989–90), of the Soviet Foreign Ministry, in an interview with William Ratliff at Hoover Institution, 17 October 1991; and Ratliff interview with Pastora, 19 March 1992.

13. Ratliff interview with Povlov, 17 October 1991.

6

Here's Mud in Your Eye

The Sandinistas knew their true political convictions, domestic agenda, revolutionary strategy, and international alliances would run into active opposition at home—though they never imagined how much—and with neighboring countries and the United States. Some of the more radical Sandinistas thought the best strategy would be to take on all problems, and take out all of their critics, at once. But the Ortegas' position in the National Directorate was to move more slowly at first and muddy the waters. They wanted to hide their objectives just enough to make it difficult for their opponents to cooperate in bringing the revolution to its knees. No one explained the Sandinista policy of deception more clearly than Bayardo Arce in what was supposed to be a secret speech in May 1984 to the Nicaraguan Socialist party. Arce concluded with the ultimate irony: the Sandinistas will so confuse the imperialists that Nicaragua will prove to be the world's "first experience of building socialism with the dollars of capitalism."[1] The degree to which this ploy succeeded is a tribute to how successfully—at least for a while—the Sandinistas manipulated the myths and realities of history, and ongoing events, in pursuit of their true, partly hidden objectives.

Militants within the Sandinista movement called this practice "manipulation." In a well-calculated and systematic way the FSLN manipulated individuals, organizations, and countries for their own ends, often by twisting facts or saying the opposite of what they planned to do or were doing.[2] This approach had been strongly recommended to the Sandinistas by Fidel Castro, though after July 1979 many militants found going slowly and being devious very hard to swallow. During the war against Somoza they had agreed to cooperate with "bourgeois" sectors of society in order to depose the dictator. It had worked. But after Somoza had been utterly routed with military force, many militants did not see why they should continue to disguise their beliefs and aims. Many Sandinistas—

including Borge, Arce, Ruiz, and others—favored moving quickly at all levels to consolidate power and socialism in the country. But these leaders and their followers did not dominate the National Directorate, and since they did not want to split the Sandinista movement now that it was in power, they clenched their teeth and went along with the Ortega-led line. Briefly, the Sandinista tactic of deception, sometimes stated with surprising clarity in little-circulated documents dating from 1977, was in varying ways and degrees to deny their fundamental positions and policies.

1. In public, they played down their conviction of the inevitability of a showdown with the United States, thus putting the onus for tensions and conflict between Managua and Washington on the Americans. The Sandinistas professed to want only peace, as discussed in a later chapter. This ploy worked very well for many years because the Sandinistas skillfully manipulated history and current politics and because the United States had repeatedly intervened in Nicaraguan affairs over the decades, and did so in the 1980s, and many Nicaraguans and foreigners were quite prepared to believe the worst accusations made against them.

2. They played down their adherence to the Castroite "new" Marxism, which they knew would alienate most Nicaraguans and many foreign governments and groups.

3. They denied a special political and military relationship to Cuba and the Soviet Union, which followed logically from their anti-American Marxism, and insisted that they were "nonaligned."

4. They denied they sought total, Leninist control in revolutionizing Nicaragua, that is, a consolidation of FSLN power to the point where they would not have to tolerate substantive dissent from anyone.[3]

Forging Unity to Dump Somoza

The manipulation of politics was critically important within Nicaragua during the late 1970s and contributed much to the fall of Somoza. Indeed, the Ortega brothers became the predominant leaders of the FSLN precisely because they were the first to recognize how political passions—the nationwide opposition to the Somoza dynasty—could be channeled and used to benefit the Sandinista objective of seizing power and carrying out a broad national revolution. But the Terceristas realized very clearly that the broad front they needed to fight "tyranny and Yankee imperialism" in the late 1970s was a temporary affair. In the words of the 1977 *General Political-Military Platform*, the Sandinistas planned to "conserve our forces' political hegemony in this *tactical and temporary* alliance."[4] This realization of the utility of a temporary alliance led the Terceristas to present themselves to the general public in a more moderate light then previously, both with respect to their ultimate objectives and their willingness to cooperate over time with the vast majority of anti-Somoza Nicaraguans. The major ideological step in implementing this strategy was the release of the "Minimum Program" in the early summer of 1978, the "democratic mask" as Douglas Payne has called it. The main institutional steps were: (1) setting up The Twelve, a group of prominent Nicaraguans all of whom were both anti-Somoza and, presumably, independent of the Sandinistas; (2) linking up with the anti-Somoza Broad Opposition Front (FAO), headed by businessman Alfonso Robelo; and (3) just before victory, founding the Government Junta, supposedly dominated by non-Sandinistas, which presumably would lead in implementation of a moderate government program of reforms in a pluralistic society with a mixed economy, as the Directorate had pledged to the Organization of American States shortly before Somoza's fall.

Humberto Ortega explained the political strategy to a colleague in a private letter in January 1979:

> The fact that we [cannot] establish socialism immediately after overthrowing Somoza does not mean that we are planning a capitalist type social-democratic or similar development policy; what we propose is a broad, democratic and popular government which, although the bourgeoisie has participation, is a means and not an end, so that in its time it can make the advance towards a more genuinely popular form of government, which guarantees the movement toward socialism. . . . [This policy] allows us to attract not only workers aware of their own class interests (which are very few due to brutal imperialist domination in our homeland, to the socioeconomic and well as cultural backwardness of our people) but mainly all the humble Nicaraguans, workers (although they are not proletarians) who, praying to Jesus Christ, are shedding their blood for the freedom of our people.

Thus, while avoiding such Marxist phrases as "all power to the workers" and "dictatorship of the proletariat," which would have put off these broad masses, the Sandinistas could, "without losing at any time our revolutionary Marxist-Leninist Sandinista identity—rally all our people around the FSLN." In fact, Sandinista references to the Marxism of the revolution were not intended for mass consumption at any time since Sandinista leaders knew both that the Nicaraguan people in general were

Christians and did not like atheistic ideologies, and that the Americans would oppose them more fiercely from the beginning if the FSLN flew its true ideological colors. Thus Humberto Ortega wrote in his January 1979 letter of the need for deceptive packaging of the movement's beliefs:

> It is right that we demand in our ranks more standards and party life, more class consciousness and more Marxist ideological clarity, but let us not do this on an open and mass level, since we run the danger of becoming sectarian and isolating ourselves from the masses.[5]

Cloaking One's Intentions in Power

After the fall of Somoza, the policy of deception was explained this way in the *72-Hour Document*:

> For obvious reasons, in a report which we want to circulate widely to all our militants, both within the country and abroad, we cannot divulge as we would like to the fundamental aspects of what was discussed [in the 72-hour meetings]. We are certain that within the party structure, the political guidelines and analyses can be expanded upon and dealt with at greater length. . . . Despite its sweeping victory, Sandinismo has not made radical moves to transform all this power once and for all into the power of the workers and peasants, because political expediency dictates that more favorable conditions be developed for the revolution and requires that first the more urgent task of its political, economic and military consolidation be obtained in order to move on to greater revolutionary transformations. . . . With some of these groups we can be frank and explain the situation; with others we should be cautious in order to achieve the desired objectives.[6]

However, even top-level Sandinista leaders sometimes found it hard to "manipulate" certain very sensitive issues with consistency. Not surprisingly, they were especially open—or careless—when they thought their words would not be circulated to the public. Arce's 1984 speech about democracy and elections quoted elsewhere is one example. Equally illustrative of this problem was Humberto Ortega's speech on 22 August 1981 to EPS chiefs and officers. Among his comments: "Marxism-Leninism is the scientific doctrine that guides our revolution." Several days later the speech was published by the political section of the army for internal circulation, but copies fell into the hands of the FSLN's enemies. Roger Miranda was immediately charged with collecting all copies of the speech and editing out this and other references to Marxism-Leninism. The FSLN then asserted that the CIA and the opposition had put those comments into the text of the speech, which it had then published and circulated, in order to discredit the Sandinista movement. Ortega was strongly admonished by the National Directorate for his carelessness.

One way to keep people from knowing the truth was to monitor all independent sources of public information, censoring them or closing them down when the Directorate deemed it necessary. The censorship, which quickly came under the direction of the Interior Ministry, was accompanied by intimidation and constant violation of the rights of media personnel. The most celebrated case in Nicaragua was the censorship of the country's main independent newspaper, La Prensa, long a severe critic of the Somoza dictatorship and later an equally tough critic of the Sandinistas. Numerous obstacles were put in the paper's way from the beginning, long before there was any threat from the Contras. Between 1982 and 1986 it published on most days, but was required to submit its entire issue to the government for prior approval and was often slowly and heavily censored; well over 12,000 items were cut out during those years and some days the paper did not appear at all. Between June 1986 and October 1987, La Prensa was closed down altogether, only being permitted to reopen as a partial concession to the demands of the Esquipulas II peace agreement of August 1987.[7] Most other critical publications, from the left as well as from the right, including radio and television stations, were censored and/or closed down even before La Prensa was. The main ploy, as the armed opposition increased in size, was to charge, usually without any proof, that the domestic opposition to the Sandinistas was allied to the Contras.

The Sandinistas also tried to convince the Nicaraguan people their policies were correct by giving the impression in Nicaragua that all the peoples and really democratic governments of the world supported them, particularly in the conflict against the United States. This was done by publishing commentaries or polls from abroad that were favorable to their position and by preventing the circulation of evidence to the contrary. Sympathetic foreigners participated in rallies and demonstrations in Nicaragua; one U.S. group staged weekly demonstrations against U.S. policy in front of the American embassy in Managua, and the Sandinistas alleged that this group represented majority opinion in the United States.[8]

Fooling Foreigners

The Sandinistas had to sell themselves abroad as well as at home. Immediately after Somoza fled, Sergio Ramírez effectively outlined precisely what the Sandinistas knew would antagonize the United States and then said the Sandinistas would not do those things:

> What would make them [the United States] react against us? If we were to say we were Marxist-Leninists, but we're not going to do that. If we were to expropriate U.S. companies, but we're not going to do that either. If we announced we were joining the Soviet bloc, but that won't happen. If we intervene in El Salvador's affairs, but that isn't going to happen either.[9]

In reality, the Sandinistas believed and did just what Ramírez said they wouldn't from the moment they took power, while denying almost everything as part of the policy of deception.

During the war against Somoza, the Sandinistas had a relatively easy time winning supporters because Somoza was so often his own worst enemy. Still it was during this period that the FSLN thought it necessary to cultivate the moderate image presented by the figurehead individuals and institutions noted above and through other actions. For example, the guerrilla commander who most often met the foreign press was Edén Pastora, a flamboyant and charismatic nationalist and social democrat, particularly after the attack on the national palace had made Pastora an international figure, the symbol of opposition to the Somoza dictatorship. As Pastora himself later put it, around the world "everyone began to know one face, a peasant face as the face of the Frente. Everyone thought that all the Sandinistas were like me and thus they supported the Sandinistas."[10]

Cultivating this moderate image, the Sandinistas promised the Organization of American States just prior to Somoza's fall that they would practice political pluralism, a mixed economy, and international nonalignment. However, discussing FSLN strategy in closed sessions with Roger Miranda and other Sandinista militants at the 72-hour meeting in September 1979, Comandante Carrión explained bluntly why Sandinista leaders had concluded it was necessary, for a while, to wear a pluralistic, nonaligned mask.

> The Americans won't believe us, except for those who are already our friends or fools. But many of the Europeans and Latin Americans will believe. And many members of the Socialist International will believe. This tactic is aimed above all else at them.

It will isolate the Americans. It may even bring us active support from some governments and groups.

The special importance of this strategy for deceiving foreigners and thereby advancing Sandinista domestic objectives was stated in Bayardo Arce's 1984 "secret speech" to the Nicaraguan Socialist party, which was published two months later in a Barcelona newspaper. Here Arce spoke of the Sandinista policy of

> bringing about revolutionary change based on three principles which made us presentable in the international context and which, as far as we were concerned, were manageable from the revolutionary standpoint. Those principles were non-alignment abroad, a mixed economy, and political pluralism. With those three elements we kept the international community from going along with American policy in Nicaragua, in fact, we got a number of governments of various tendencies to back the position of Nicaragua, the position of the Sandinista Front.

Arce continued to explain the use the Sandinistas made of the 1984 elections and other aspects of "bourgeois democracy" to advance their strategic objectives.

> What a revolution really needs is the power to act. The power to act is precisely what constitutes the dictatorship of the proletariat—the ability of the [working] class to impose its will by using the means at hand [without] bourgeois formalities. . . . For us, then, the [1984] elections . . . are a nuisance, just as a number of things that make up the reality of our revolution are a nuisance. But from a realistic standpoint, being in a war with the United States, these things become weapons of the revolution. . . . We are using an instrument claimed by the bourgeoisie, which disarms the international bourgeoisie, in order to move ahead in matters that for us are strategic.[11]

The effectiveness of a policy of deception always depends on the other party's willingness to be deceived or inability to see through the propaganda. For a variety of reasons, most of the FSLN's supporters proved incapable of seeing, or unwilling to see, through Sandinista claims. Also, some FSLN critics made such preposterous and counterproductive allegations they provided the Sandinistas and their allies perfect targets to use in discrediting those making legitimate criticisms.

Three examples of deception will be noted here to illustrate the application of the strategy: one relating to FSLN support for the Salvadoran guerrillas and two burrowing to the heart of the Contadora and Esquipulas II peace plans, all of which are discussed in detail in other chapters.

1. Support for the Salvadoran guerrillas was a key if sometimes shifting aspect of Sandinista foreign policy from the time the FSLN took power. Denying this support began simultaneously with the policy itself; it was a repeated strategic lie intended generally to deceive the gullible and specifically to discredit the U.S. government and undermine any efforts Washington might make to thwart FSLN policies. A typical statement of that lie was Daniel Ortega's in early 1981, "If we have intervened in any way, in some form, in El Salvador, it is only with the example of our victory." But perhaps the classic international denial was made before the World Court in 1984 by Sandinista foreign minister Miguel D'Escoto: "In truth, my government is not engaged, and has not been engaged in, the provision of arms and other supplies to either of the factions engaged in the civil war in El Salvador," a claim we examine in detail in a later chapter.

2. The FSLN repeatedly manipulated the popular desire for peace to disguise its support for war abroad and to weaken those who resisted Sandinista policies, from the Nicaraguan peasants who came to form the vast majority of the Contras to the Reagan administration. The Sandinista announcement in September 1984 that it would sign the Contadora draft treaty was an act of carefully calculated cynicism, for the Sandinista government had no intention of abiding by its strictures, as we show in detail in a later chapter. But the Sandinistas guessed correctly that their agreeing to sign—like the signing of the Esquipulas II accords—would make the unimaginative United States seem inflexible and warlike in the eyes of the world.

Consider the FSLN's first major deception supporting its signing of the Contadora draft, the "good will gesture" by Daniel Ortega in one of his first acts as elected president of Nicaragua. On 27 February 1985 Ortega announced three "unilateral initiatives and decisions" in response to the Reagan's administration's "campaign of calumnies and lies" about the Sandinistas. The announcement was made "to the governments, parliaments, international organizations and people of the world." The three initiatives were: (1) sending home 100 Cuban advisers, an apparent response to one of the main Contadora objectives; (2) a unilateral "indefinite moratorium in the acquisition of new arms systems," a specific reference to the U.S. concern that the Soviet Union might send MiG-21 fighters or other sophisticated arms to Nicaragua; and (3) an invitation to a bilateral commission of U.S. congressmen to visit Nicaragua. The initiative was intended "to rob Mr. Reagan of his pretexts," said Alejandro Bendaña, first secretary of the Foreign Ministry, adding that "the ball is once again in Mr. Reagan's court."[12]

The first two points had been drawn up by a top-level five-man EPS commission headed by Humberto Ortega and including Roger Miranda. The ploy was to appear to give up a lot in an effort to achieve peace under Contadora when in fact the FSLN was giving up nothing at all. First, an EPS internal study had shown that several other Central American countries—particularly El Salvador—were far more dependent on foreign advisers than the Sandinistas. Thus what the first offer didn't say was that the FSLN knew the comparative advantage of the withdrawal of foreign advisers tilted strongly toward themselves. What is more, the 100 Cubans were scheduled to go home in three months anyway. Even more important, the Tripartite Commission of Nicaraguan, Soviet, and Cuban military chiefs had just concluded the 1986-90 military protocol. While some analysts guessed that the Cubans were scheduled to go home soon, no one knew the cynicism behind Ortega's offer to give up the advanced systems. The Sandinistas desperately wanted these systems, but their Soviet supplier had just told them behind closed doors they could not have them. Thus neither concession was a concession at all, and the proposed Congressional visit was a throw-away.

3. In August 1987, as the presidents of five Central American countries—among them Daniel Ortega—were signing the Esquipulas II Peace Plan in Guatemala City, the Sandinistas were negotiating the largest military expansion program ever conceived for Central America. The planning for this massive top-secret buildup had been underway since July, just before the Guatemala meeting, in a tripartite commission including Nicaraguan armed forces chief of staff Cuadra and top-level officials from the Soviet and Cuban ministries of defense. The entire plan, accepted by the Sandinista National Directorate in October 1987, was a gross violation of the Esquipulas II Central American Peace Plan President Ortega had signed just two months before.

Winning the War in Washington and Waukeegan

As shown in Daniel Ortega's words quoted above, while manipulating international opinion generally was important, the United States was always the main target because it posed what the Sandinistas considered the immediate direct and indirect threats to their existence. "Nicaragua's most important war," Tomás Borge said in 1983, "is the one that must be fought inside the United States. The battlefield will be the American conscience and its fundamental objective will be to avert a U.S. intervention here. . . . When they [the visitors to Nicaragua] return to the United States they have a multiplier effect on the public opinion of your country."[13]

The Sandinistas' most important "allies" in the United States—whether these individuals and groups always realized or intended it or not—were in the government, universities, churches, political parties, and media, often informed and/or coordinated to varying degrees by solidarity committees. These people were, or acted as if they were, receptive to Sandinista objectives and/or propaganda.[14]

The CIA traced some political ties with the Sandinistas to the offices of several U.S. congressmen, though most of the aid to the Sandinistas came from a lower level and outside the government.[15] According to U.S. government sources, by early 1986 the Nicaraguan Committee of Solidarity with the Peoples (CNSP) was reporting that it had established ties to solidarity committees in Great Britain (10), Ireland (6), France (53), Switzerland (19), Scotland (12), Luxemburg (8), West Germany (120), and Spain (48), among others. The CNSP added that at the time of the report, there were some eighteen hundred "Brigadistas" in Nicaragua, including more than six hundred Americans, involved in harvesting, construction and other activities.[16]

These and most other Americans who visited Nicaragua during the 1980s were predisposed toward the Sandinista government and openly critical of the United States as well as of the armed and the nonarmed opposition to the FSLN.[17] They needed less guidance than open-minded visitors, because they could usually be expected to conclude that criticism they might encounter of the Sandinistas was inspired by "reactionaries" and "imperialists." Many visiting groups were photographed for the FSLN/government newspaper *Barricada*, a not so subtle form of flattery that more often than not had a positive impact. *La Prensa* editor Jaime Chamorro has written that many of the groups and individuals who visited his paper's office "asked questions solely to obtain compromising statements that could then be used against us." And Chamorro noted the double standard applied routinely into the mid-1980s by many political activists and influential organizations in the free world:

How we remember the international support we received when Somoza censored or closed us. There was an incessant cry of outrage from governments and other international bodies. Sustained world opinion contributed to freedom in Nicaragua. But as a dictatorship of the left, the Sandinistas did not have to worry about this; they merely had to proclaim a lie to make it officially true.[18]

During the 1980s about one hundred thousand students, church activists and others visited Nicaragua for a few days or longer, the vast majority returning home to give interviews to local media in which they knowingly or unknowingly repeated Sandinista propaganda. Former MINT investigator Alvaro Baldizón, who reported directly to Tomás Borge, has described some of the techniques used to impress foreigners. Official visitors were escorted by professional members of the diplomatic corps and the FSLN's Department of International Relations. They never were allowed to talk with political prisoners in the jails, to see the warehouses full of arms for the regional insurgents, or visit with dissident members of the indigenous communities on the Pacific coast. Tours involving groups of foreigners were arranged in advance: after the area to be visited was selected, probable troublemakers were picked up and security agents sent along as guides or photographers. Church delegations were often taken to meet Borge in his office decorated with pictures of poor children, crucifixes and a Bible, which is not his real working office. Poor people often showed up "spontaneously" and were given assistance by Borge. Privately, Borge referred to these visitors as temporary allies and useful idiots.[19]

New York Times correspondent Stephen Kinzer reported how a frustrated market vendor in Managua exploded at him one day:

You Americans, I can't believe how stupid you are! . . . You come here for a couple of days or a week, you live in some nice hotel, and maybe you go up north to pick coffee for a day. . . . Then you go home to your little solidarity group or your church group and tell everyone how wonderful the revolution is. You people are so blind! You're forcing Communism on us Nicaraguans, don't you see? The Sandinistas are leading you around by the nose! You think everything looks so nice here, but we can't afford to eat in those places where you people eat. Poor people are suffering in this country! We don't have food for our children, but you don't see that because the Sandinistas don't show it to you! You're living in nice apartments in New York or Europe, and the idea of a revolution seems so nice to you from over there. Open your eyes! Don't keep telling lies! Don't be useful idiots.[20]

When the visitors this vendor had in mind returned home, their observations and conclusions were passed on as eyewitness accounts of Nicaraguan conditions and the horrors of U.S. policy. This was the "multiplier effect" Borge said was central to Sandinista policy. They helped throw a web of disinformation over Nicaragua and U.S. policy in the region, profoundly complicating the lives of policymakers in Washington, who set many traps for themselves by making their own serious mistakes and sometimes passing on their own deceptions. The Sandinistas knew that the United States often had fairly good intelligence on their activities. Thus these obfuscators were all the more necessary to discredit the findings of that intelligence whenever possible.

Taking Aim at the Contras

Many themes were manipulated during the 1980s. One of the most important, "peace," is examined later and references to others occur throughout this book. But special note must be made here of the heavy propaganda campaign to discredit the Contras, to hide the fact that by 1983 what had originally been a force dominated by former national guardsmen had become one made up overwhelmingly by disaffected peasants and ex-Sandinistas. The objective of the FSLN campaign against the Contras was twofold: (1) to disguise the fact that the Contra War had became a peasant insurrection against the FSLN, a fact most Sandinista leaders themselves had great difficulty understanding for years; and (2) to so confuse and divide Americans on the makeup and activities of the Contras as to discredit the Reagan administration generally and, specifically, to end U.S. funding of the armed opposition.

Several points need to be made here. There is no question some of the Contras committed serious human rights abuses, some of which have been documented by Amnesty International, Americas Watch and in books by Glenn Garvin, Sam Dillon, and Christopher Dickey. But they did not commit nearly as many as was reported abroad and believed in the United States largely because of Sandinista propaganda and American naïveté, ignorance, and gullibility. There were probably no more than one would expect in a nasty civil conflict of this sort, and no more (and less calculated) than those committed by the Sandinistas.

One of the most notorious incidents, which illustrated the nature of Sandinista tactics, occurred in December 1983. A group of Miskito Indians, a priest, and a Catholic bishop, Salvador Schlaefer, who had lived for decades in Nicaragua, decided to flee the resettlement town of Francia Serpe to Honduras with the help of some Contra guerrillas. The

Sandinista government announced that the Miskitos and the clergymen had been kidnapped by the Contras. The EPS was ordered to follow the fleeing group and use whatever means necessary to make sure that none of them reached Honduras. Daniel Ortega then announced that Schlaefer had been murdered by the Contras during the march. But despite being fired on by the EPS troops, who were held off by the Contra rear guard, the Contras and Miskitos arrived in Honduras after several days march. Once there, the Miskitos told the press the Contras had saved them and Schlaefer, who had not been killed after all, said he had joined the exodus because these people were his friends.

One source of confusion was that few Americans realized that the Sandinistas had two types of military forces in the field: the EPS forces, which were streamlined as the years passed, and the militias, which defended the cooperatives in the countryside. The militias were poorly armed and trained, but they were part of the Sandinista armed forces and sources of intelligence on Contra movements. The Sandinistas often reported militia losses, which sometimes were heavy, as civilian casualties from Contra attacks, though in fact they were military forces; the general population of the villages often supported the Contra actions against the militia because the latter represented the FSLN. At times civilians were killed, including women, children, and the elderly, and the fact is that Humberto Ortega was pleased when this happened because of its enormous propaganda value. The deaths of civilians seemed to prove that the Contras were nothing but barbarians and savages, as the Sandinistas—and some American congressmen and others—were saying. As military leader, Ortega realized that the killing of those civilians contributed more to the ultimate defeat of the Contras than EPS attacks on rebel fighters ever could.

Occasionally, this common ploy was exploded. For example, in March 1987 several American journalists were allowed to visit a village after the Sandinistas charged the Contras had conducted a "terrorist attack" on several trucks filled with civilians. But when the reporters talked with peasants in the area, and even survivors of the attack, they found the Contras had let one of several trucks pass when it was obviously carrying unarmed peasants; they had then attacked a truck of rifle-carrying loggers, many wearing government uniforms. "I was dressed like a soldier," one survivor admitted, and another said, "I think they fired on us because they could see we were armed."[21]

Sometimes unexpected deaths—as in a helicopter crash that killed several score women and children during a peasant resettlement operation—were charged to Contra attacks on civilians. In these cases, too, the impact was greater on the outcome of the war than the loss of many more lives would have been on the field of battle. Finally, as noted in the chapter on the Contra War, the Contras were blamed for mining roads, destroying power lines, killing international volunteers, and other things actually done by the Sandinistas.

Notes

1. Arce's speech, published in *La Vanguardia*, Barcelona, 31 July 1984, is reprinted in Leiken and Rubin, *Central American Crisis Reader*, 297.
2. The anti-Sandinista writer and democrat Pablo Antonio Cuadra described this policy as "never calling things by their proper names, always denying and hiding behind false colors." See Cuadra's "Notes on Culture in the New Nicaragua," in Leiken and Rubin, *Central American Crisis Reader*, 243.
3. On the use of "cloaks of deception," see Douglas Payne, "The 'Mantos' of Sandinista Deception," *Strategic Review* (Spring 1985): 9-20; and Payne, *The Democratic Mask* (New York: Freedom House, 1985).
4. National Direction, FSLN, *General Political-Military Platform*, 16, 28, emphasis added.
5. Humberto Ortega to Francisco Rivera (Rubin), 7 January 1979, published in *Novedades*, 19 April 1979, cited in Nolan, *The Ideology of the Sandinistas*, 67-68. Since this letter was originally published in a Somoza-owned newspaper, its authenticity has sometimes been questioned. Privately, members of the FSLN accept its authenticity.
6. *72-Hour Document*, Falcoff and Royal, *The Continuing Crisis*, 494, 497, 506.
7. On the censorship of *La Prensa*, see the books of two editors of that period: Roberto Cardenal Chamorro, *Lo que se quiso ocultar: 8 años de censura sandinista* (San Jose, Costa Rica: Libro Libre, 1989), which is a detailed study of what items were censored out; and Jaime Chamorro, *La Prensa: The Republic of Paper* (New York: Freedom House, 1988). Cardenal's collection of 95 percent of the material censored out of *La Prensa* now is housed in the archives of the Hoover Institution at Stanford University.
8. See cable from U.S. embassy in Managua to Department of State in Washington, P 051840Z, December 1986.
9. Warren Hoge, "Junta Moves to Feed Nicaraguans and Bids Civilians Surrender Arms," *New York Times*, 22 July 1979.
10. Ratliff interviews with Pastora, 18 March and 19 March 1992. Pulitzer Prize winning correspondent Shirley Christian has documented the media's fascination with Pastora in "Covering the Sandinistas: The Foregone Conclusions of the Fourth Estate," *Washington Journalism Review*, March 1982. Joshua Muravchik discusses why foreign journalists were unable to cope with "the elaborately planned and painstakingly executed campaign of deception that was an integral part of Sandinista strategy," in his *News Coverage of the Sandinista Revolution* (Washington: AEI,

1988), 107; also see Robert Leiken's forthcoming book on Nicaragua and the U.S. media.

11. See Arce's comments in Leiken and Rubin, *Central American Crisis Reader*, 289-97; quotes from 291-93.

12. See long article by John Lantigua, "Nicaraguan Says 100 Cuban Advisers To Be Sent Home; Freeze on Arms Is Also Pledged," *Washington Post*, 28 February 1985.

13. Borge quoted in Juan Tamayo, "Sandinistas Aim Soft Sell at Activists," *Miami Herald*, 14 December 1983.

14. See William Ratliff, "East Confronts West in Central America," in Bruce D. Larkin, *Vital Interests* (Boulder, CO.: Lynne Reinner, 1988), 91-112; Ratliff, "Latin American Studies: Up from Radicalism?, *Academic Questions* 3, no. 1 (Winter 1989-90), 60-74.; and Paul Hollander, "The Newest Political Pilgrims," in Falcoff and Royal, *The Continuing Crisis*, 453-64.

15. See David Johnston, "Spying Data on Sandinistas Involved U.S. Congressmen, Ex-Officials Say," *New York Times*, 15 September 1991; Benjamin Weiser, "Fiers Describes CIA's Eavesdropping on Congressional Calls to Sandinistas," *Washington Post*, 20 September 1991; North, *Under Fire*, 270.

16. Figures cited in cable from U.S. embassy in Managua to Department of State in Washington, December 1986.

17. See Paul Hollander, *Political Hospitality and Tourism* (Washington: Cuban American National Foundation, 1986).

18. Jaime Chamorro, *La Prensa*, 101, 134.

19. Baldizón was chief investigator of MINT's Special Investigations Commission from December 1982 until he defected in July 1985. See Baldizón, *Inside the Sandinista Regime*, 11-12. Also see, Edward Cody, "Nicaragua Jousts With U.S. for Hearts and Minds of World Media," *Washington Post*, 3 April 1983.

20. Kinzer, *Blood of Brothers*, 152.

21. See reports by Julia Preston, *Washington Post*, 28 March 1987, and Richard Boudreaux, *Los Angeles Times*, 28 March 1987.

7

The Godfather and the Poor Brother in the Family

Humberto Ortega has acknowledged publicly that from the early 1960s Cuba provided support and assistance to the FSLN.[1] But the details of that relationship—which ranged from safe haven and training to international contacts and aid—have been widely misunderstood and misrepresented in the United States, both by the right and by the left.

From Nobodies to Castro's Comrades

Prior to the end of 1978 the Sandinistas had important personal ties to Cuba, but they were with low level functionaries of the America Department. Similarly, there was some financial aid, but it came to no more than several thousand dollars, according to Edén Pastora.[2] Top FSLN leaders were totally isolated from contacts with important members of the Cuban government, the only exception being periodic encounters with Che Guevara—who was killed in 1967—which seemed to be more on the personal initiative of the Argentine than a result of Cuban government policy.

Sandinista leaders knew that realistically speaking they did not then pose a serious threat to Somoza and thus could not be a high-priority group for the Cubans when compared to the seemingly more viable revolutionary movements in Venezuela, Guatemala, and Colombia. This was a matter of judgment and hierarchy of interests the Sandinistas themselves had to face in their relations with other guerrillas beginning in mid-1979.

And yet the tensions existed, particularly with the Ortegas. On the way home from a lavish visit to Cuba in 1982, and a session with Fidel Castro,

Humberto Ortega raised the subject of Cuban/Sandinista relations with
Roger Miranda:

> Miranda, what do you think of the attention we received in Cuba?

> It seemed excellent to me, Comandante. I think the Cubans have always shown
> comradeship and solidarity to the Sandinista movement.

> Don't believe it, Miranda. Things have not always been like this. Before 1978 we
> were looked on as secondary allies. I lived for years in Havana and always traveled
> by bus. When I was under medical treatment for gun wounds received in Costa Rica,
> I had to stand in long lines to get the physical therapy recommended by the doctor.
> Now that we are in power, they treat us differently. But you should know that until
> 1978 relations were so distant that Carlos Fonseca, though he too lived in Cuba for
> many years, died without knowing Fidel.

After this opening blast, Ortega complained at great length about the
Cuban leaders and their early relations with the Sandinistas.

The Ortegas were particularly unhappy with the Cubans because prior
to Edén Pastora's seizure of the National Palace in Managua in August
1978, and the insurrections that followed in September and October, the
Cubans had lined up with the Fonseca/Borge Prolonged People's War
(GPP) faction within the Sandinista movement. What might have been a
break for the Terceristas came in March-April 1978, after the murder of
Pedro Joaquín Chamorro in January and several developments that came
in the wake of the assassination: nationwide strikes and Tercerista attacks
on the military bases in Rivas, led by Edén Pastora, and Granada. The
attacks on the military bases in particular drew the Cuban leader's
attention. Castro contacted Panamanian General Omar Torrijos, who had
been in close touch with the Terceristas through his friendship with
Pastora, and said he wanted to talk in Havana with a delegation from the
faction. The delegation, consisting of Daniel Ortega, Carlos Coronel,
Oscar Pérez Cassar and Pastora, went to Havana where it explained the
Tercerista line to dozens of Cuban political and military leaders. They
won almost no support, for the Cubans, like the Prolonged War faction,
looked on the Terceristas as an ideologically flabby mix of Marxism and
social democracy that drew much of its outside support—political,
financial, and military—from such "bourgeois" or "politically ambigu-
ous" governments as those of Venezuela and Panama. The only Cuban
official who supported the idea of Tercerismo was Julián López, an
important member of the America Department, though the Terceristas
did not talk with him directly.[3] After Pastora's seizure of the palace, and

serious Cuban aid to the FSLN began, López coordinated that aid through Cuba's DA office in Costa Rica. After July 1979, he became Cuba's first ambassador to Nicaragua.

When the delegation met with Castro, the Cuban leader was pleased with the attacks on the military bases, which reminded him of his own far less successful attack on the Moncada military barracks in Cuba in 1953. Then another parallel came up, though a less important one in Castro's mind. Pastora mentioned that he had proposed an attack on the national palace in Managua, but that the FSLN Directorate had ruled against it. Castro didn't like the idea either and compared it to the disastrous attack on the palace in Havana in early 1957 by the Directorio Revolucionario. "But Comandante, you are telling me about Havana," Pastora said. "I am talking about Managua."⁴

Fidel changed his tune toward the end of 1978 simply because Pastora went ahead with the seizure of the National Palace and it proved to be an enormous success, a pivotal action in the war against Somoza. With the insurrections that followed in September and October, the Terceristas proved that they rather than the moribund GPP were the dominant faction within the FSLN and a serious challenge to the Somoza government. Only then did Castro personally zero in on the FSLN, and on the Ortegas in particular, to strengthen his own hand in Nicaragua and to diminish the influence of Panama's chief, Omar Torrijos, and Venezuela's president, Carlos Andrés Pérez, who was in any event leaving office at about that time.

When Fidel first met with the three top Sandinista leaders (who became ruling comandantes) in September 1978, they were GPP leader Borge and two Terceristas, Daniel and Humberto Ortega. Thus it was from late 1978 that Castro made a special effort to cultivate the Ortegas. During early 1979, Cuban support became important as Havana shipped substantial quantities of arms to the FSLN, but managed so as to benefit mainly the Leninist-Stalinist members of the faction, not the social-democrats. Pastora had originally arranged with Torrijos to have the arms shipped through Panama, where he and the Panamanian leader could direct more of them to the social democratic sectors of the Terceristas like Pastora. But Costa Rican security minister Johnny Echeverría, who had great influence on Costa Rican President Rodrigo Caraso, went to Havana and convinced Castro to send the supplies through Costa Rica. There up to half of the arms were diverted to Costa Ricans and the rest divided out by López and others, usually away from the social democrats in the Tercerista movement. Looking back, Pastora branded Echeverría—a Fidelista second only to Fidel himself—"the prime cause of all that happened in Nicaragua."[5]

Immediately after the triumph of the revolution, the Cuban presence and influence were felt at all levels in the new government and society, sometimes even in excess of what some FSLN Leninists wanted, and far more than the majority of the people wanted. According to Edén Pastora, whose first position with the new government was as vice minister of the interior, the first Cuban advisers went to work setting up security jails and all that went with them. These and other advisers worked to strengthen the Leninists in the FSLN and the old families with members who supported the Directorate—the Cuadras, the D'Escotos, the Cardenales.[6]

The Best of Allies, Up to a Point

Cuban teachers and military advisers began arriving in July 1979 and other forms of aid, much of it discussed in later chapters, accompanied them. These Cuban advisers worked with Borge in Interior, Ortega in Defense, and at all levels in health and education programs. In 1986 some 20 percent of university professors in Nicaragua were foreigners, most of them Cubans. Each year approximately six hundred fifty Nicaraguans between the ages of twelve and twenty-five received full scholarships to study in Soviet bloc countries, about a third of them in Cuba, usually for approximately six years. A news item in 1986 said that Cuba had "attended to more than 3000 students a year."[7]

Nicaraguan State Security (DGSE), which is described in more detail in a separate chapter, was modeled on its Cuban counterpart and depended on a large number of Cuban and Soviet bloc advisers to detect and deal with any actual or potential threat to the FSLN's power. (The Nicaraguan army had its own counterintelligence force to handle problems within its own ranks.) State Security officials were educated at the outset mainly in Cuba and their procedures were basically the ones used there as well as others long characteristic of Latin American dictatorships. Cuban counterintelligence officers remained important in the DGSE over the years. In mid-1985, according to Alvaro Baldizón, Cuban advisers were assigned to interior minister Borge, each of the three vice ministers, the chief of the central general staff, each of the three chiefs of general directorates, and each of the thirteen chiefs of directorates. There were forty-three at the level of chiefs of department in Managua and others in regional MINT offices, as well as more than fifty at MINT training schools.[8]

Cuban involvement was critical in the military as well, both in terms of aid and advice. While the Soviet Union sent the Sandinistas arms, and some military and technical experts, and to a lesser extent provided training in its academies, the Cubans were primarily responsible for providing military and other advisers on the spot in Nicaragua and more extensive training in Cuban academies. By the end of 1987 the Cubans had trained almost ten thousand five hundred officers in their academies and sent several thousand of their advisers, most of whom had been trained in the Soviet Union, to serve with the EPS in Nicaragua for periods of one to two years. At their peak in September 1984-85, when Nicaragua signed the Contadora draft treaty, there were about twelve hundred fifty Cuban military advisers and instructors in the country. In quality, the Cuban advisers generally fell below the level of their Soviet counterparts, with notable exceptions. One of the important military-related projects with Cuban involvement was the construction of the large airfield at Punta Huete intended to accommodate the MiG-21 fighters the Soviet Union promised in 1981 and again in 1987, but never delivered.

From the beginning there were aid limits beyond which neither the Cubans nor the Soviets would go. Neither country ever set up a military base in Nicaragua, and neither ever sent active combat troops. When Humberto Ortega pointedly asked Fidel Castro to send a brigade of Cubans trained in irregular warfare in 1983, Castro refused to do so.

The highest ranking Cuban to die in Nicaragua as a result of the Contra War was a colonel named Leliebre, the chief of the Cuban military mission in Puerto Cabezas. He and other Cubans were wounded in a Contra ambush in a small village near Puerto Cabezas. His wounds were in the right lung, the arm, and foot and he could have survived had it not taken almost twenty hours to move him out of the Atlantic Coast which has no adequate hospital. Twice, planes sent from Managua could not land because of the weather. He was finally picked up by a plane flown in from Havana and taken to Cuba where he died during an operation.

And there were times when Cuba proposed more than it carried out. Two projects, for example, which would have had commercial value, as well as military importance, should be mentioned. In 1982 Cuba offered to construct a new port on the northern Atlantic coast at the city of Puerto Cabezas. The proposal remained on paper, however, because of the expanding civil war in the north and because the Sandinistas worked out a joint venture with Bulgaria to build a port farther south at Bluff near Bluefields, through which 95 percent of Soviet and other arms subsequently entered the country. In 1983 Cuba began talking about building a "dry canal," an interocean railway, from the Pacific port of Corinto to the Atlantic port of Rama. In July Vice President Sergio Ramírez announced the beginning of the first stage—the track from Corinto to Managua—which was to be finished by the end of 1984 and then followed immediately by the Managua-Rama link. But again, nothing happened.

Cuba's Men in Managua

For the first five years, the dominant Cuban in Nicaragua was Castro's distinguished ambassador, Julián López, who was in charge of both political/economic matters and the strategic aspects of military relations between Nicaragua and Cuba. López had particular prestige among the Sandinistas because he had directed Cuba's military aid passing through Costa Rica to the Sandinistas in 1979; he was introduced to the delegates at the final session of the seventy-two-hour meeting in Managua in September 1979 with more honors than any other visitor.

From the time of his arrival in Managua, López was the most important ambassador serving in the country. He was considered a personal representative of Fidel and thus a man with considerable power. He also was a source of information the Sandinista leaders wanted and needed, such as what Soviet leaders thought about the development of the Sandinista revolution, who the key players in the Soviet power structure were, how the Soviet Union would react if the Sandinistas took specific international political steps, and what products could be solicited from which Soviet bloc countries. Thus it was commonplace to see the cars of the comandantes parked in front of his residence.

López was about fifty years old. He spoke slowly and with dignity. He was not easily angered or caught off guard and often responded with such phrases as "could be" and "perhaps." He was discreet and led a solitary life; his only son was in Cuba. His relations with his subordinates were good and, though he had the direct phone lines of both Ortega brothers, he usually followed the regular channels to make an appointment to see either of them. He was respectful to all of the comandantes, but particularly to the Ortegas. Customarily he—and through 1985 Soviet ambassador to Nicaragua German Shliapnikov as well—would have Christmas dinner with Humberto's family. Humberto's invitations were carefully reasoned and had a subtle impact in the early years of the revolution; while individual comandantes were still trying to secure their positions of power within the National Directorate, the fact that both of these Soviet bloc representatives routinely had this holiday meal with Humberto in its small way seemed to signal a special tie between the younger Ortega and both the Soviets and Cuba.

After several short trips to Nicaragua in 1983, Cuban Division General Arnaldo Ochoa arrived in Managua in 1984 to help reform the Sandinista military. His arrival brought a shift in Sandinista relations with Cuba. As a senior military officer, Ochoa considered himself in charge of the military mission, which had previously been under López's control. López remained the main political adviser of the Sandinista leadership, despite the loss of his military portfolio, and Ochoa never challenged him on political grounds since such matters did not interest him. Still, during 1985 tensions between the two became increasingly obvious.

A military man, about six feet two inches tall and of strong build, Ochoa was not as respectful as López. And yet, though he had less formal education and the style of a peasant, Ochoa had extensive experience and knowledge of military affairs and, except for Raúl Castro, he had the highest visibility and reputation of anyone in the Cuban military. In fact, he was the pride of the Cuban military, for he had recent and very impressive experience as a field commander in Ethiopia and Angola, which Raúl did not.

He was not given to discussing political affairs for he believed that politicians made politics and the military made war. Although he never expressed anti-Marxist sentiments, he could not be characterized as a fervent partisan of Marxism, as the earlier representatives of the Cuban military mission had been. Indeed, privately Ochoa was critical of the inflexibility that prevailed among military leaders, of the lack of creativity among officials, and of the subordination of military leaders to partisan structures. Often one heard him say, alluding to López, "Look, friend, politicians are just that, politicians; what business do they have sounding off on military matters?" And yet the reforms Ochoa promoted in the military had political and other repercussions throughout Nicaraguan society. In effect, as noted below, Ochoa introduced Nicaraguans to the Cuban program that developed after the U.S. invasion of Grenada at the end of 1983, the War of All the People, which Humberto tagged the Patriotic People's National War (Guerra Nacional Patriótica y Popular).

Relations on a Roller Coaster

Fidel Castro's critical inspirational role in the Nicaraguan revolution has been noted above. But in the mid-1980s, even as tensions between Cuban representatives in Managua increased, FSLN relations with Fidel came into increasingly difficult times. Ochoa's arrival in Managua was followed by an important event in Cuba, which in time had repercussions in Nicaragua. During 1985 Raúl Castro became Fidel's official heir apparent. This signaled increased power for Cuba's military mission in Nicaragua, as distinct from the DA, which had long meddled in military matters. Since Ochoa represented the military in Nicaragua, and López spoke for the DA (among other things), the former's stock went up in Managua.

Fidel was directly and negatively involved in one of the most controversial undertakings of the Sandinista government, the effort to obtain Soviet MiG-21 fighters; the tensions among Moscow, Havana, and Managua that resulted from this are discussed in a separate chapter. The MiG affair, taken with Castro's debt crusade that followed shortly thereafter, taught Sandinista leaders that despite Cuba's strong support for the Sandinista revolution, there were times when Castro's national and personal interests clashed with those of the Sandinistas, and when they did, Fidel would try to maneuver the FSLN into doing things his way, whatever the Sandinistas's own interests might be.

Fidel Castro had noted the danger of the foreign debt to Latin Americans off and on since 1971, but during 1984-85 he launched a relentless campaign calling for the renunciation of this debt. As the campaign soared in 1985, with a rash of continental conferences in Cuba for women, youth, journalists, labor leaders, and politicians, the Sandinista leaders concluded that Fidel had become so obsessed with the debt issue that he had lost touch with or interest in the real and pressing problems faced by the Sandinistas.[9]

These tensions between the comandantes and Castro reached a peak during and after a meeting between the Castro brothers and Humberto Ortega in early 1985. Humberto had gone to Cuba highly concerned about the U.S.-sponsored Contra War and specifically to discuss the new five-year plan for military cooperation between the Soviet Union and the Sandinistas. After a session during the afternoon with Raúl, devoted to military matters, the trip ended with a meeting with Fidel. Only seven people—Fidel, Raúl, Ochoa, Julián López, Manuel Piñeiro, Humberto, Joaquín Cuadra, and Miranda—attended the meeting, which lasted from 10:00 P.M. to 5:00 A.M., adjourning just in time for the Nicaraguans to catch their plane home.

Fidel entered the room at 10:00 P.M. impeccably dressed, his beard neatly trimmed, in olive green uniform with awards on collar and shoulders. He wore a cheap wristwatch, in contrast to the gold Rolex sported by his brother. Fidel gave Humberto a strong, warm embrace and everyone else a friendly greeting. The meeting was like one involving a holy man and his apostles. Fidel's monologue was uninterrupted except once in a while when Raúl raised his hand and asked permission to speak: "Chief, may I make a few comments?" Raúl would petition, or "Chief, may I be permitted to speak?" Fidel would respond, "Speak, Raúl" or "Please, tell me what you think, Raúl." And Raúl invariably seconded his brother's message. Only rarely would Fidel ask anyone else for an opinion.

The conversation quickly touched on the political, economic, and military situation in Nicaragua. At first Fidel seemed concerned with the development of the war, specifically noting that if it dragged on it might bring about the collapse of the weak Nicaraguan economy and of the Sandinista government, his close ally in the region.

But very soon he tied Nicaraguan economic problems to his concern over the debt in Latin American generally and forgot Nicaragua's specific needs. He spoke emotionally and at great length, trying to win partisans to his cause. He paced around the room, raised his hands to his head as if grieved by the atrocities imperialism had done to the hemisphere with its money. He sat down and pounded the table for emphasis. He cited figures and argued that the debt could not be repaid. Then he went over to Humberto, put his left hand on Humberto's right shoulder, looked into his eyes and said:

Humberto, the gringos have not taken full account of this problem of the foreign debt, how at any minute it could explode like a time bomb. We revolutionaries must be ready when the explosion occurs for it is going to shake the foundations of imperialism in Latin America and change forever the relations between imperialism and the Latin American people. We should lead the debtor's strike.

But Fidel had totally misjudged Ortega, and the consequences were felt for some time to come. Castro evidently believed that if he gave Humberto an extended oration on the importance of the debt, he would win his outspoken support. But it didn't work. In the first place, Humberto was openly bored by long meetings, especially ones that lasted all night. Second, he believed Fidel was overestimating the importance of the debt at that moment, and that the Cuban leader was trumping up the cause in order to make himself a leader of hemispheric stature. In fact, if anyone were to lead such a campaign, Humberto thought, it should not be Fidel, because of his well-known hatred of the gringos, but a more popular nationalist like Peruvian President Alán Garcia, with whom Fidel had been fighting. Finally, and above all else, Humberto was deeply offended that Castro seemed to ignore precisely the problems of Sandinista survival in wartime that the Nicaraguan delegation had gone to Havana to discuss. For Humberto, the Sandinistas' critical problem was not the weight of the debt but the war he argued was financed and directed by the United States.

Julián López later told Humberto that the Nicaraguan response to the meeting had greatly disturbed Fidel, who felt abandoned by those he had helped so much, those who had been the firmest allies of Cuba's policy in Latin America, those who might have helped rally Latin American support for Castro's campaign. López was one who later felt the aftershock of this conflict.

In February 1986, during the first session of the Third Congress of the Cuban Communist party, López was named an auxiliary member of the PCC Central Committee. In Nicaragua this was interpreted as a move by the Cubans to balance the powerful figure of General Ochoa in Managua. Then in April Ochoa unexpectedly informed Humberto that he was being recalled to Cuba in May. Even though his basic reforms had been put into practice, and had saved the EPS and the Sandinista government, Humberto wanted Ochoa to stay at least a year longer. Daniel took this request to Castro in early May but to no effect, for Ochoa returned to Cuba on 12 May. Humberto saw the sudden recall of Ochoa as both Fidel's revenge for the Sandinistas' failing to support him on the foreign debt issue and the handiwork of Raúl, with whom he had never been on good terms.

In midyear relations with Cuba took another turn for the worse. A telephone call López made to a subordinate in the embassy was recorded, a common practice among the Cubans. In the conversation López said that Raúl was a square, inflexible, and politically limited man. In response to a comment by the other person, López said, "and what is it to me what Raúl thinks?" The tape cassette was flown immediately to Cuba and López was told to report to Havana.

No one in Managua knew what the terms of López's dismissal were, but after a couple of days he returned to Managua where he told Daniel Ortega, without much explanation, that he been relieved of his duties in Nicaragua. The National Directorate immediately asked Fidel not to recall López. But Fidel, still brittle after the rebuff at the debt crisis session, told the Nicaraguan ambassador in Havana that the matter was closed: the Politburo had decided, he said, and there was nothing he could do. The Directorate knew this was nonsense since Fidel could override any decision the Politburo made if he wanted to. Just before López left, the Sandinistas slapped back at Fidel by awarding the long-time ambassador the Carlos Fonseca Order, the highest honor given by the Directorate. In fact, the award was made despite Castro's request, made to the Nicaraguan ambassador in Havana, that it not be given. López packed and on 26 November was gone. Nothing was heard of him for almost a year, when it was finally learned that he had been politically ruined and given a very minor position in the America Department.

But things got still worse at the beginning of 1987 when Cuba nominated General Sergio Pérez Lezcano—who had been the first chief of the Cuban military mission in Nicaragua—to be ambassador in Managua. It was assumed that he would be accepted, and the Cuban general threw a big party at his house in Cuba to celebrate the appointment, among those present being Raúl Castro. But the Sandinistas turned him down, for three reasons:

1. The Directorate wanted to show Fidel that it too could refuse proposals from an allied government.

2. Humberto was still miffed by recent events and he believed that a refusal would be a rebuff to Raúl, who he was sure was behind the proposed assignment.

3. The DN felt that the appointment of a general as ambassador would give the impression that Cuban military clout would now reach beyond the strictly military sphere.

In May 1987 Humberto went to Cuba to meet with Raúl to talk about various aspects of the military protocol. Humberto and Raúl, each with his advisers, sat across from each other at a large table in Raúl's office. Humberto began the meeting by explaining that as the military situation developed, it became clear that the EPS needed some things that had not been considered in the previous protocol: more irregular warfare advisers, some construction units to put roads into war zones (that is, Brigades for the Construction of Roads, known by their Spanish acronym, BICOCAS), some types of grease and oils for some artillery units. As Humberto finished, Raúl looked him in the eye and said, "Humberto, how can you ask me to increase the number of advisers in Nicaragua when you refuse to accept a general as ambassador?" Humberto paused for a moment, collected himself, and then went on, ignoring what had been said. At a break, Humberto took Raúl's arm, said something quietly to him, and Raúl's attitude changed completely. It seemed that once again Humberto had decided to play the role of the "poor brother in the family." And in September General Lezcano came to Managua to receive the Camilo Ortega award, presented by Humberto. But Cuba had no ambassador in Managua for a year.

Sticking Together When Things Get Tough

And yet even during this period of high tension, Castro came through on important occasions for the Sandinistas. For example in late 1986, the Sandinistas made their most extensive incursion into Contra camps in Honduran territory in several years, though publicly denying they had done so. More important, for the first time EPS troops remained in Honduras after the Contras had retreated and even when the United States mobilized forces and condemned the Sandinista action in the strongest terms. Humberto was so enthusiastic about what he considered this military victory he planned to keep Sandinista troops in Honduras while he negotiated with the Hondurans on the latter's support for the Contras in their territory. His thinking was that Reagan's hands were tied by the Iran/Contra scandal, which had just come into the open, and he concluded that the mobilization of U.S. troops—which included the use of American troops and aircraft in moving Honduran soldiers to the front lines—was meant to intimidate the Sandinistas, nothing more.

Suddenly, at the end of the first week of December, Cuban General Ochoa turned up in Managua with a different perspective in the form of a message from Fidel, which he passed on privately to Humberto:

> Chief, the commander in chief in Cuba is very worried about how long Sandinista troops have stayed in Honduras and the deployment of U.S. troops there. Fidel believes that a confrontation with the United States would not be favorable for the EPS and keeping the EPS there any longer now plays into their hands, giving them a pretext for a confrontation. We do not think the EPS can be successful militarily in a showdown with the gringo army, which has besides the support of the Honduran army. And to make things worse, the EPS will seem in public opinion to be the aggressor, being dislodged after invading a neighboring country. Politically and militarily the EPS is at a disadvantage.
>
> Besides, Chief, there is something very important Fidel has authorized me to tell you. Through intelligence sources we know that prior to the Iran/Contra scandal the Reagan government had decided to invade Nicaragua militarily. The Iran-Contra matter has debilitated Reagan in trying to get support from Congress. But believe me, Chief, for the first time we know that Reagan has decided to invade. If you remain in Honduran territory, you are giving him the pretext he needs to rally the support of Congress. Besides, chief, remember that your troops are totally unprotected against any air attack, and if the Hondurans or the gringos decide to hit you from the air you will take many casualties and a humiliating defeat.

This was in fact the first time the Cubans had spoken to the Sandinistas of American invasion plans—which are denied by then Secretary of State George Shultz—in such specific terms.[10] Humberto was very preoccupied by Fidel's message and the more so because Ochoa had delivered it personally. Humberto had the greatest respect for Ochoa on military matters. Ochoa retired at about 9:00 P.M. and Humberto immediately called Daniel, Arce, and Borge to tell them about his meeting with the Cuban general and persuaded them that the EPS should retire overnight from Honduran territory. Humberto then called Lt. Col. Javier Carrión and personally ordered the immediate retreat from Honduras, insisting that they must not even wait until dawn. And the next morning, sure enough, the Honduran Air Force did launch massive attacks against the positions the EPS had occupied for several days, but by then the EPS troops were moving back into Nicaraguan territory. Now deeply con-

cerned about possible U.S. intentions, and to show the United States the
Sandinistas would exact a high price for an American invasion, Ortega
ordered the largest maneuvers of the war, called Subtiava '86, in the
Pacific coast department of Chinandega bordering on Honduras.

Nicaragua a Second Cuba?

There has long been a debate as to whether the Sandinista revolution
is simply a copy of the Cuban Revolution or whether the former, despite
close ties to the latter, retained its own character and independence. On
28 February 1980, Daniel Ortega told the fourth Congress of Ecumenical
Theology in São Paulo that "with the passage of time it has become clear
that the Cuban revolution can not be replicated in the same way here."
Most comandantes, and particularly the Ortega brothers, spoke of maintaining a differentiation between the Cuban and Sandinista revolutions,
and sometimes they tried to follow up their words with actions.

Perhaps the most important difference was that the FSLN had no Fidel.
That is, there was no single, overwhelmingly dominant leader, but rather
a group, though throughout the 1980s several comandantes sought successfully to make themselves far more important than their colleagues.

And the Sandinista revolution was more gradual than the Cuban. Fidel
himself had advised the Sandinista leaders to move more cautiously in
their policies than he had. Indeed, the Cubans wanted the Sandinistas to
avoid potentially debilitating political and ideological ties to Havana, at
least in the beginning. For this and other reasons, when Fidel attended
the first anniversary of the revolution in 1980, he praised the Sandinista
leaders for their wisdom in avoiding the policies that had brought quick
isolation to the Cuban revolution. It was bound to make it easier for them
to get allies, at least for a while, in the Western world, which would
strengthen their hand against the United States.

But the Sandinista leaders' talk and in some degree hopes of differen-
tiating their revolution from Cuba's turned out to be mainly propagandistic, the perceived need to maintain an image distinct from Cuba on the
international stage. If we consider the characteristics of the society and
government sought by the Sandinista leaders, it was fundamentally a
copy of the Cuban model, save for certain differences in form and, at
times, structure.

Undoubtedly the most important thing the Sandinistas shared with Fidel and cultivated under his direct and indirect influence was his bitter anti-American sentiment, the conviction of inevitable confrontation with the United States and all that followed therefrom in terms of militarization, domestic policies generally, and international alignments. Both countries had a long record of American military and other intervention in their internal affairs and the soil was fertile for anti-American nationalism of an extreme variety. And flowing from the intense anti-Americanism in the very shadow of U.S. imperialism was the formation of international alliances with the other side in the East/West conflict that again made Cuba dependent on a superpower.

Edén Pastora tells of a poignant experience with Fidel Castro at the end of 1981 which brought home the Cuban leader's intense but internal frustration at changing dependence on one country for dependence on another. When Pastora delivered his letter of resignation to Humberto Ortega in mid-1981, the National Directorate asked Castro to confine the popular leader for a while in Cuba, luxuriously, which Fidel did. Just before Pastora left Cuba at the end of the year, Castro visited him for the last time. The conversation was almost a discourse, Pastora recalls.

> Fidel said this was one of the most difficult times of his life. "You are constantly talking to me about Sandino," he said. "What do you mean by 'Sandinismo'?" I said I could put it in three words: nationalism, sovereignty and shame. I paused for a moment and added, "national shame when one's country is invaded." Fidel stood up, came over to me, put his hand on my shoulder, and said as if it were a secret: "Maintain that position throughout your life."[11]

Many observers have noted that Sandinismo permitted a more open, multiparty political system than existed in Cuba. That is true, but if put in the proper context it was, for many years, less significant than it appeared.

• The essence of the Sandinista political system was the same as Cuba's. The existence of other political parties besides the FSLN in Nicaragua was permitted in order to create a false image internationally—part of the deception Arce described—rather than to develop a truly democratic system. The opposition parties had to operate within a very repressive, though never totalitarian, system. They existed under conditions that were highly advantageous to the Sandinistas, who controlled all the resources of the nation, including finances, mass organizations, the EPS, security forces, television, and the centralized propaganda apparatus. Still they did continue to exist in a stunted form and became a rallying point for opposition to the Sandinistas, especially in the late 1980s.

• The organs of executive, legislative, and judicial power, as well as the army and security apparatus, were subordinated to the governing party: in Cuba to the Politburo—or, in reality, to Fidel—and in Nicaragua to the FSLN, in reality to the National Directorate. In this sense, as in Cuba, the ruling body was a single force whose "sacred duty" was to govern the destinies of the country forever.

• As in Cuba, it was impossible to control the abuses of power committed by the governing party and the state, which were the same. In Cuba the citizen generally had two options: he could be a member of the government and/or an open supporter of its actions, or he could be a counterrevolutionary. The same was true in Nicaragua where during much of the decade one was, in effect, either a Sandinista or a Contra. Even Cardinal Miguel Obando y Bravo, when he suggested negotiating with the Contras, was branded the second face of Ronald Reagan. This required a mass organizational system to maintain strict control over the population. In Cuba this included the control structure of the central government and the Committees for the Defense of the Revolution (CDRs); in Nicaragua it was the parallel control structure and the Sandinista Defense Committees (CDS).

• After 19 July 1979 Cuban influence was decisive in creating new government structures. The FSLN had no experience in these matters and believed that what Cuba had done often could be adapted to Nicaraguan needs, nowhere more so than in the control apparatus and the EPS. Concern over lack of flexibility and a certain patronizing attitude among the Cubans came later, as the Sandinistas got more experience of their own and the Cubans stayed on.

To some degree Cuba reciprocated in the early 1980s by proclaiming Nicaragua the model revolution for Latin America. In early 1982, for example, Manuel Piñeiro, the head of the America Department that had helped the Sandinistas defeat Somoza in 1979, addressed an international conference on the future of revolution in Latin America. He emphasized the need for a unified strategic outlook and tactics and pointed to the FSLN's struggle against Somoza as the model. The Sandinistas had shown how to take advantage of "any, even the smallest, opportunity of winning a mass ally, even though this ally is temporary, vacillating, unstable, unreliable and conditional." And he concluded that "the Sandinista triumph reaffirmed the crucial value of the unity of the vanguard as the nucleus providing cohesion and orientation to the anti-dictatorial, democratic, anti-imperialist and revolutionary forces as a whole."[12]

On balance, the relationship with Cuba was a disaster for Nicaragua since it promoted policies that created, above all else, domestic stagnation and decline and domestic and international warfare. In the late 1970s the Tercerista faction of the FSLN had adopted the more flexible, conciliatory line—similar to Castro's during 1957-58—that had made victory over Somoza possible and could have led to domestic growth and peace in Nicaragua after July 1979. But that line, which in the beginning Fidel Castro had considered downright "social democratic" was, in the words of Tercerista Víctor Tirado, "postponed" after 1979 as the Sandinistas pursued their "anti-imperlialist revolution. . . . We allowed ourselves to be guided by the ideas of the Cubans and the Soviets," Tirado wrote shortly after the 1991 FSLN Congress.[13]

Notes

1. See Humberto Ortega interview, *Verde Olivo* (Havana), 6 November 1986.
2. Ratliff interview with Pastora, 20 March 1992.
3. Ratliff interview with Pastora, 18 March 1992.
4. Ratliff interview with Pastora, 18 March 1992.
5. Ratliff interview with Pastora, 18 March 1992; also see Frank McNeil, *War and Peace in Central America* (New York: Scribner's, 1988), 113.
6. Ratliff interview with Pastora, 19 March 1992.
7. Figures cited in cable from U.S. embassy in Managua to Department of State in Washington, December 1986.
8. See Álvaro Baldizón, *Inside the Sandinista Regime: A Special Investigator's Perspective* (Washington: Office of Public Diplomacy, February 1986), 16.
9. See William Ratliff, "Castro's Debt Crusade," in Robert Wesson, ed., *Coping with the Latin American Debt* (New York: Praeger, 1988), 155-60.
10. In an interview with William Ratliff at the Hoover Institution, Stanford University, CA., 16 January 1992, George Shultz said: "There was never a plan or decision to invade Nicaragua. If others wanted to think we had one and squirm, we let them think it and squirm."
11. Ratliff interview with Pastora, 19 March 1992.
12. Manuel Piñeiro, "Imperialism and Revolution in Latin America and the Caribbean," in *New International: A Magazine of Marxist Politics and Theory* (New York), Spring-Summer 1984, 125, 124.
13. Víctor Tirado López, "Revolution is Creativity," *El Semanario* (Managua), 1-7 August 1991, trans. in *FBIS* (Latin America), 21.

8

The Soviet Union and the Sandinistas

The first contact of a "Sandinista" with the Soviet Union came in 1957, before the FSLN existed. During the summer and fall of that year, Carlos Fonseca, who several years later founded the FSLN, visited the Soviet Union twice and Eastern Europe once. He was the only Nicaraguan to attend the Sixth World Youth Festival in Moscow, cosponsored by the Soviet-front World Federation of Democratic Youth (WFDY) and the International Union of Students, which focused on youth from developing countries, as well as the Fourth Congress of the WFDY in Kiev. In Kiev he was invited to attend the Fourth Congress of the World Federation of Trade Unions in Leipzig, and in Germany Soviet workers invited him to return to Moscow, Kiev, and Leningrad, which he did. Fonseca's *A Nicaraguan in Moscow* is a wide-eyed description of these visits, as well as what he considered the overflowing international brotherhood of the exploited and the magnificent efficiency and productivity of state-run governments and enterprises.[1]

But none of this implied formal relations between the Soviet Union and the FSLN before 1979. Indeed, before the July revolution, the Sandinista leaders were disappointed that the Soviet Union would never agree to accept official FSLN representation in Moscow. They did not resent this, however, for they knew the Soviet Union did not have that sort of tie to other Latin American guerrilla movements either.

The first formal contacts came just days after the revolution. They were in Havana, for Cuba immediately played the role of intermediary between Managua and Moscow. At first the National Directorate appreciated this, since it had no experience dealing with the Soviets, and since the USSR was bound to prefer dealing with a potential new ally through an established old one. The Directorate considered this Cuban relationship transitional, however, as discussed elsewhere. But even when the Sandinistas felt it was time for a change, it was difficult to raise the matter, for Moscow seemed as satisfied with the Cuban channel as Fidel Castro, and the latter could not imagine it any other way.

Military Agreements and Aid

During the early years of the revolution, Cuba was included in all strategic decisions regarding the Soviet Union and Nicaragua. It was well known that the Soviet ambassador in Managua did not communicate directly with Moscow, but with the Soviet ambassador in Havana. Similarly, the Soviet Military Mission in Managua dealt with the mission in Cuba. Military and economic discussions were conducted by tripartite commissions, which included representatives of the three countries. In military cases, a Soviet delegation would visit Nicaragua in preparation for the lowest-level tripartite meetings in Managua. Then the proposals of the tripartite sessions involving EPS chief Joaquín Cuadra and the chiefs of the Cuban and Soviet military missions in Nicaragua would be taken to a higher level of tripartite meetings in Havana, those involving Humberto Ortega, Raúl Castro, and the chief of the Soviet military mission in Cuba, a three-star colonel general named Vladímir Konchis. After this commission reached its conclusions, Humberto would go to Moscow for the pro forma signing of the protocol with Soviet Minister of Defense Dimitri Ustinov.

In military and other affairs, there was a natural division of labor between the Soviets and the Cubans posted in Nicaragua. Moscow and its allies provided military aid to the Sandinistas free of charge, but its representation in Managua was in the hands of relatively low-level officials who met only with the top Sandinista officials. On several occasions Humberto Ortega invited General Konchis to visit Nicaragua, but he never came. To Ortega this was one of many "slights" that demonstrated to him that the Soviets never considered Nicaragua a really high priority in their foreign and defense policies. The Cubans, on the other hand, provided the bulk of the advisers, from officers of the renown of Arnaldo Ochoa down to the level of battalion chiefs, but almost no weapons.

After July 1979, the first Soviet arms came to Nicaragua by way of Cuba. A few weapons went exclusively to the Ministry of the Interior, among them a half dozen small, very destructive double-barreled derringers that used the same 7.62 ammunition as the AK-47 rifle and were intended for close-up assassinations and other dirty work. But most arms went to the EPS.

The first Sandinista delegation to visit Moscow to discuss military matters went in May 1980 and consisted of Defense Minister Ortega, Interior Minister Borge, and Henry Ruiz. It was decided that the Soviet Union would arm and equip the EPS, but that the details would have to be presented in a draft protocol prepared by a tripartite commission of Nicaraguans, Soviets, and Cubans, as described above, that would begin discussions in May 1981 in Managua. The protocol was completed in June 1981 and on 20 November 1981, Humberto Ortega signed the treaty in Moscow with Marshal Ustinov, though in fact heavy weapons (tanks and artillery) had begun to arrive at Port Bluff the previous July. It was called the Danto Plan in honor of FSLN fighter Germán Pomares, known as Danto, who was killed in 1978.

The treaty drew up three guidelines and laid the groundwork for years of intensive military development: (1) defining the enemy the FSLN would confront, (2) deciding on the type of army needed to engage that enemy and how it should be organized, and (3) determining what arms the Soviet Union should provide.

As discussed in the chapter on military doctrine, the FSLN and Soviets agreed that the primary enemy was the United States and preparations had to be made to meet the inevitable confrontation with Washington. The confrontation was inevitable, it was reasoned, because the United States would try to prevent the FSLN from building a communist society in Nicaragua and because Washington could not ignore Sandinista efforts to overthrow Central American governments and replace them with governments similar to the FSLN's. The FSLN recognized that this plan carried with it the probability of conflicts with the armies of other Central American countries, but in preparing to confront the Americans, the FSLN consciously was preparing to take on its neighbors as well.

With this main enemy, the EPS would need a massive modern army with extensive firepower and counterattack forces that would be capable of annihilating at least the first forces the enemy would send into Nicaragua. An early difference with the Soviets emerged. While the FSLN said it could build an army of 210,000 men with 20,000 on active duty in the first stage of development, the Soviets wanted 120,000 total with 22,000 on active duty. The Soviet position won out.

In the first treaty, the Soviet Union agreed to deliver the following arms, among others, during the 1981–1985 period:

• 100,000 AK rifles, about 3,000 light and heavy RPK and PKM machine guns, and RPG-7 rocket launchers;

• 4 T-55 tank battalions and 4 BTR-60 and BRDM-Z armored vehicle battalions;

• 4 152mm cannon groups, 3 122mm cannon-shell groups, 2 BM-21 repeat artillery groups, about 62 82mm mortar batteries and some other types of smaller caliber land artillery;

• a MiG-21 squadron (12 planes), a MI-8 squadron, and other AN-2TP single-engine airplane squadrons, as well as C-ZM and ZU-232 anti-aircraft weapons;

• 8 1400 ME Griff patrol boats.

The treaty also included communications and technical advisers for logistics, military engineering, transport, radar systems, construction of the MiG-21 airport, and training for officials in different specialties with courses lasting from six months to four years.

In 1984 the Managua-level Tripartite Commission began to develop the bilateral military protocol for 1986–90. The chief officials involved were Cuadra, Ochoa, and the Soviet representative, Major General Pablo, who came with the basics of the protocol already decided. The Sandinistas wanted any of several new arms systems, but the Soviets wouldn't even discuss the possibility. The Soviet decision was only to augment existing systems. The EPS did get some new infantry arms useful against the Contras, including the automatic AGS-17 hand grenade launcher; the largest single item was three squadrons (twelve units each) of MI-17 combat/transport helicopters.

The chief disappointment in Soviet aid became Moscow's failure to deliver the MiG-21 fighters it promised in 1981, discussed in detail in the next chapter. At the end of 1984, when it had became clear the planes would not be delivered as promised, a border incident raised Sandinista hopes high in a different direction. Unidentified planes attacked FSLN communications equipment in the northern part of the country, and the Soviets quickly sent a military commission to Managua. The Tripartite Commission recommended that sophisticated Pechora (SA-3) missiles be sent to Nicaragua to shoot down planes at low and medium altitudes. Directorate members saw this as a welcome compensation on the part of the Soviets for their failure to deliver the MiGs. At the end of 1985 a group of EPS officials under Captain Aldo Briones went to Cuba for six-months training in the Pechora, but in January 1986 word came to Managua that the missiles would not be sent, that 100mm cannons would be provided instead. Humberto moaned, "I'm not surprised. Every day I am more convinced that we're not first, we're not second, we're not even tenth priority to the Soviets!"

Still, by October 1987, a sampling of what the EPS had received included: some sixty Soviet-made helicopter gunships, including a dozen MI-25 HIND-D "flying tanks" and seventeen MI-17 helicopters; eighty-seven T-55 tanks and forty-three T-54 tanks, the critical element being the durable and easily-maintained T-55, which had strong fire power in certain tactical engagements but also could serve to intimidate the Nicaraguan population; sixty 152-MM cannons and thirty-six 122-MM cannons; thirty-six BM-21 rocket launchers ("Stalin's Organ"); and more than 250,000 rifles, from the Soviet Union (157,000), Korea (70,000), Iran, Bulgaria, Libya, RDA and Cuba.[2] By the tenth anniversary of the victory over Somoza in 1989, the EPS had a total of 250,000 soldiers on active duty, in the militias and the reserves. The FSLN had an armored force of some four hundred Soviet-made tanks and other armored personnel carriers—Somoza had had two dozen—which was about twice the number of armored vehicles in all other Central American countries combined.

The Last Soviet Hurrah

Sandinista military stock seemed to take off once again in July 1987 when negotiations began on a major new military escalation not just backed but initiated by the Soviet Union. The negotiations began a month before the Esquipulas II Central American peace agreement was concluded in Guatemala and continued after the signing of that document, which the Central American presidents (aside from Ortega) expected would reduce military forces and threats in the area.

On 19 October Humberto Ortega, accompanied by Joaquín Cuadra and Roger Miranda, explained the details of the Soviet offer to the National Directorate, as described elsewhere. Army Chief Cuadra gave a briefing on the technical and military aspects of two plans, called Diriangen I and II after a rebel who fought against the Spanish crown in the colonial period. The first plan focused on what was needed to defeat the Contras by 1990 and the second on a massive expansion thereafter.

Diriangen II was intended to at least double the size of the Nicaraguan military (regulars and reserves) to 600,000 between 1991 and 1995, even though the Sandinistas were convinced that the Contras and the Reagan administration would both be gone by then. This expanded military would include 100,000 regulars who would be used to mobilize the others in case of need. The details included the delivery of the long-awaited MiG-21s, mobile surface-to-air missiles, 400-ton warships, and other items. Although everyone wondered what the Soviets were expecting from this deal, Humberto argued that they obviously were thinking in "strategic terms" and that the unprecedented emphasis on the navy suggested they might be considering construction of an interoceanic canal through Nicaragua. Humberto then concluded, only partly in jest, that with a force of this size "we can sit down and seriously negotiate the San Andres Island issue with the Colombians," an island claimed by Nicaragua but long held by Colombia. Diriangen II was not only contrary to the Esquipulas II accord, it was against the spirit of Soviet glasnost.[3]

The objective on the Nicaraguan side still was to obtain a Soviet defensive "umbrella" and develop the capability to respond militarily to a U.S. invasion. But what was the Soviet Union up to offering this kind of military aid when it was talking publicly about easing tensions around the world? When asked about the plan several years later, then Soviet Foreign Minister Eduard Shevardnadze said he did not remember it at all, seeming to confirm Humberto's conclusion that Nicaragua didn't mean much to the Soviets. But a senior Soviet diplomat, Yuri Povlov, remembered it well, though he could not explain how it came about. It did not have the authorization of the foreign ministry, he said, but rather seems to have been hatched by the Soviet military hard-liners seeking to safeguard their own influence and foreign bases in competition with reformers in the central government.[4]

Moscow's Military Men in Managua

Daniel Ortega ended the discussion of the Diriangen II plan in 1987 by saying the Soviets knew what they were doing. But, in strictly military terms, did they really? Certainly for years Soviet military advisers stationed in Managua had created little confidence in their grasp of either military doctrine suitable to the Nicaraguan situation or more practical matters such as types of arms and fighting tactics. And since the tripartite meetings were managed by the Soviet delegate, one must assume that at least on the basics, the Soviet advisers in Managua represented the positions of the leaders in Cuba and Moscow.

The FSLN had started pressing for a resident Soviet military adviser in 1980, but none arrived until the end of 1981. Humberto speculated that the delay could be explained by a certain conservatism on the Soviet part: Moscow did not want to leap into what was traditionally considered an American sphere of influence as an ally of a government that had not yet even proven it could hold on to power. The first adviser—all of whom were known to the Sandinistas by Spanish-language pseudonyms—was Alejandro, a one-star general who had fought against the Germans in the Second World War. Unlike the Cubans, he spoke little, watched a lot, and refused to make judgments before he knew something about the subject. But he could not understand nor adjust to Nicaragua's needs.

In late 1983, as the war against the Contras was becoming a major challenge to the Sandinistas, Alejandro was replaced by Pablo, a totally different personality. Pablo was a rude bore who would crash into a meeting unannounced, a heavy smoker with withering breath who insisted on talking loudly into your face, the very model of an Ugly Soviet. Within the upper level of the EPS he was known as "manimal," the man-animal. When Miranda would ask Pablo's translator, Nicolai, how the general was, the aide would respond, "unbearable." Pablo would sit up all night watching videos and Nicolai would have to stay up with him to translate.

More important, however, negotiating with the Soviets under Pablo was even more difficult than before, though on major issues at least he undoubtedly was not so much negotiating as representing Moscow's predetermined wishes, as demonstrated in the 1984 discussion of the bilateral military protocol for 1986–90. But even discussions of conventional weapons could be unsuccessful. When the Sandinistas said they needed 100,000 rifles to arm the people's militias, Pablo responded that militias—which in the Soviet Union meant police—don't use that type of arms. In any event, he concluded, that would be a matter for the Interior Ministry not the Defense Ministry. Cuadra tried to explain to Pablo that the militias in Nicaragua were different, but all he could elicit was a wagging of the head and a progression of "niet, niet, niets." In the end the request was denied. Humberto was furious and wanted to go to the Soviet ambassador and ask that Pablo be sent home. Ochoa held Humberto back: "Look, chief, you have no idea what problems that would cause. On the contrary, you must try to work more with Pablo, develop more friendly ties and persuade him to change his mind."

Then in 1985, when the Contras were attacking the Sandinistas in larger forces, General Ochoa suggested that some of the Soviet artillery could be moved closer to the front lines and used against them. Pablo was furious and said he was there to make sure the FSLN used Soviet aid properly. With a rough voice and wild gestures, he told Cuadra: "Comrade, this is crazy. Artillery was made to be used in regular warfare, not against guerrillas." Cuadra tried to explain why the ministry had made the decision, but to no effect. Pablo stormed out of Cuadra's office shouting he was going to inform Moscow. But Humberto was more impressed by Ochoa's experience and advice than Pablo's rantings, and went ahead with the plan. The unorthodox use of artillery, even if not totally effective, served to break up the larger concentrations of Contra forces.

It May Be Junk, but It's Something and It's Free

Nicaragua could not have survived the damage caused by its own domestic and international policies for nearly as long as it did without Soviet economic aid. If there was never enough aid to meet the needs of Nicaragua's continuously worsening situation, any complaints had to be measured against three facts: Moscow's military aid was free, economic aid was virtually free, and the Soviet Union bought Nicaraguan products at above-market prices.

As in the case of military support, Sandinista leaders often felt the economic aid was not selected with adequate attention to Nicaragua's peculiar needs. One serious problem was the type of low-quality petroleum the Soviets provided, which was difficult to process with the technology available in Nicaragua. Also, the canned food was low quality, with a high grease content, and had to be eaten as quickly as possible because expiration dates often had already passed. Members of the EPS in particular complained repeatedly about the quality and many got sick from eating it. In general, the Soviet goods were of very low quality. Indeed, the Nicaraguan people distinguished three classes of quality in products: good, bad, and Soviet. One day Bayardo Arce arrived at Humberto Ortega's office for a meeting with several other comandantes who were already there. When he reached out and grabbed the door handle, it came off in his hand. He threw it aside with disgust, remarking "This must have been made by the Soviets." There was knowing laughter all around.

But there was also an important political angle to Soviet economic aid. FSLN leaders sought Soviet aid to enhance Nicaraguan separation from the non-communist world. One illustration of this was the FSLN's effort to increase its independence from two of its major neighbors—Mexico and Venezuela—that had long supplied much of Nicaragua's petroleum. When these two countries began applying economic pressures in the mid-1980s, the National Directorate concluded that these economic demands in fact demonstrated that Caracas and Mexico City had caved in to U.S. political pressures. Daniel Ortega wrote several letters to Soviet leaders arguing that Moscow should guarantee petroleum aid so that the level of dependence on Mexico and Venezuela could be broken for good; this would have involved the construction of a new refinery in Managua that could make better use of the Soviet petroleum. Indeed, at times the Directorate felt the petroleum problem put the very survival of the revolution at stake because irregular deliveries forced the FSLN to dip into EPS strategic reserves to prevent the collapse of the economy. In the event of a crisis, this dipping might have prevented the EPS from adequately performing its military plan.

At Cross Purposes with the Soviets

With few exceptions, for ideological and practical reasons the FSLN supported Soviet policies on the international level, privately, and in such public forums as the United Nations. But diplomatic differences and even tensions arose at times. The most serious was over the MiGs, which is discussed in the next chapter. Other matters included the cases of Israel and Iran, and Soviet bilateral relations with other countries reminded the Sandinistas that they were, with the Soviet Union too, "the poor brother in the family."

In 1984 the FSLN considered establishing diplomatic relations with Israel. There were several reasons for this. The Israelis had offered to drop the Nicaraguan debt to them in exchange for recognition. But even more important for the Sandinistas was the effort to neutralize a strong U.S. ally. Daniel Ortega explained to the Soviet ambassador that the Directorate thought if Nicaragua recognized Israel, the latter would not become involved in subverting the FSLN on behalf of the Americans. This was especially important just then because the U.S. Congress was turning against sending aid to the Contras and the Reagan administration's need for surrogates increased correspondingly. Several days after talking to Ortega, the Soviet ambassador received a cable from Moscow saying, among other things,

> the Soviet Union considers it useless to try to neutralize Israel's support for U.S. war policies in the region. The Nicaraguan government has the sovereign right to establish relations with Israel it if wishes to, but it should consider that such an action would not contribute to strengthening either cooperative ties with some Arab countries nor the bonds of friendship and solidarity between Nicaragua's government and our own.

No diplomatic ties were pursued.

A second instance of tension related to Iran and demonstrated how politics, even among ideological allies, could stand in the way of important domestic and international policies. When Vice President Sergio Ramírez visited Iran in 1984, the Iranians told the Sandinistas they would give them thousands of rifles and antitank missiles. Since it was deemed inadvisable for the Iranis to deliver the arms directly to Nicaragua, it was decided that they could be dropped off in Korea, which had recently promised a substantial arms donation to the FSLN, and the two shipments could be delivered to Cuba, which had agreed in advance to send an equal number of weapons to the Sandinistas in exchange for the arms from Korea and Iran.

Then the trouble began. At the end of 1984 Roger Miranda met with the Soviet ambassador in Managua to arrange for Soviet ships to transport the Korean and Iranian arms contributions to Cuba. As soon as Iran came up, the ambassador looked down, which he rarely did when speaking, but finally said: "Tell Commander Humberto that I will send the message to Moscow and that there should be no major problem, although the Iranian point may be misunderstood." When Ortega heard this he said, "Miranda, I think we have stuck our foot in it this time by mixing the Korean and Iranian donations." And sure enough, several days later a message arrived from Moscow: "The Soviet Government does not consider it appropriate to transport the arms donated by Iran because they are Soviet arms that were donated to Iraq and captured by Iran. We will, however, transport the Korean arms to Cuba as soon as the Koreans ask us to send a ship to do so." The Korean government responded that the Soviet ship could land, but that Moscow had to ask permission. Both parties said it was a question of sovereignty and neither would budge. The stalemate continued through 1985 and into 1986. The matter was finally resolved when Fidel Castro visited Korea in March 1986 and arranged for the arms to be sent to Cuba on a Cuban ship.

Notes

1. Carlos Fonseca, *Un Nicaraguense en Moscú* (Managua: Departamento de Propaganda y Educación del F.S.L.N., 1981).
2. Figures from "Equipo Militar Suministrado a Nicaragua Hasta La Fecha (Octubre de 1987)," in Roger Miranda archive, Hoover Institution.
3. The content and objectives of Diriangen I and II are spelled out in detail in top secret documents Roger Miranda carried out of Nicaragua at the end of 1987, materials now available in the Miranda collection at the Hoover Institution. See in particular: "Principales Lineamientos Para el Perfeccionamiento Orgánico, Fortalecimiento y Equipamiento del Ejército Popular Sandinista Para el Período 1988-1990, y Lineamientos Preliminares Para el Quinquenio 1991-1995" (Octubre 1987); and Ejército Popular Sandinista: "Pedido Complementario de Armamento, Técnica y Aseguramiento Técnico Material Para el Período 1988-1990: Diriangen I)" and "Pedido Preliminar de Armamento y Técnica Para el Quinquenio 1991-1995 (Diriangen II)"; and "Informe de la FAS-DAA para la Reunión Tripartita: 1987."
4. William Ratliff interviews at the Hoover Institution, Stanford, CA, with Eduard Shevardnadze, 18 May 1991; and Yuri Povlov, 17 October 1991.

9

The MiG Umbrella That Never Was

One of the key issues affecting and elucidating relations among the Sandinistas, the United States, Cuba, and the Soviet Union was the matter of the possible placement of Soviet MiG-21 fighter planes in Nicaragua. The issue requires separate attention because it played a major role in Sandinista attitudes toward, and relations with, all three governments.

The Sandinistas wanted MiGs for two overlapping military and political reasons that shifted in importance with the consummation of the military reforms in 1984:

1. Prior to that year, the MiGs were considered mainly in military terms, as critical for defending the country against an attack by the United States and/or its allies;

2. During and after the Ochoa-led reforms, the MiGs were still considered critical for defending Nicaragua against a U.S. attack as well as important in intercepting Contra supply planes. But the political significance of the planes became even more important, for the National Directorate hoped that their placement in Nicaragua would constitute a firm Soviet commitment to defend the Sandinista revolution, comparable to the "umbrella" Castro got after the Missile Crisis of 1962.

How Would You Like Some MiGs?

In 1981 Humberto Ortega and Soviet armed forces chief Marshal Dimitri Ustinov signed the first Nicaraguan/Soviet military protocol in Moscow. In this agreement, the Soviet Union committed itself to deliver a squadron of MiG-21s to Nicaragua early in 1985. Moscow also agreed to conduct the final training of the pilots and send specialized equipment for the construction of a military airport near Managua, the airfield to be built with the help of the Cubans.

The young Nicaraguans chosen to be trained as pilots ranged in age from seventeen to twenty-two years and had to go through a rigorous screening process, covering everything from health to political views, with the direct involvement of Soviet officials. The training period consisted of three years in Bulgaria and one in the Soviet Union. Only a couple of recruits caused difficulties and had to be returned to Nicaragua. One was a student who had spent two years studying in Bulgaria before it was discovered that he had been born in Costa Rica. He was recalled because only native-born Nicaraguans were allowed to participate in the program.

The construction of the airfield posed many more problems, but at least it went ahead slowly. Cuba, which had invaluable experience building airfields at home and in other countries, sent a team of advisers and some equipment, but refused to contribute cement, a critical component that was in short supply in Cuba as well. The construction was begun in 1981 at Punta Huete on the shores of Lake Managua and for years used a high percentage of the national production of cement, at the expense of other important national projects.

But the planes themselves were never delivered and the matter of the MiGs became the single most serious source of tension and mistrust ever between Managua, Havana, and Moscow. This is how it went. Toward the end of 1982 the possible delivery of the MiGs became an international issue when U.S. Secretary of State George Shultz told the OAS in Washington that Nicaragua was getting a squadron of the fighters. Humberto called a press conference in which he neither denied nor affirmed Shultz's story. Typical of his comments was one that the government of Nicaragua had not tried to buy arms in recent months, nor would it in the weeks or months ahead. The escape was that the protocol had been signed a year earlier—not in recent months—and the planes would be given to Nicaragua, not bought. But the Sandinistas were not really bothered by the American position, and indeed early in the decade the State Department was not particularly concerned that the Soviets would actually send MiGs to Managua.[1]

Fidel Horns In

Everything seemed to move smoothly for the Sandinistas until early 1984 when Fidel Castro unexpectedly began suggesting to Sandinista leaders that they should tell the Soviets to forget the MiG-21s and send a squadron of MI-25 helicopters instead. His effort to shift Sandinista preferences was so intense, in a field of such vital interest to the Nicaraguan leaders, that it had strong negative repercussions on Nicaraguan-Cuban relations.

Fidel began his campaign in January 1984 during an all-night session in Havana with Comandante Henry Ruiz. His argument was:

1. The Reagan administration was pressuring Moscow not to send MiGs; if the Soviet Union sent them, the U.S. air force would attack and destroy the planes on the ground, in what would be a very embarrassing development for the Soviets.

2. The most important task now for the Sandinistas was to defeat the counterrevolution. This was the period of greatest Contra strength; they had grown so much that Castro argued they had to be dealt a profound blow or they would become a serious threat to the government. The MiG-21s were of no value in fighting the Contras because their speed and armaments meant they were intended to intercept and fight enemy aircraft not to battle guerrillas. The helicopters, however, could contribute a great deal to the anti-Contra struggle. Fidel said that if the Sandinistas agreed, he would send instructors to Managua to retrain the MiG pilots who had studied in Soviet bloc countries so that they could fly the helicopters.

Fidel then explained a new Cuban defense strategy developed since the U.S. invasion of Grenada, which he felt was suitable to Nicaragua as well. (It was the strategy General Ochoa introduced in Nicaragua beginning in that year, which is discussed in the chapter on military strategy.) For two decades, Castro said, the Cubans themselves had mistakenly thought they could fight the Americans in conventional warfare: land, sea, and air. After Grenada, Castro realized that that strategy was ridiculous. And if the Cubans couldn't defeat the Americans in the air, how much less could the Nicaraguans. "But we can defeat them on the ground," he said, "using a combination of conventional and unconventional warfare. We are much better in the latter than they are. The Americans are not going to try to kill millions and millions of Cubans who are defending their country. That is why we are launching The War of All the People, as the Vietnamese did before us."

When Ruiz returned to Nicaragua, he passed Castro's analysis on to the National Directorate, with his own full support. There were more pressing issues to discuss in the Directorate at the time, but Daniel and Humberto sat back puzzled: what signal was Fidel trying to send? A month later the message Fidel had given to Ruiz was repeated in a speech to top-level Cuban government officials. Suddenly every contact with anyone from Cuba was an occasion for the same message. It came from Fidel and Raúl and others to anyone who visited Cuba, and it came from every Cuban stationed in or visiting Nicaragua, including Ambassador López, General Ochoa, and Manuel Piñeiro. Meanwhile, no one ever said what the Soviets thought or wanted, including the Soviets themselves.

Differences of Opinion in the Directorate

As the barrage continued, the National Directorate debated the idea. Humberto was the most outspoken in opposition to Fidel's position. He acknowledged that it was true a successful confrontation with the Yankees would have to rely more on people than technology and that the helicopters would be more useful in fighting the Contras than the MiGs. But, he added:

1. Nicaragua still does not have the protection of a Soviet "umbrella," as the Cubans have had since 1962. So far the Sandinistas had received only modest military aid and a military mission in Managua of no more than eight people. The FSLN needed to move the Soviets step by step toward a full commitment to the Nicaraguan revolution, to accepting it as their own, to agreeing to defend it in the event of a U.S. invasion. The issue of the MiGs might move the Soviets in that direction. If Washington tried to intimidate Nicaragua by threatening to strike the planes on the ground in Nicaragua, it would be intimidating the Soviet Union as well. If the United States attacked the planes, it would be violating Nicaraguan sovereignty, but even more importantly, it would be defying Moscow and this might bring the Soviets to a firm agreement to defend the revolution. Thus the Sandinistas had to point to this matter of the MiGs as a confrontation between the United States and the Soviet Union; they had to press the Soviets to send the planes, playing on their pride. Humberto concluded, "I am hoping that for the United States and the Soviet Union, this point of the MiG-21s will become the counterpart of the Cuban missile crisis of 1962."

2. Cuba is not telling us exactly that the Soviet Union wants us to take helicopters instead of MiGs. Humberto continued:

> It doesn't seem at all unlikely to me that the Soviets, lining up their international interests, have asked Castro to persuade us to give up the MiG-21s. But we must never renounce them, nor must we allow Cuba to continue being an intermediary between ourselves and the Soviets. If the Soviets think they can't send the MiGs, for whatever reasons, they must tell us that directly. We can not let our strategic relationship with the Soviets be run any longer through Havana, no matter how profound the ties of friendship have been between ourselves and the Cubans.

The debate in the National Directorate was hot, with Ruiz and Borge much more inclined to accept Fidel's argument than the Ortegas were. But in the end all the comandantes recognized the concerns of the Ortegas and decided that

1. the Sandinistas would not accept the role of the Cubans as messengers of the Soviets on the MiG affair;

2. the FSLN would not renounce the MiGs promised in the 1981 protocol;

3. Humberto Ortega, who had agreed to take a trip to North Korea in April, would pass through Moscow and find out from Marshal Ustinov what the Soviet position was;

4. Humberto would be authorized to talk with the Czech government about getting L-39 hunter-interceptor planes, which the Sandinistas considered second best to the MiGs, if the Soviet deal fell through.

In early March, shortly after the National Directorate meeting, Roger Miranda met with the Czech ambassador to Managua and informed him that Ortega wanted to visit Czechoslovakia during an upcoming trip to the Soviet Union and North Korea. The ambassador was delighted and said he would get full honors. But the Czech Ministry of Defense wanted to know if Ortega had specific business to transact. When the Czech ambassador informed Prague that the FSLN defense minister wanted to explore the possible acquisition of L-39 planes, communication was broken for several weeks and finally the reply came back that the Czech minister was sick and the trip would have to be postponed. No one believed he was sick and Ortega was not only angry but personally insulted. He concluded that the Czechs had talked with the Soviets and the latter had felt Prague should not discuss the possible acquisition of L-39s with the Sandinistas.

Ortega, Miranda, and the delegation left Managua for the Soviet Union and North Korea on 29 March and spent the night in Havana in the special protocol house no. 14 called El Lagito. The Cubans knew Humberto had been invited to Korea as the personal guest of Kim Il Song, but they did not know that the stopover in Moscow was to talk about the MiGs. Humberto met with Ustinov in Moscow and the latter said the Soviets, as honorable allies, would supply the planes by 1985 as promised in the protocol. When the Managua-level Tripartite Commission began to develop the second bilateral military protocol (for 1986–90) in 1984, the FSLN again raised the matter of the elusive MiGs. But when the protocol was finished, no MiGs were mentioned and delivery according to the original agreement never occurred.

Aftershocks

Several bizarre twists occurred in the MiG story after that, among them the following.

In September 1986 Daniel Ortega and Fidel Castro met with Moammar Qaddafi at the VIII Nonaligned Conference in Zimbabwe. At that meeting, the Libyan leader offered to send Nicaragua 20,000 AK rifles and 3 Czech L-39s. When Daniel told Humberto, the latter responded, "Are you sure there wasn't a problem of translation?" but Daniel responded, "I said the same thing but Fidel was at the meeting and that's the way he heard it too." Since the EPS then wanted such fighters, Roger Miranda pursued the matter with Libyan representatives. It was decided the Cubans would send a ship to pick up the arms, but when Cuba did so, it came back with only 800 rifles and a message to come back again for the rest. In January 1987, as soon as the ship reached Cuba, Fidel sent Brigadier General Alejandro Ronda Marrero, chief of the Special Troops in Cuba's Ministry of the Interior, to Managua. Ronda Marrero's arrival was totally unexpected and he asked to meet immediately with Humberto to deliver a personal message from Fidel. Ronda Marrero told Humberto that, on hearing about the size of the delivery from Libya, Fidel had shouted out that Qaddafi was an "asshole sonofabitch" and proclaimed that he would not send another ship back to get anything more.

The MiG-21s came up again in late 1987 when Soviet negotiators turned up in Managua to urge the Sandinistas to accept these planes—as if urging were necessary—as part of the broadest EPS expansion program yet proposed, as related in detail elsewhere in this book. According to the new offer, delivery would be in 1992. The Sandinista leaders wondered what lay behind the new offer—the MiGs and all the rest— even as they questioned the timing. But they accepted the Soviet proposal, and again received nothing.

The prolonged MiG affair raised a lot of questions and prompted the Sandinista leaders to draw a variety of sometimes tentative conclusions with respect to their two closest allies in Havana and Moscow. Among the most important were the following.

• With respect to the Soviet Union, Sandinista leaders were confirmed in their belief that the Nicaraguan revolution was a rather low priority concern in Moscow. Why had MiGs been offered in 1981 and never delivered, and offered again in 1987. Were both offers, the second totally out of line with Gorbachev's glasnost policy, simply ploys intended as bargaining chips in general Soviet relations with the United States? Was the unexpected 1987 offer, most of which was not followed up on, indicative of internal conflict within the Soviet Union; between Gorbachev, for example, and the military, with the latter wanting to maintain a much more active profile abroad than the former?

• With respect to Cuba, Castro sometimes had an agenda that did not coincide directly the Sandinistas' own interests. Because this was so, and because the Nicaraguan revolution had to stand independently in the world, the Sandinistas could not allow Castro to continue his original role as middleman between Managua and Moscow.

Note

1. Ratliff interview with Charles Hill, former chief of staff of the State Department and executive aide to Secretary Shultz, at the Hoover Institution, Stanford, CA, 1 August 1991.

10

Beyond Nicaragua's Borders

One of the primary elements of Sandinista foreign policy was revolutionary internationalism, or ties to "anti-imperialist" revolutionary movements around the world. The term meant everything from verbal defense of revolutionary groups to arming, training, and otherwise tangibly supporting guerrilla movements seeking to overthrow established governments in the Third World, especially Latin America. During the 1980s priority was given to the Central American region generally and El Salvador specifically, where it was particularly easy to pinpoint the United States as the principal enemy.

The Sandinista leadership engaged in this form of revolutionary internationalism for a variety of interrelated reasons. It felt a sacred duty to revolutionary comrades abroad, many of whom had helped the Sandinistas overthrow Somoza. Also, it promoted the long-term objective of weakening the United States by bringing to power other groups that had the same domestic and international objectives as the Sandinistas. In a secondary way it might enhance security by destabilizing regional governments that were allies of the United States, thus diverting U.S. attention from Nicaragua, and by strengthening revolutionary groups in the region that could be counted upon to harass the Americans if Washington dared to invade Nicaragua, directly or indirectly.

In a sense this was the Sandinista implementation of Che Guevara's call in his 1967 "Message to the Tricontinental":

How close and bright would the future appear if two, three, many Vietnams, flowered on the face of the globe, with their quota of death and immense tragedies, with their daily heroism, with their repeated blows against imperialism, obliging it to disperse its forces under the lash of the growing hate of the people of the world![1]

During the euphoria of the early years, there was never any question as to whether the Sandinistas would aid neighboring guerrillas; the only questions were which ones and how? Foreigners who think the National Directorate did not send some support abroad immediately and continue over the years as a matter of policy, or think they would have ended this support through the mid-1980s in exchange for a U.S. pledge not to support a counterrevolutionary movement, to give more economic aid, or whatever, simply have no idea how the comandantes then felt and thought. Revolutionary internationalism was not up for discussion at that time; it was a given.

But it was publicly denied. Uninformed foreigners believed these denials while the Sandinistas' allies abroad either believed in ignorance or went along with the lies as a form of revolutionary solidarity. For example, on 12 March 1980, Tomás Borge told the Chamber of Deputies in the Dominican Republic: "We are not responsible for what is happening in El Salvador. . . . We are only guilty of our example and we can not help it if our example reaches other places. . . . There will never be any aggression from our country against any other country." On 23 June 1980, just as the guerrilla network operating out of Managua was coming on line *under his personal supervision*, Bayardo Arce said the charges that the Sandinistas were supplying arms to the guerrillas in El Salvador were absurd and slanderous.

The Sandinistas gave priority to Central America for several reasons: the geographic proximity of the region, the strategic importance of those countries to the United States, and the history of relations between the Sandinistas and guerrillas in the area. The ties went back to the 1960s and for some time were closest to the Revolutionary Armed Forces (FAR) of Guatemala under Luis Augusto Turcios Lima, a prominent participant in the 1966 Tricontinental Conference in Havana who died in October of that year. During the final years of the war against Somoza, the Salvadoran guerrillas—chiefly the Armed Forces of National Resistance (FARN)—donated several million dollars gained from ransoms in El Salvador.[2]

Guerrilla Central in Managua

Consequently, the FSLN promoted the destabilization of neighboring governments and, by the end of 1979, Nicaragua had become the center of revolutionary activity in Latin America. Managua hosted representatives from guerrilla movements of Colombia, Guatemala, El Salvador, Argentina, Uruguay, Chile, and other countries. At first the relations were informal, but by the end of 1979 they were handled by the Secretariat for International Relations (SRI), headed by Doris Tijerino and directly supervised by Bayardo Arce, modeled on and advised by the Cuban America Department. The Secretariat was soon enlarged and strengthened to become, in September 1980, the Department of International Relations (DRI). Tijerino was replaced by a more powerful person, Julio López Campos, who reported directly to the National Directorate as the America Department did to Fidel in Cuba.

With Cuban help, a new structure was formed in Managua under Arce's control to accumulate, warehouse, pack, and dispatch military supplies to different Central American guerrilla movements. By July 1980 the structure was fully operational. It was based in a villa confiscated from a Somoza supporter in the old quarter of León. The supply operation was headed by Arce's right-hand man, Luis Armando Guzmán. Guzmán's pseudonym was "Ernesto" and the new apparatus, called the "Buro," soon was known as the "Buro Ernesto." It pulled together all activities that linked the supply of arms and other materials to guerrilla forces. Cuba played an active role in setting up the Buro with its professional core in underground transport of military supplies, communications, service personal, etc. But the Buro also depended on the active and official support and resources of the two largest ministries in the Nicaraguan government—Defense and Interior.

During 1981 the Buro consolidated and developed its activities, providing various sorts of military supplies to guerrillas in all Central American countries, as well as some in South America, including the Colombian M-19. Ernesto had gained the respect and admiration of those who knew about his work and he had become a key staff member in the Sandinista administration.[3] Still, in the end, the success of the "Buro-Ernesto" system must be seen as a reflection of the skill of Bayardo Arce.

Simultaneously, in early 1980, responsibilities were assigned for feeding and training the guerrillas, a task of immediate importance since the Cuban, Sandinista, and Salvadoran leaders planned to launch broadly based actions in early 1981. A natural division of responsibility was adopted: Nicaragua would be the center for the reception and supplying of arms and munitions and a large warehouse in Managua was reconditioned for this use near what is known as Casa Pellas. The main training would be done in Cuba, where experience was greater and conditions better, though some units and groups were trained also in Nicaragua. Those trained in Nicaragua attended the recently formed Carlos Agüero School, where original basic courses of six months were later extended to one year.

Focus on El Salvador

The Directorate considered El Salvador the most likely location for a successful guerrilla war for several reasons: (1) the government was showing signs of internal crisis and divisions; (2) the army was not prepared to confront large-scale guerrilla warfare; (3) there was a large, dense population living in very poor conditions, which was considered compensation for the relative lack of mountains.

The first step undertaken in cooperation with the Cubans was to apply pressure on the Salvadoran guerrillas to unify, an effort which bore first fruits in December 1979, when the Communist party of El Salvador (PCES), the Popular Liberation Forces (FPL) and the Armed Forces of National Resistance (FARN) coordinated actions. In the first months of 1980, the People's Revolutionary Army (ERP) and the Revolutionary Party of Central American Workers (PRTC) joined them to form the Unified Revolutionary Directorate (DRU), which was later called the Farabundo Martí Front for National Liberation (FMLN).

By the end of 1979, with the help of Cuban military advisers, the FSLN had drawn up a still somewhat vague "Victory Plan" to transform its guerrilla army into a regular army, the EPS, the first steps being taken in 1980. With arms taken from Somoza's defeated National Guard, and those the FSLN had received from other countries during the war against Somoza, the Sandinistas on taking power had some 20,000 rifles of different makes of Western manufacture: M-16, FAL, GARAND and M-1 SPRINFEL, among others, not all of which were in good condition, as well as various artillery pieces of different calibers; by 1987 some 18,000 had been passed on to guerrillas abroad. Every weapon the FMLN received went through Nicaragua.

Thus the Sandinistas had the Western infantry weapons the Salvadoran guerrillas needed, but they could not provide them to the FMLN until they were sure the EPS would get replacements. For their part, the

Cubans had a great quantity of armaments, but most were of Soviet manufacture. They had reserves of infantry arms of Western manufacture, but always less than were needed by the various guerrilla movements. Thus the Cubans advised immediate joint actions including "the cousins," as they affectionately called the Salvadorans, with the Communist bloc countries, especially Vietnam, to obtain Western arms. But the Cubans, Sandinistas, and Salvadorans knew that this process would not bear fruit for at least a year and, given the need to acquire arms for the 1981 actions, something else had to be done in the meantime.

Therefore at the beginning of 1980, the Cubans proposed sending a high-level Sandinista delegation to Moscow with the following goals:

1. Explore with Soviet leaders their willingness to arm and equip the nascent Sandinista People's Army;

2. Inform the Soviets of the general strategies reached with the Cubans with respect to Central American guerrilla movements, and in particular the Salvadoran guerrillas, thus the urgency of acquiring Western arms;

3. Inform the Soviets that the Cubans would be ready to provide Soviet-made infantry weapons to the EPS if the Soviets would replenish the Cuban stock of arms with weapons the Soviets were ready to send to the Sandinistas. The Sandinistas could then send their Western arms immediately to the FMLN. This program of three-way aid and exchange was known as "triangular trade."

The Sandinista leadership responded positively to the recommendation and on 17 May 1980 the Military Commission of the National Directorate of the FSLN, made up of Borge, Humberto Ortega, and Henry Ruiz took off for Moscow. The Soviet and Sandinista negotiators agreed:

1. The Soviet Union would arm and equip the EPS, as described above.

2. The Soviet Union would send AK rifles to Cuba between 1981 and 1985 enabling Cuba immediately to send Soviet weapons from its supplies to the Nicaraguans. This guaranteed, the FSLN could send Western infantry weapons immediately to the FMLN.

Thus the Sandinistas, with critical Cuban and Soviet support, began a covert war against the Salvadoran and other Latin American governments through the triangular military aid program. The National Directorate received a daily war report prepared by the Directorate of Military Intelligence (DIM) in conjunction with the FMLN representative in Nicaragua.

While Nicaragua provided arms and other support, the FMLN usually planned its own actions. But FMLN leaders were expected to discuss any significant new tactical move in advance with the Sandinistas. Proposals and reactions were presented, whether in El Salvador or Nicaragua, with mutual respect. Once this did not happen, when the FMLN assassinated four U.S. Marines in the Zona Rosa of San Salvador in June 1985, and the tensions were palpable. The U.S. government sent a note to the Sandinistas saying the Americans had heard plans were now being made to attack U.S. citizens in Honduras as well. Considering Sandinista relations with these groups, the U.S. source warned, Nicaragua would be held directly responsible for any such attack that occurred. Arce put his foot down: "No more of that," he warned the Salvadoran and Honduran guerrillas.[4]

The Sandinistas had sent arms to El Salvador during the last half of 1979, but shipments had been irregular and disorganized. In January 1980 Joaquín Cuadra met with FMLN leaders on behalf of Humberto Ortega to plan the official, coordinated supply program. After that time Nicaragua sent arms and munitions systematically to the Salvadoran guerrillas, though not always as many or as systematically as the guerrillas wanted, part of the problem at times being continuing disunity among the guerrillas themselves.[5]

The main routes were by sea and land since air would have allowed easy tracking of the supplies. The sea route at first used "cayucos" (small launches with outboard motors) that left the Nicaraguan coast from the Gulf of Fonseca at night; in a few hours they arrived on the Salvadoran coast of Usulutan which was sparsely patrolled by the Salvadoran army. This form of transport had the advantage of not leaving evidence of the cargo's origin if discovered en route. If a boat was stopped, the weapons would be thrown overboard; if the supplies were seized on Salvadoran territory, they would already be in the hands of the FMLN.

The usual point of departure was from the Padre Ramos creek, about 50 kilometers north of Corinto Port. In January 1984 one of the Sandinista supply ships was captured by a Sandinista marine patrol, which had not been informed of this activity. Immediately thereafter, Humberto Ortega delegated Roger Miranda, accompanied by Gustavo Moreno, who had taken over as head of the "Buro Ernesto" in 1983, to brief the two top heads of the marines, Commander Ricardo Lugo and Captain Manuel Rivas, on this activity and stressed the need to prevent such incidents from recurring. It was decided that Lugo would be notified in advance of any ship's leaving for El Salvador, and he in turn would inform the deputy chief of the marines who would instruct the patrol boats operating out of Corinto that day. This was called the "butterfly operation."

The land routes used commercial trucks or private vehicles called "ants," with double undercarriages that made it difficult to determine whether or not the truck was carrying arms. Chances of discovery were remote also because the inspection process needed to find arms was lengthy and uncommon since there were long lines of vehicles waiting to cross the borders.

During 1980 the Salvadoran guerrillas received at least two thousand automatic rifles and sufficient munitions for their operations, some siege machine guns, RP-G-2 rocket launchers and explosives. They operated a radio station that supposedly transmitted from El Salvador but actually was in a house on Villa Panama in Managua, only meters from the home of Foreign Minister Miguel D'Escoto.

At the beginning of 1981, according to plan, the Salvadoran guerrillas were able to launch a major campaign that has come to be known as the "final offensive." Some in the FMLN, Nicaragua, and Cuba thought this offensive would overthrow the Salvadoran government, but some did not. Miguel Castellanos, a member of the Political Commission of the Popular Liberation Forces, and chief of the FPL Urban Front, did not believe the offensive would be final and attributes this optimism to a "triumphalist" attitude of some Cuban and Nicaraguan supporters.[6] The FPL and some advisers abroad did not believe that conditions were yet sufficiently ripe for the seizure of power. The strategy was to build the FMLN into the strongest guerrilla force in Latin America, to exhaust the army, to sabotage the economy, and to attract increasing support from abroad, particularly in and from the Western democracies.

Shipments could not be maintained at that level and they fell briefly after the "final offensive." But the temporary decline was in no sense because the Sandinistas had changed their minds or were waiting for a conciliatory gesture from Washington. During the year, the Buro continued to supply the guerrillas with reserves from the EPS as well as arms sent by Cuba. The most important shipment came from Vietnam. It arrived at Port Corinto, on the Pacific side of Nicaragua, in July 1981, and consisted of 1500 M-16 rifles, each with 1000 cartridges, as well as 120 pistols—.38 calibre—and some light machine guns. The Vietnamese

142   The Civil War in Nicaragua

donation had been made at the beginning of the year, but was delayed because the Vietnamese authorities required that the Nicaraguan government send a high-level delegation to Vietnam to confirm that the Nicaraguan party agreed to receive the weapons earmarked for the FMLN. In March of 1981 Humberto Ortega headed a delegation to Vietnam. In May, Captain Augusto Montealegre, then secretary-general of the Defense Ministry, traveled to Vietnam to finalize the shipment with the Vietnamese secretary of defense. On Humberto's instructions, the shipment was recorded under the code name, "Operation KDV," for "cargo from Vietnam."

The united and well-equipped guerrillas had a great impact in El Salvador, where the army had never faced such a challenge. Among their major exploits was the destruction of the important Oro bridge on the Lempa River. In response, the United States stepped up military aid to El Salvador and neighboring countries, charging Sandinista involvement with the FMLN, though the Sandinista government denied any role. On 12 March 1981, for example, Daniel Ortega directed Foreign Minister D'Escoto to categorically deny that the Sandinistas were sending any arms to El Salvador. The document concluded: "Consequently, the Nicaraguan government has not made any commitment to suspend sending arms, because it has never sent any."

At the beginning of 1982, the Directorate drew up a balance sheet on the activities of the FMLN, weighing the levels of success in El Salvador with the international political cost of continuing support. On the one hand, the facts seemed to prove the Ortega brothers had been right; the guerrillas, receiving support from their Sandinista comrades, had become a formidable force. Contrary to some pessimistic predictions, the guerrillas had started the year stronger than ever. Indeed, if members of the Directorate hoped for a guerrilla victory, it was in 1982. Consideration was even given to reinforcing the Salvadoran guerrillas with EPS squadrons headed by such leaders as Hilario Sánchez and Walter Ferrety, an idea that was finally rejected because of the possible repercussions if they were captured or killed on Salvadoran territory.

Increasing Doubts, but Aid Continues

But the FMLN's failure to make greater progress, and its internal weaknesses, increasingly caused concern among the comandantes. Be-

ginning in August 1981, the United States launched diplomatic initiatives, discussed below, and carried out a joint U.S.-Honduran military
maneuver called "Halcon Vista" on the east coast of Honduras. Other
maneuvers followed, the United States expanded its military presence in
Honduras and improved the Hondurans' military infrastructure. In light
of these actions, the Directorate had to reconsider, ever more seriously,
whether supporting the FMLN was really an effective way of preventing
or countering an American attack. Or might it in fact significantly
increase the prospects of open U.S. intervention in El Salvador and then
Nicaragua?

But buoyed by the continuing hope of a guerrilla triumph, and unwilling to back down on the principle of revolutionary internationalism, the
aid continued throughout 1982. Doubts were even greater in 1983.
Despite continuing support for the guerrillas by the Sandinistas and the
Cubans, the government in San Salvador had shown signs of moving
beyond the crisis stage; if President Duarte couldn't defeat the guerrillas,
he was no longer in danger of being overthrown. Also, in January 1983
the governments of Mexico, Colombia, Venezuela, and Panama launched
the Contadora peace movement, which meant greater obstacles to the
delivery of aid as well as opportunities for exploiting the peace movement.

Beginning in 1983, expectations of a quick military victory began to
diminish and by 1985 some members of the Directorate—particularly
the Ortegas—looked increasingly on the FMLN as a bargaining chip in
the FSLN effort to stop the expansion of U.S. military activity in the
region, to get the U.S. and Honduran governments to stop supporting the
burgeoning Contra rebels, and to negotiate an end to U.S. aid for the
Salvadoran army. But even if some comandantes were losing confidence
in the prospects of the FMLN, this did not bring an end to the Sandinistas'
military and other support for the FMLN. During the first six months of
1984, the Sandinistas increased arms shipments to the guerrillas because
they expected more pressures on them for peace during the last half of
the year. Also, as the year progressed it became more difficult to get
weapons into El Salvador because of improving security procedures
introduced by the Salvadoran military.

Notwithstanding doubts about the FMLN's prospects, aid continued
through the decade at irregular levels. An incident in January 1985—just
days after Castro had visited Managua and proclaimed that "revolutions

can not be exported"—illustrated the continuing Cuban and Nicaraguan involvement in the Salvadoran war and threw light on the personal sacrifices Nicaraguans and Cubans made to help their ally. On 20 January a Soviet-built IL-18 took off from Havana's José Martí Airport with only forty passengers on board, among them the wife of Nicaraguan ambassador to Cuba Marcos Valle and the couple's two-year-old daughter. Most of the plane's seats were empty. It was common knowledge among military leaders that any large Cuban passenger plane with few passengers, like this one, was carrying arms and munitions in its baggage compartment. The arms in this shipment, which had been donated by Cuba, Bulgaria, North Korea, and East Germany, were intended for the FMLN. Marcos Valle was waiting to meet his wife at the Sandino Airport in Managua, as was Commander Omar Halleslevens, chief of military counterintelligence, who was responsible for moving the arms to clandestine military warehouses near the Casa Pellas. But this day, just fifteen minutes out of Havana, the heavy cargo, which had been carelessly packed, began to shift. The pilot got permission to return to Havana, but at San José de las Lajas, twenty miles south of Havana, he lost control and the plane crashed. There were no survivors. The report of the accident in *Barricada* said nothing about the cause of the crash or the plane's cargo.[7]

Cayetano Carpio and Ana María

Another dramatic personal drama, which the Sandinistas tried to turn into a campaign against "U.S. imperialism," calls for special attention. This incident occurred in 1983 and reflected the ever-present tensions within the FMLN, which had in some degree decreased its effectiveness and lessened FSLN confidence in ultimate victory. This was an explosion of sadistic violence within the FPL, the most substantial of the five FMLN guerrilla groups, and the biggest scandal among the Salvadoran guerrillas since Joaquín Villalobos was in the hit squad that killed guerrilla poet Roque Dalton in 1975.[8]

On 6 April 1983, just south of Managua, the second-in-command of the FPL, Melida Amaya Montes, known as Ana María, was murdered by multiple stabbings. The National Directorate's first reaction to the murder of this model woman revolutionary was to try to hide it from the media on the grounds that it confirmed U.S. charges that the Salvadoran guerrilla leaders lived in and worked out of Nicaragua. But after consultations with other FMLN leaders in Managua, including Joaquín Villalobos, the head of the ERP, who had good ties to Ana Maria, they decided to publicize her death. Because of the treacherous and sadistic nature of the crime, and because preliminary investigations suggested it had been committed by the CIA, the Directorate decided that more was to be gained than lost by pinning the murder on the CIA and trying to capture the perpetrators.

The offensive against the United States was launched in *Barricada* on 7 April in a communique signed by the leadership of the FMLN, supposedly written in San Salvador but actually composed in Managua. It stated: "This treacherous crime, committed by the shadowy bands of the Central Intelligence Agency, shows in a palpable manner the desperation of imperialism . . . to avoid the certain revolutionary triumph of the Salvadoran people." The next day, the lead headline of *Barricada* said: "Confirmed: the CIA Assassinated Ana María," with a smaller headline saying, "The Fruits of Reagan's Policy." Beneath the headlines there were two photographs, one of Ana María's bare, mangled body and the other of a beaming Ronald Reagan. The story, reporting on a press conference by Tomás Borge and Lenín Cerna, charged that the assassination was "another bloody landmark of imperialist aggression" and "can not be seen outside the context of Reagan's plans against the people of Nicaragua and El Salvador." On behalf of the Directorate, Borge provided numerous details presumably implicating the CIA. On 9 April a long editorial in *Barricada* argued that "the manner of the brutal assassination . . . is not a criminal act produced by the emotions of the political moment in Central America," but a calculated action that is part of a global plan by U.S. imperialism to destroy Sandinismo, a perfect reflection of the inherent brutality of the CIA and imperialism. For days the Sandinistas reported that the whole world was clamoring against the Americans.[9]

The leader of the FPL was its founder, the old man of the Salvadoran revolutionary movement, Salvador Cayetano Carpio, known as Marcial. He was a short, tough, inexpressive man with a beard like Lenin's. At the time of the assassination, this legendary figure on the Salvadoran left was in Libya discussing military and financial aid for the FMLN with Qaddafi. After the news broke, Marcial returned immediately to Managua, arriving on 9 April. During the burial ceremony and honors to Ana

Maria, he seemed particularly pained, for Ana Maria had been his principal supporter in the development of the FPL over many years, though more recently their relationship had turned very sour indeed and only shortly before her death they had had several nasty confrontations at meetings of party leaders.

The investigations continued, with the help of Cuba's America Department chief, Manuel Piñeiro, and after several days Borge reported the clear, unexpected, and unwanted results to the Directorate:

1. The intellectual author of the assassination had been Cayetano Carpio himself, who just days before leaving for Libya had personally approved the assassination plan, confident that no trace could be found and that everyone would blame the CIA.

2. The man who had committed the assassination was Rogelio Bazzaglia, twenty-eight, known by the pseudonym "Marcelo," who was a member of the FPL Central Committee and in charge of intelligence and had the absolute confidence of Marcial. Also implicated were FPL militants Walter Elias, Andrés Vázquez, and Julio Soza.

The National Directorate members were shocked and concerned that they would lose credibility for having blamed the CIA. Borge was appointed to inform Cayetano Carpio of the results of the investigation, and the FSLN's determination to bring the perpetrators to justice. Miguel Castellanos, then one of the top FPL leaders, reports that Daniel Ortega also talked with Marcial and condemned him for the action and for doing it on Nicaraguan territory. Shortly after Borge's visit, Carpio committed suicide. Marcelo told a three-member FPL delegation briefed on the affair in Managua immediately after the suicide that Marcial had ordered the murder. Castellanos concluded that Carpio's suicide resulted from Cuban and Sandinista pressures and the old guerrilla's losing his mind because he believed that his role in the FPL, already greatly reduced, would be nothing in the future.[10] Marcial was buried privately with no honors, the only people attending the burial being his widow, Borge, and Daniel Ortega. There was no official representative of the FMLN leadership.

On 21 April *Barricada* reported Cayetano Carpio's suicide and that Ana Maria's murder had been committed by members of the FPL. But the Directorate still didn't come clean, for it reported that Bazzaglia was "the intellectual author and organizer of the criminal action." Marcial, who was still portrayed as a great hero in an accompanying article and in an FPL communique, reportedly committed suicide because he was so depressed by the "enemy activities carried out by a man who had his confidence." Both the MINT statement and the FPL communiqui still hinted at some CIA involvement in these actions, which they implied were so "characteristic of the Agency."[11]

There undoubtedly were personal, leadership, and other reasons why Carpio decided to have Ana Maria killed, but the most important were differences over the course of the war in El Salvador, foreign involvement in Salvadoran affairs, and Carpio's declining authority within the organization. Marcial, among the most conservative leaders in the FPL, had been unenthusiastic about the Cuban-engineered unity of the FMLN and in 1981 wanted the FPL to get out. This was opposed by Ana Maria, whom Marcial accused of making deals with the Cubans, who in fact did quietly support her. In Nicaragua, Marcial's closest ally was Tomás Borge. In 1982 and early 1983 Cayetano Carpio opposed increasing pressures within the FPL and the FMLN generally for greater cooperation among the guerrillas, broader national alliances against the government, and ties to Cuba and Nicaragua. Marcial's stubbornness, especially after the vast majority of the FPL central committee voted against his positions, seemed to have driven the intense man to strike out in this desperate way against the woman he perceived as his chief adversary.[12]

The FMLN and the Missiles

From 1983 on, the FMLN asked repeatedly for ground-to-air missiles, but the Sandinistas put the guerrillas off, fearing possible political repercussions while they were increasingly bogged down in the Contra War. In August 1987 Daniel Ortega confronted the matter of FSLN support for the FMLN head-on with Salvadoran President Napoleón Duarte during a break at the presidential summit in Guatemala that produced the Esquipulas II accords. As Daniel later related it to Humberto:

I did something to change Napoleón Duarte's attitude. I told him frankly that we acknowledge that we are still arming the FMLN but we think we have come to the moment to negotiate this point within the context of a regional accord. I also told him that for some time the FMLN has asked us to send anti-aircraft missiles to them, but that we have not done so even though the United States is sending them to the Contras, as a way of showing our willingness to negotiate this point.

"You told him that?" Humberto responded. "Yes, it seemed to me stupid at these high levels to continue denying it to Duarte. It's all very well to deny it publicly, but at this level of discussion, we would lose respect," the same reasoning that lay behind Daniel's admission of involvement in talks with U.S. diplomat Thomas Enders in August 1981, discussed below.

It was shortly after this that Salvadoran Communist party chief Shafik Handal got Humberto Ortega to promise privately that the Sandinistas would supply missiles, an agreement that caused a showdown in the National Directorate, as described earlier. The Sandinistas backed off the agreement but since a promise had been made, and all the comandantes were sympathetic with the FMLN's problem, a compromise of sorts was struck. In late 1987, after Humberto consulted with the Castros in Havana, fifteen Salvadoran guerrillas were taken to Nicaragua for training in the use of the missiles. No missiles were sent at that time, in part because they would have had to come from Cuba, the FSLN not having any extras, though some were sent at the end of the decade.[13]

Aid to Non-Salvadoran Guerrillas

While emphasis in the 1980s was on supporting the Salvadoran guerrillas, relations were maintained with groups in and from Honduras, Guatemala, Costa Rica, Colombia, and Chile, among other countries, sometimes involving the shipping of some arms. Early in 1983, for example, the Directorate experimented with increasing support for the Honduran guerrillas and for using Nicaraguan territory as a base for incursions into Honduras. The objective was to put pressure on the Honduran government while looking for a time to negotiate the aid away in exchange for Honduran government support against the Contras. Of course, the FSLN did not tell the Honduran guerrillas that the Directorate's interest in supporting them was because they might later become a useful bargaining chip.

The Honduran guerrilla situation was just the opposite of the Salvadoran. Even though Honduras is the poorest country in Central America, guerrillas had not won over important social sectors; repeated military coups combined with some democratic reforms seemed to have impeded the growth of a strong guerrilla movement. The Honduran group whose interests most nearly corresponded to the plans of the Directorate was the Revolutionary Party of the Central American Workers of Honduras (PRTCH), headed by Secretary General José Maria Reyes Mata, which had the Armed Forces of the People (FAP) as its military arm. Reyes Mata was an old figure on the Honduran left, with longer-standing ties to the Cubans than to the Sandinistas.

The Buro Ernesto, working with the Cuban America Department, began seriously training military units of the FAP in 1983 with the expectation that they would operate out of Nicaragua. By August military units of the PRTCH, which amounted to no more than seventy men, were prepared to move into Honduran territory. But problems arose, for Reyes Mata had his own ideas about how he would conduct his operation, perhaps even suspecting the FSLN's objective. He believed that in the east of Honduras he had sufficient peasant support to survive without the use of Nicaraguan territory and besides, he wanted to establish his own autonomy. Thus he refused to operate out of Nicaragua. But on 18 September, just a few days after he returned to Honduras, Reyes Mata and his men were killed by the Honduran army in the Piedras Azules sector of the Atlantic Zone of Honduras.

Sandinista relations with the Guatemalan guerrillas date back to the 1960s. They were strengthened during the early 1980s by some supplying of arms and through ties to the top leaders of Guatemala's three main guerrilla organizations who lived much of the time in Nicaragua and had periodic meetings with Humberto Ortega in the latter's office. These three were Pablo Monsanto of the Revolutionary Armed Forces (FAR), Rolando Morán of the Guerrilla Army of the Poor (EGP), and Gaspar Ilón of the Armed People's Organization (ORPA). Humberto Ortega provided a house for Moran near his own home. Many of the Guatemalan guerrillas in command positions spent time with the Irregular Warfare Battalions (BLI), while others studied conventional war in the Carlos Agüero School.

Humberto Ortega's ties to Costa Rica were particularly strong since he had lived there for several years during the Somoza period and had contacts with people at all levels of society. The Costa Ricans had taken some of the Cuban arms shipped through their country before the Sandinista victory, as noted a above, and after July 1979 the Sandinistas provided some hundreds of weapons and explosives to the People's Vanguard Party (PVP) of Manuel Mora Valverde through the latter's son

Manuelito. Many Costa Ricans were given basic guerrilla training in Nicaragua and Cuba.

Notes

1. Che Guevara, *Che Guevara Speaks* (New York: Merit Publishers, 1967), 159.
2. Ratliff interview with Edén Pastora, 20 March 1992.
3. Guzmán had previously been the political official for the Sandinista daily newspaper, *Barricada*. In October 1982 he was transferred to the Department of the Interior, rose to the rank of deputy commander, and was appointed deputy chief of the intelligence branch of Interior known as Directorate V. Under the Chamorro government he became chief of immigration in Nicaragua.
4. The Sandinistas believed the note was from the State Department, but a top official at State says none was sent. He speculated that the message may have come from Oliver North at the National Security Council. Interview with Charles Hill, 1 August 1991.
5. One example of guerrilla irritation over delays is the four-page "Informe Sobre Viaje," an FMLN report on a trip to Nicaragua to get arms in July 1980; in a three-page letter of 31 August 1980, Jonas, Eduardo and Marcial (see below) argue that the fundamental task of the moment is for the guerrillas to unify. Documents in Salvadoran guerrilla collection, Hoover Institution Archives.
6. Javier Rojas U., ed., *Conversaciones con el Comandante Miguel Castellanos* (Santiago, Chile: Editorial Adelante, 1986), 53.
7. *Barricada*, 12 January 1985, 20 January 1985.
8. Villalobos admitted his involvement in Dalton's murder in an interview with Barcelona's *La Vanguardia* shortly before the FMLN's November 1989 offensive; see *Transitions*, May-June 1990, 19.
9. See *Barricada* of 7, 8, and 9 April 1983.
10. Rojas, *Conversaciones con Miguel Castellanos*, 82, 83.
11. *Barricada*, 21 April 1983.
12. On the Marcial/Ana Maria affair, see Rojas, *Conversaciones con Miguel Castellanos*, 67–84; Ratliff discussed the incident with Castellanos in San Salvador, El Salvador, on 10 December 1987.
13. William Ratliff and Roger Miranda, "The Cold War Is Still Burning Hot in Central America," *San Diego Union*, 10 December 1989.

PART III

The Enemy of Humanity

11

The Gringo Imperialists

Between July 1979 and the late 1980s, the major points of conflict between Managua and Washington remained basically unchanged: 1) Sandinista support for foreign insurgencies, particularly in El Salvador, and, from the early 1980s, U.S. support for the Nicaraguan resistance; 2) the militarization of Nicaragua, particularly through the expansion of the EPS, and the U.S. military buildup in the region; and 3) Nicaragua's alignment in the East/West conflict. As Costa Rican President Oscar Arias said in late 1987, "The United States knows that the Sandinistas are on the side of the Soviet Union—that is the whole problem."[1] Nicaragua's domestic political system was not an issue at first, though it became so later in the decade, and was the major component of the Arias peace initiative and Esquipulas II agreement.

Was Jimmy Carter Different?

As noted earlier, the Sandinistas believed both the Republicans and Democrats had an imperialist mentality; they had the same objectives even though they sometimes tried to get what they wanted in different ways. Thus, predictably, the conflict between the two countries began as soon as the FSLN took power during the administration of Democrat Jimmy Carter. On 24 September 1979 Daniel Ortega made his first personal contact with President Carter in the White House. Carter emphasized his desire for friendly relations with Nicaragua and his intention to give aid and support to the new government, but he also noted three U.S. concerns: that the Sandinistas not intervene in the affairs of neighboring countries, that they maintain true international nonalignment and that they respect human rights in a democratic atmosphere, a long-standing Carter concern that had led to the termination of aid to both Somoza and El Salvador's leaders several years earlier. Ortega responded that the

153

FSLN was interested in U.S. support and added: "Nicaragua is not a factor in the radicalization of El Salvador—now, in the past, and it will not be in the future." As he was leaving the White House, Ortega said to Carter, "We will not link you with the past."[2]

Ortega's public account of the meeting several years later had a similar ring, for he said, "we had to admit that it was possible to initiate then an effective dialogue" and he noted a "mutual disposition to readjust and improve relations between Nicaragua and the United States," which "was brusquely set back in January 1981 when the new [Reagan] administration took office."[3]

This juxtaposition of possible cooperation with the Carter administration and conflict with the Reagan is one of the great myths of the 1980s, not only as it touches U.S.- Nicaraguan relations but for what it says about the Sandinista worldview and FSLN policy in general. Ortega's visit to the White House took place one day after the Sandinista National Directorate had finished presenting its *72-hour Document*, discussed above, to FSLN militants in Managua. During the Carter administration—the FSLN's first eighteen months in power—the United States was the world's most generous donor to Nicaragua, providing $118 million in direct aid, encouraging international loans of $262 million and supporting large adjustments in debts. And yet it was during these 18 months that the Sandinistas began and institutionalized all the domestic and international policies that challenged both the United States and all other countries in Central America, including precisely the involvement in El Salvador that Daniel Ortega had personally assured Carter would not happen. The reality is that Sandinista policies toward the Carter administration were in line with basic Sandinista beliefs and not with either Ortega's private words to the U.S. president or subsequent statements in public. Those policies during the Carter years led directly to the armed confrontation during the Reagan administration.

Already in the Carter years, U.S. intelligence reports on Sandinista aid to the Salvadoran guerrillas were detailed enough to force the Democratic president to be the first to turn on the FSLN. In mid-January 1981 Carter reluctantly resumed the military aid to El Salvador that he had cut in 1977, one of two main reasons for doing so being because of Sandinista support for the FMLN. And Carter suspended aid to Nicaragua itself, explaining the latter action this way:

I had no alternative but to cut off aid to the Sandinistas before I left office, because there was evidence that was clear to me that the Sandinistas were giving assistance to the revolutionaries in El Salvador, and the law required me to stop the aid. I was very eager to give the people of Nicaragua economic aid after the revolution, but it was not possible under those circumstances.[4]

Taking on the California Cowboy

Notwithstanding Ortega's comment about a "setback" in January 1981, Sandinista leaders thought the policies of the Reagan administration were essentially a continuation of those developed by the Carter administration. And contrary to propaganda in the United States and abroad, the new president did not take office with the Sandinistas at the top of an international anti-communist hit-list. In reality, the Reagan administration also tried for a negotiated settlement that would recognize the Sandinistas's freedom to do what they wanted to in Nicaragua but halt the escalation of military threats or conflicts within the region. Indeed, at first, Reagan's terms for an agreement were even more flexible than Carter's, since they dropped the latter's concern for human rights and democracy within Nicaragua.

In fact, prior to mid-1981 the Reagan administration was so concerned with El Salvador that it thought very little about Nicaragua. This changed after mid-year when then Assistant Secretary of State Thomas Enders, NSC Latin Americanist Roger Fontaine and others began drawing up the plans which resulted in Enders's critically important visit to Nicaragua in August 1981. That trip and Enders's offers were a test. "I wanted to give the Sandinistas every opportunity to react," Enders said some years later, "before we got serious about the Contras." His offer, summarized by the State Department, was: "bilateral nonaggression agreement and renewed economic assistance if Nicaragua stops aid to Salvadoran guerrillas and limits its military buildup."[5]

Enders's discussions in Managua, first with Foreign Minister D'Escoto and Bayardo Arce, and then with Daniel Ortega, were heated and truly frank on both sides. Enders found the Sandinista leaders

totally hostile toward the United States. The ones I saw spoke with great bitterness about U.S. intervention in the past and were convinced that that model would be repeated. Ortega said they were sure they were going to have to fight the United States in the end, so they were helping to arm the Salvadoran guerrillas, whom they considered a shield, to keep the fighting away from Nicaragua.

Enders responded that Washington knew very well what help the Sandinistas were giving the Salvadorans and that while the FSLN could do whatever it wanted within Nicaragua, the aid to El Salvador had to stop. Otherwise, Enders warned, "we are ready and able to resist it." Bayardo Arce told Enders the Sandinistas would retreat into the mountains, if they had to, and fight again as guerrillas; he drew a parallel to Indochina, where he said determined and well-armed guerrillas had stood off the United States. Enders responded that Arce shouldn't be too confident of that since Vietnam was a large country and far away from the United States while Nicaragua was small and nearby. In the end, Enders and Ortega agreed to "call a halt to the polemics and exchange proposals."[6]

Enders and those around him prepared three detailed proposals, sending each one off as it was finished, touching on everything from Sandinista aid to the Salvadorans to renewed U.S. aid to Nicaragua. The public polemics did stop for several weeks, but Enders got no response to the proposals. He sent a message to ask why there was no response, but got no reply. Then in early October, Daniel Ortega launched a bitter attack against the United States at the United Nations and the truce was off. At the end of the month, D'Escoto wrote Enders to say the proposals were "sterile. "The U.S. proposals," Enders concluded,

> were knowingly and willingly shot down by the Sandinistas themselves. They had had a gameplan from the beginning for a revolution in the isthmus. They were not expecting me. Perhaps because of differences within the Directorate, it was easier for them to maintain their gameplan than to become involved in complex and time-consuming negotiations with the United States.[7]

According to Edén Pastora, who was present, Daniel Ortega gave the following account to Fidel Castro in Havana just after the meeting with Enders: the U.S. envoy said President Reagan was willing to live with a communist Nicaragua but that the United States could not tolerate Nicaraguan involvement in the East/West conflict or its arming the guerrillas in El Salvador. Castro asked Ortega how he had responded to Enders's statements. Ortega replied that he said the Sandinistas had nothing to negotiate since they were not involved in the East/West conflict nor in El Salvador. And how did Enders react to that, Castro asked? By saying, "Negotiate with us, Comandante, or we will crush you," words Enders said he did not use though they undoubtedly represented the Sandinista reading of his message. Fidel's response: "Don't negotiate."[8]

Sandinista bitterness and commitment, which made an agreement impossible at that time, is recalled in the retrospective comments of Bayardo Arce and some other Sandinista officials. In mid-1985 Arce told Roy Gutman, "At the time, we didn't think that Enders was very serious. In retrospect, we consider him as the most serious person who spoke with us." A Sandinista Foreign Ministry officer, looking back in 1986, simply said, "We were not so pragmatic in those days." When Stephen Kinzer asked Bayardo Arce if the Sandinistas had come to regret turning Enders down, Arce replied,

> You can't put it in those terms. . . . We made our decision based on principles. It was not a matter of cold analysis, or else the choice might have been different. Remember what was the climate at that time. We were still in a wartime mentality. . . . Enders's proposal did not meet the requirements of that moment.[9]

Weeks later Reagan signed the secret "finding" that officially authorized military support to the armed resistance.

In August 1981 the Sandinista revolution was in a blooming stage, self-confident and unbending in its rejection of the United States and support for both Cuba and the Salvadoran guerrillas. As Arce said above, the National Directorate was not remotely interested in meeting anything like the basic terms of the Enders mission, as rational as they may have seemed in retrospect. The United States "genuinely tried to build a new relationship with Nicaragua," wrote Larry Harrison, the head of the U.S. AID mission in Managua between 1979 and 1981, under Jimmy Carter. But "the Sandinistas could not live with a positive view of the United States. They bear the responsibility for the confrontation."[10]

The matter of Sandinista intervention in El Salvador came up again on 2 December 1981 during nearly two hours of conversation between U.S. secretary of state Alexander Haig and Nicaraguan foreign minister Miguel D'Escoto at a meeting of hemispheric foreign ministers. Commenting on their conversation, D'Escoto said:

> They [U.S. officials] talk of the principle of reciprocity which means that if we intervene in any Latin American country they, on the basis of this principle, would be obliged to take appropriate measures, implying intervention. I responded that reciprocity should always be between the attacking state and the state attacked. He said that the United States can not tolerate intervention anywhere in the world.

D'Escoto responded, "This is very interesting to hear because for many countries in the world the United States is synonymous with intervention." Haig's warning, and D'Escoto's rejection, came two weeks after Reagan's secret "finding."[11]

In October 1983 former secretary of state Henry Kissinger visited Managua as head of President Reagan's Bipartisan Commission on Central America and met for forty-five minutes with Daniel Ortega in the César Augusto Silva Center. The atmosphere was oppressive and unfriendly from the beginning, in part because both sides already had made up their minds about the other. On the Sandinista side, the hostility was all the greater because the visit had been preceded by large-scale Contra attacks in different parts of the country—in particular one on Port Corinto fuel storage facilities—which were interpreted as U.S. pressure on the FSLN. Ortega's attitude toward Kissinger was aggressive and demanding throughout, but the tensest moment came when, during Ortega's presentation, Kissinger took off the headphones through which he was receiving an English translation of the comandante's comments. Ortega was infuriated by this seeming put-down and became even more strident. Nothing positive came of these sessions. Oliver North noted that "we were clearly talking past each other."[12]

A week later the United States invaded Grenada. The U.S. invasion, in the wake of U.S. military maneuvers near Nicaragua—including "Big Pine" with Honduras in February 1983 and an increase in naval presence of the Pacific and Caribbean coasts of Central America in July—made the Sandinistas fear that Washington was on a roll and would invade Nicaragua next. For the first time, the FSLN decided it was time to talk seriously.

But the United States failed to move until the middle of 1984, by which time things had changed again: the CIA had launched the counterproductive mining of Nicaraguan harbors, for which action Nicaragua had taken the United States before the International Court of Justice. Washington, in a flurry of foolish legalisms, then refused to make the case against Nicaragua at the World Court. By mid-1984, the Reagan administration's hand had been further weakened by Congress, which responded to the mining incident by cutting aid to the Contras.

At the same time, though the Sandinistas were no longer so concerned about an immediate U.S. invasion, the situation had deteriorated for them. The Contra War had expanded so rapidly that some FSLN leaders now admitted privately that it was a broadly based peasant insurrection, part of a general picture of rapidly deteriorating economic and other conditions in the country as a whole. Also, support for the Salvadoran guerrillas did not seem to be working and the FMLN looked like it might never be able to overthrow the government in San Salvador. On the brighter side for the Sandinistas were the far-reaching and basic reforms being planned and implemented under Cuban General Ochoa.

Thus, when U.S. secretary of state George Shultz visited Managua at the beginning of June 1984 and launched the nine bilateral "Manzanillo" talks that lasted through mid-December, the Sandinistas were no longer as fearful as they had been immediately after Grenada. The two sides were again talking past each other. The Sandinistas played their improving international hand: they argued that they were living up to their 1979 pledge to the OAS by holding an election in November 1984, that they were anxious to find peace, as was demonstrated both by their agreement in September to sign the Contadora draft treaty and by the "concessions" proposed by Daniel Ortega in early 1985, discussed above. No progress was made. Secretary Shultz's executive aide at the time, Charles Hill, put it this way: "We didn't see the Sandinistas as negotiating seriously at any time. We had our demands, they had theirs, and there was no common ground."[13]

From 1985 into 1987, Nicaragua was in increasingly desperate condition; suffering from domestic economic collapse, a civil war that was expanding and far longer and more arduous than the Sandinistas had expected, and all sorts of international pressures. And the Ortegas felt power slipping from their hands. Thus the two brothers, more than most other comandantes, were ready to talk to Washington. Some in the U.S. government—Secretary of State George Shultz and Special Envoy Philip Habib, for example—were interested as well, if they had believed the Sandinistas were serious.

A variety of trial balloons were launched in Managua during this period. In November 1986 there was a large military parade seen by the U.S. military attache commemorating the birthday of Carlos Fonseca. The street was heavy with Soviet arms and technology. There was only one American vehicle, a Jeep Renegade. Its passenger, Humberto Ortega. "I want to show the Americans that despite all this Soviet hardware, I can ride in a Jeep," meaning that he did not have his mind closed with respect to the United States. In early 1987, Panamanian leader Manuel Antonio

Noriega's envoy to Managua, Didio Souza, gave Humberto his periodic briefing on conditions in Panama. When he had finished, Humberto asked Souza to see if Noriega could get him a meeting with the head of the U.S. Southern Command stationed in Panama. "We military men understand each other better," Ortega said. At about the same time, when the U.S. changed its military attaché in Managua, Humberto took the unprecedented step of inviting the new U.S. attaché to visit him. (Previously the U.S. attaché had been received by the army general chief of staff.) Although Humberto did not mention his interest in talking with the head of the Southern Command, the visit itself, taken with the fact that Ortega gave the attaché a gift—a teapot and cups he had been given recently by the Polish military attaché in Havana, which he didn't like—was meant to convey a message. But there was no American response to any of these overtures. "Daniel Ortega got to the point where he would set ambushes for American officials," said former top Sandinista leader Moisés Hassan. "He would lurk in dark corners until an American official showed up, and then jump out and try to engage him in conversation."[14]

But the messages didn't get through. Shultz's executive aide, Charles Hill, said innumerable politicians, clergymen, businessmen, and others brought back "feelers" from Managua, but they could not be confirmed. Secretary Shultz decided that if the Sandinista leaders were serious about talks, they would approach the administration clearly, even if privately, through proper channels. Some feelers, according to Shultz's chief aide, may well have ended up at other branches of the government.[15]

In one respect, the heat was briefly off the Sandinistas with the signing of the Esquipulas II peace agreement in August 1987: with the war against the Contras ending, attention could be turned to improving the domestic situation. The peace agreement applied pressures on the United States and Honduras, and thus on the Contras.

Dealing Drugs for War and Profit

In 1982, shortly after the Enders visit and President Reagan's official approval of aid to the Contras, the Sandinistas became involved for several years in the narcotraffic business. Fidel Castro's influence was strong, originally through his argument that in war anything is permitted, and the Sandinistas like the Cubans were at war with the United States.[16]

And, as Humberto said to Miranda, it seemed to be an easy way to get a lot of money. Ricardo Bilbonick, a drug dealer testifying at the trial of Manuel Noriega in Miami in late 1991, said that Noriega introduced the Medellín Cartel to the Sandinistas, though plans launched in May 1984 to send Inair planes to Nicaragua evidently fell through. According to Carlos Lehder, a convicted former chief of the Medellín Cartel who testified in Miami, "the Cubans were in charge of that cocaine conspiracy in Nicaragua. It was not the Sandinistas." Lehder added that the Sandinistas would not "lift a finger" without first getting a go-ahead from the Cubans. Daniel Ortega rejected Lehder's comments on Sandinista involvement, saying his "evidence" was all an effort to cover up U.S. involvement in peddling drugs to supply the Contras.[17]

The narcotraffic activities were directed by Tomás Borge, while Humberto gave his personal approval to the National Directorate plan through the authorization of permits for drug traffickers to make refueling stops and overflights, which were controlled by the chief of the air force. The Sandinistas pulled out of the business of drug trafficking in mid-1984 after the United States launched heavy criticism of their activities. Above all, they were concerned that their involvement in drug trafficking might give the United States a pretext for intervening in—perhaps invading—Nicaragua. As Humberto Ortega remarked to Miranda, returning to the theme that was behind so much of his thinking and planning—"Nicaragua isn't Cuba. It has no Soviet umbrella."

Problems with U.S. Policy

The critical problem with U.S. policy toward Nicaragua was that it was in a constant state of flux; indeed, there was no firm policy. In early 1986 the confusion and dissension in Washington literally walked into Humberto Ortega's office one day in the person of departing U.S. ambassador to Nicaragua, Harry Bergold, whom the Ortegas thought of as a friend of Tomás Borge. Bergold told Ortega that Reagan's policy of arming the Contras didn't have support in Congress and would have very rough sailing ahead. He added that some sort of negotiations seemed in order. When Bergold left, Ortega turned to Miranda and asked: "What does he mean? What is he trying to tell me?"

In August 1987 Jaime Chamorro, co-owner of the opposition paper *La Prensa*, put it this way: "Factfinding missions from Congress always come down here to ask what we think of U.S. policy. But I reply, 'What policy?' The basic trouble is that the President and Congress can't agree and thus the United States has no policy." But the problem was even deeper than Chamorro suggested, for the divisions were not simply between the president and Congress, but everywhere, including within Congress and among the president's own staff. Indeed, U.S. policy flipped and flopped to the point that by August 1987, Chamorro, Alfonso Robelo, and other Nicaraguans long basically friendly to the United States said Washington's policies were so vacillating as to be "immoral."[18]

Indeed, President Reagan's effort to push the Sandinistas into a corner and force them into making political concessions was often seriously hampered or thwarted by some of his administration's own policies. These included such military/ economic mistakes as the aforementioned mining of the harbors, which brought an end to Congressional support for the Contras and much criticism from the World Court, and the May 1985 economic embargo, the latter less an economic impediment—except to the private sector—than a propaganda boon to the Sandinistas. Finally, there was the desperate Iran-Contra scheme. When that one broke in late 1986 it virtually assured the demise of the Contras just as the $100 million the U.S. Congress finally gave the guerrillas in mid-1986 was beginning to pay off. And yet even so, in the end, the prolonged pressures the guerrillas exerted, along with the deepening economic chaos, were the major reasons Daniel Ortega signed the Esquipulas II accords in 1987 that resulted in the 1990 elections.

Notes

1. Oscar Arias, interview in *Die Zeit* (Hamburg), 11 December 1987, in FBIS (Latin America), 11 December 1987.
2. Robert A. Pastor, *Condemned to Repetition* (Princeton: Princeton University Press, 1987), 206-7. Pastor was Carter's Latin Americanist on the National Security Council.
3. Ortega's account in his 25 March 1982 talk to the United Nations Security Council mentions a meeting with Carter in September *1980*, though there was no meeting at that time; he unquestionably meant the meeting Pastor referred to in September *1979*. Ortega, *El acero de guerra*, 60. It was in September 1980 that U.S. Deputy Assistant Secretary of State James Cheek went to Managua for the Carter administration to warn the Sandinistas of the dire consequences of their support for the Salvadoran guerrillas.

4. Pastor, *Condemned to Repetition*, 223-28, quote from 228. Also see *Revolution Beyond our Borders: Sandinista Intervention in Central America* (Washington: U.S. Department of State, September 1985), esp. 15-13.

5. U.S. Department of State, *Revolution Beyond Our Borders*, 38. Ratliff interviews with Thomas Enders, 8 May 1992, by phone, and with Roger Fontaine, 6 May 1992, in San Francisco, CA.

6. Ratliff interviews with Thomas Enders, 5 and 8 May, 1992, by phone, and with Roger Fontaine, 6 May 1992.

7. One journalist has written that National Security Adviser Richard Allen and NSC Latin Americanist Fontaine took Enders's proposal, changed the demands and made it so tough it gave the hard-liners on the National Directorate "the perfect excuse to stall Ortega's peace initiative." Clifford Krauss, *Inside Central America* (New York: Summit Books, 1991), 143. It is true that there was not full support within the Reagan administration for Enders's offer. One member of the National Security Council called his visit a State Department "end run" around the president's policy, "without inter-agency agreement." See Constantine Menges, *Inside the National Security Council* (New York: Simon & Schuster, 1988), 104. But Enders says the people he needed in the NSC cooperated fully in drawing up, and in no way subverted, his proposals. Ratliff interviews with Enders, 5 and 8 May 1992. To speak of "Ortega's peace initiative," as Krauss does, is nonsense.

8. Ratliff interviews with Pastora, 19 March 1992 and 2 June 1992, and Enders, 5 and 8 May 1992.

9. Roy Gutman, *Banana Diplomacy: The Making of American Policy in Nicaragua, 1981-87* (New York: Simon & Schuster, 1988), 72; Kinzer, *Blood of Brothers*, 96.

10. Lawrence Harrison, "The Confrontation with the Sandinistas: Myths and Realities," *St. Louis University Public Law Review*, VI, 1 (1987): 39.

11. D'Escoto's comments are in *Barricada*, 3 December 1981. Limited aid had been given to the opposition during the Carter administration, but this "finding" was the formal declaration that set larger events in motion.

12. North, *Under Fire*, 229.

13. Ratliff interview with Hill, 1 August 1991.

14. Ratliff interview with Moisés Hassan in Palo Alto, California, 2 May 1991.

15. Ratliff interview with Hill, 1 August 1991.

16. Edén Pastora recounts a visit he made in late 1980 or early 1981 to a luxurious marina in Havana filled with the abandoned yachts of narcotraffickers. With him were Fidel Castro, Raúl Castro and General Arnaldo Ochoa. At one point Fidel remarked: "I'm getting tired of being the policeman of imperialism. The narcotraffickers have offered to pay me to let them use Cuba and I am thinking of doing it." When in 1989 Pastora heard that Castro had executed Ochoa for ties to drug dealers, the remarks of that earlier day fell into place. Ochoa was indeed involved with drugs, but only the general himself knew the order came from Fidel. With him out of the way, there was no one to talk. Ratliff interview with Pastora, 18 March 1992.

17. See David Lyons, "Ex-envoy: Noriega Introduced Cartel to Sandinistas," *Miami Herald*, 19 November 1991; David Lyons, "Lehder: Cuba OKd Drug Flights," *Miami Herald*, 21 November 1991. Ortega's comments were made to NOTIMEX (Mexico City), 23 November 1991, in *FBIS* (Latin America), 25 November 1991, 28.

18. Ratliff interviews with Jaime Chamorro, in Managua, Nicaragua, 29 August 1988, and Alfonso Robelo, in San José, Costa Rica, 1 September 1988.

PART IV

The Democracy of Violence

12

Framework of Control

The Nicaraguan people have been ruled by dictators for most of the twentieth century. The Somozas, who governed between 1933 and 1979, were followed by the comandantes between 1979 and 1990. What difference did the change in 1979 make? "We used to have only one dictator," one common phrase on the streets during the 1980s had it, "but now we have nine." This expression was complemented by another: "We're worse off now than we were before." That is, there were similarities, but in the end more people suffered more during the Sandinista than during the Somoza period.

The most important similarities relate to the exercise of power and maintenance of control. In terms of the exercise of power, the Sandinistas were in many respects typical Central American despots, though they acted as a group instead of individually, and more than most dictators in such small countries they played in the big leagues of world politics as dictated by their ideology. The common features included the following, though in each case the Sandinistas carried the characteristic farther than the Somozas had done.

- The hierarchy of power was similar. There was no significant separation of powers under either regime. There was no independent judiciary that could impartially defend the individual against the state acting on behalf of the regime in power. In reality, both were above the law. Bureaucratic and financial resources of the state were used freely to promote the objectives of the governing individual or clique.

- The military, police, and intelligence services were tools of the ruling individual/clique and were used accordingly. Intimidation, imprisonment, and death were used against critics of the government. Both regimes even had their goon squads: under the Somozas it was the Nicolasa headed by Nicolasa Sevilla, and under the Sandinistas, the turbas divinas, the "divine mobs." Some Nicaraguans started calling the turbas the Nicolasa

167

Sandinista, and indeed some of the thugs in the Somocista mobs turned up again in the turbas.

• Major portions of the economy were owned and/or controlled by the dominant individual/clique, with all the influence that control carried with it.

• Freedom of the media was limited or forbidden.

• Patronage, corruption and abuse of power were extensive.

The main differences between the Somozas and the Sandinistas were the following:

• Significant political and many other decisions during the Somoza period were made or acquiesced in by the one Somoza in power, while during the Sandinista period decisions were made by a clique of nine, with some of the nine having more political clout, if not more votes, than the others. In practical terms this meant no official in the Sandinista period attained the unchallenged individual power and wealth of the Somozas, though a very few dominated the country. As a result, under the Sandinistas many times more leaders and bureaucrats had their hands in the state coffers. What is more, during its final months in power, the Sandinistas looted the country of funds, property, enterprises, and other goods. And whereas Somoza's looting of Nicaragua was "rectified" by the state's seizure of the dictator's property in 1979, before leaving office in 1990 the Sandinistas passed legislation to "legalize" their ownership of their spoils of power, an action that led to substantial ill-will throughout the country during the Chamorro government.[1]

• The Somozas were allied to the United States, though relations with Washington had their ups and downs. The Sandinistas, though claiming to be "nonaligned," had been aligned to Cuba from the early 1960s, and from the first day in power looked for aid and inspiration to Havana, Moscow, and the Soviet bloc generally, also with some points of tension. This Sandinista tie to the Soviet bloc sucked the Cold War for the first time into the heart of Central America and gave Sandinista Nicaragua an international significance Somoza never could have imagined, or wanted.

• Although Somoza's troops occasionally violated the borders of neighboring countries, and Nicaraguan territory was used by dissident Guatemalans (in the mid-1950s) and Cubans (in the early 1960s), there was no concerted, ongoing government program to subvert neighboring regimes under the Somozas as there was under the Sandinistas.

● While the Somozas at times had a populist image, by and large they did not systematically justify their control of the country by saying they were serving the masses of the Nicaraguan people. The Sandinistas loudly claimed to be the people's government, a claim that as time passed was accepted far more widely among admirers abroad than people at home.

● Sandinista institutions of control were more pervasive and systematic than those of the Somozas, the former trying to remake the country and individuals while the latter sought mainly to prevent challenges to the dictator's political and in some respects economic dominance. This meant that across society—from labor to education to religion—the Sandinista leaders actively sought not only to present the ideas of the National Directorate but to enact them in such a way as to destroy or at least neutralize all even potentially opposing positions across the political, economic and social spectrum.

Structure of Control

The Sandinistas sought to enforce the decisions of the National Directorate through a variety of decrees and institutions. At the upper level, enforcement was carried out by the Ministry of the Interior, the Sandinista People's Army, and through control of the national economy, each of which will be examined in separate chapters below. Also there was a variety of lesser formal and informal institutions, often related to one of the above three divisions. On the medium and lower levels was a network of vertically structured mass organizations of workers, youth, women, and others; the Sandinista Defense Committees, directly modeled on the Cuban Committees for the Defense of the Revolution; as well as informal groups, most importantly the Interior Ministry's mobs.

Within this institutionalized structure of influence and control, opposition groups like the church, independent labor unions, many businessmen, part of the media, and increasingly the population as a whole, were pressured to abide by the dictates of the National Directorate. If adherence could be gained by commitment to the same cause, that was ideal. But those who had different goals, all or even part of the time, had to be brought around through inducements, deception, intimidation, psychological and/or physical force, though repression was not always as absolute as the Sandinistas wanted or as U.S. administrations claimed.

The *72-Hour Document* spoke of the need to "lay the foundation of a system of power that will not endanger the stability of our revolution." It noted the supreme importance of ensuring "the influence, education, organization and guidance of the most revolutionary classes, turning them into the driving force of the revolutionary process." This process was to be guaranteed by a highly politicized EPS, "the armed organization par excellence of the revolutionary masses." The new economy would have to "adhere to comprehensive national planning whose hub must be the State Sector."[2] A confidant of one of the comandantes, who asked for anonymity, put it more bluntly: "The state decided to keep the land for political purposes. Consolidation of power would be based on the [Sandinista] army and control of the economy."[3]

Sandinista control and repression were carried out within the framework of a series of increasingly severe political and economic states of emergency. The first was between the month Somoza fell and February 1980; the second, a state of economic and social emergency, was imposed in September 1981 and was strengthened by a more far-reaching military state of emergency in March 1982. This was relaxed in August 1984, in anticipation of the election in November. After the election, however, the screws were tightened again, culminating in the October 1985 state of emergency, which was the most repressive of all. There was a certain ebb and flow to the repression, though one of the late high points was during early and mid-1988, after the Esquipulas II peace agreement, with its pledges to democratize the country, had been signed.

In August 1980, long before the Contras were any challenge whatsoever, the Sandinistas established prior censorship on matters of "national security." According to *La Prensa* editor Jaime Chamorro, by May 1982 "the Sandinista regime had already surpassed Somoza in censorship and repression."[4]

Overlooking Repression

One of the chief criticisms legitimately leveled at the Somoza government was its violation of human rights. Indeed, that is what led the Carter administration to freeze U.S. aid to Somoza in 1977. But there was a new angle to the problem of human rights when the Sandinistas took power, an angle that brought greater suffering to the Nicaraguan people and simplified the FSLN's move to consolidate power in its own hands.

For many years some outsiders refused to believe that the FSLN would violate human rights, or at least that the FSLN would do it systematically as government policy. This was reflected in the experiences of José

Esteban González, the founder of the independent Permanent Commission on Human Rights (CPDH). During the Somoza government, González had considerable success collecting money in Europe and America to support his human rights activities critical of Somoza. But when the Sandinistas took over, the World Council of Churches and most of his other sources dried up. They evidently assumed that the Sandinistas, a popular movement when it was fighting Somocista repression, would not behave as Somoza had, and the González they had trusted a year before could not convince them otherwise.[5] Around the world, eyes and minds were closed to Sandinista actions, and with a strong program of conscious deception, discussed above, the FSLN tried very hard, and for a long time quite successfully, to keep them that way.

It is often very difficult, sometimes impossible, for outsiders to collect reliable information on some kinds of government repression simply because the truth is withheld or obscured in a closed, or secretive, society. Other forms of repression and control are more easily documented. All can be noted in some degree, however, if the observers are not working under a political bias for or against the government that makes it impossible for them to accept what they don't want to see. This self-induced blindness seems to have been the case with a number of usually reputable individuals and organizations who for many years, some even into the 1990s, failed to understand what the Sandinistas did during the 1980s.

Among the important human rights organizations that failed to report adequately on Nicaragua was Americas Watch. A member of the Permanent Commission on Human Rights in Nicaragua commented as follows on the Americas Watch report issued in early 1985, and on its chief investigator, Juan Mendez:

> The Sandinistas are laying the groundwork for a totalitarian society here and yet [when he came here recently] all Mendez wanted to hear about were abuses by the contras. How can we get people in the U.S. to see what's happening here when so many of the groups who come down are so pro-Sandinista?[6]

Not until the late 1980s, after military aid had ceased to be a burning issue in Washington, did Americas Watch manage to find a "pattern of abuse" by the Sandinista government.

Amnesty International's reporting on Nicaragua was better but uneven. AI's evasion of Sandinista practices was so blatant in the widely circulated 1984 *Torture in the Eighties* that we must draw attention to it as an example of this blindness. Even in 1991 this was one of the most prominently advertised books—a "major study"—in AI catalogues and was found on reference shelves in libraries around the world. Half of this volume consists of background essays on human rights issues, with innumerable references to Chile, El Salvador, Guatemala, and some other Latin American countries; the one reference to Nicaragua is to the Somoza period. In the global survey, the second half of the book, fifteen Latin American countries are covered in some detail. Several additional American countries on which AI "received some reports of torture or ill-treatment" are discussed briefly, among them Costa Rica, the United States, and Canada. There was nothing in the entire book about Sandinista Nicaragua.[7]

The bias was not found in human rights organizations alone. In the United States it was widespread on most university campuses, the order of the day for many lay church groups, and fairly ingrained in much of the media, matters which are discussed elsewhere. It was widespread in Latin America, Western Europe, and beyond.

But as the years passed, it became ever more difficult to ignore Sandinista abuses. The FSLN was embarrassed by the critical reports of the Permanent Commission on Human Rights (CPDH), even though most people abroad never heard of the organization. So in 1980 the Sandinistas formed their own group, the Commission for the Protection and Promotion of Human Rights (CNPPDH), which had little more access to the prisons than the CPDH and focused mainly on downplaying criticism of the government while emphasizing real and contrived atrocities of the Contras. The government was highly embarrassed in March 1985 when CNPPDH's executive director, Mateo Guerrero Flores, defected and condemned the subservience of the organization to the propaganda of the government; indeed, Guerrero reported that the commission even published, under its name, documents prepared by the Interior Ministry.

Another shoe fell in 1985. This was Alvaro Baldizón, who had for several years been chief investigator of the Interior Ministry's own Special Investigations Commission on human rights. Baldizón, who had reported directly to Interior Minister Borge, had even more to tell about systematic human rights abuses—"special measures"—against the Miskito Indians, opposition political leaders, and others by the Sandinista government. Each violation alleged by an international organization was investigated, Baldizón said, and some form of plausible denial was concocted; as demonstrated below, deaths deliberately or accidently caused by the Sandinistas, were often blamed on the Contras.[8]

Conclusions

Once in power, the level of at least outward unity maintained by the National Directorate, and the conformity it imposed on the nation, made it possible for the Sandinistas to withstand many pressures from inside and outside the country, at least for some years. In this sense enforced conformity prolonged the life of the National Directorate and Sandinista government. But as the years passed, the negative side of the closed society kicked in more and more, becoming in the end (what it always had been in fact), a prolonged and painful suicide. Sandinista politically correct thinking automatically rejected, often on the most righteous grounds, the possibility of active participation by non-comandantes in decision making. That is, the National Directorate refused to allow the kind of give-and-take in political, social, and economic discussions that would have made possible a wider variety of policies that were outside of the ideological framework of Sandinista thinking. But these were just the ideas the new government desperately needed to hear. Thus in a real sense the FSLN's imposed conformity within narrow limits, taken with inexperience, incompetence, corruption, and enormous domestic and international pressures, turned people against the Sandinistas, made the country ungovernable, and in the end brought the regime down.

Notes

1. See William Ratliff, "Out of Power, Sandinistas Still Act Like Kings," *The Wall Street Journal*, 26 July 1991.
2. See *72-Hour Document*, in Falcoff and Royal, *The Continuing Crisis*, 502, 505, 508, 511.
3. Quoted in Forrest Colburn, *Managing the Commanding Heights: Nicaragua's State Enterprises* (Berkeley: University of California Press, 1990), 43.
4. Jaime Chamorro Cardenal, *La Prensa* (New York: Freedom House, 1988), 17–18, 62.
5. See remarks by González in Shirley Christian, *Nicaragua: Revolution in the Family* (New York: Random House, 1985), 280–82.
6. Quoted in David Asman, "Despair and Fear in Managua," *The Wall Street Journal*, 25 March 1985. Rita McWilliams analyzes the failures of Americas Watch in "Who Watched Americas Watch?," *The National Interest*, Spring 1990, 45–58.
7. Amnesty International, *Torture in the Eighties* (London: Amnesty International Publications, 1984). When challenged on this omission, AI released a mild, single

sheet "Update," which disappeared as "Updates" tend to do. On AI's virtues *and* political biases, see William Ratliff, "Call it Amnesia International," *New York Times*, 20 March 1989, and a letter by Mark Keith Benenson, the son of the founder of AI and for fifteen years a member of the American section's board of directors, in *New York Times*, 6 April 1989. On the other hand, Ratliff participated in a seminar on contemporary Nicaragua at San Francisco State University in 1984 at which the representative of Amnesty International was shouted down by Sandinista supporters when he tried to give even a mild account of FSLN rights abuses.

8. Guerrero and Baldizón interviews with Douglas Payne; see Payne, "Human Rights in Nicaragua," St. Louis University, *Public Law Review*, no. 1 (1987): 57–58. Several years later Baldizón died mysteriously after eating in a Nicaraguan restaurant in Los Angeles, California.

13

Promoting Poverty

For two decades prior to the 1972 earthquake that leveled Managua, Nicaragua had enjoyed considerable economic growth. From 1950 to 1977, Nicaraguan economic output increased by an impressive annual average of about 6.5 percent, though the growth was not spread out evenly across society. About three-quarters of Nicaraguans worked the land, often at subsistence level; the country was largely self-sufficient in the basic grains. The export economy focused on traditional, particularly agricultural, products, including coffee, cotton, bananas, and meat, produced by small growers and some relatively modernized industries.

Still, economic factors played a major role in the fall of Somoza. Persisting poverty was a factor, but even more important was the dramatic aftermath of the great earthquake. Substantial amounts of humanitarian aid came in from abroad, but most of it was squandered, so that in 1979 what was once "downtown" Managua was still rubble overgrown by weeds. There was no identifiable new "downtown," as indeed there wasn't when the Sandinistas left office. Some of the aid funds were immediately pocketed by the Somozas and others in positions to get their hands on them. But much aid found its way into those same pockets by more devious routes that turned some sectors of society that had previously coexisted with the dictator into open critics and opponents of the government. Most importantly, Somoza moved into the fields of construction and banking, which he had previously left to others, and thus through manipulation in these fields "legally" absorbed even more of the foreign aid.

Somoza was never popular. But taking large portions of the international emergency relief funds, which were desperately needed to rebuild the country and the lives of the people, turned the vast majority of Nicaraguans ever more vigorously against him. And as the people protested, Somoza became increasingly repressive, which in turn created

175

greater animosity toward the regime. In brief, Somoza was thrown out in July 1979 because (1) he drove a wedge between himself and his clique, on the one hand, and virtually every other Nicaraguan; (2) his domestic policies, particularly after the earthquake, including human rights abuses, alienated the United States, particularly the Carter administration, and other foreign countries; and (3) the Tercerista branch of the Sandinistas had the opportunity, foresight, and good luck to achieve hegemony over what it forged into a united national opposition to the dictator.

When the Sandinistas came to power, they had the full or at least conditional support of the vast majority of Nicaraguans. And in the beginning they had substantial economic support from abroad, too, from such diverse countries as the United States, West Germany, Mexico, Venezuela, Libya, Cuba, and the Soviet Union. During their first thirty months, the Sandinistas received a variety of economic packages, ranging from new loans to better terms for repaying Somoza's foreign debt for a total of more than $1.5 billion in foreign support, only about 20 percent from the Soviet bloc or Third World.

But the FSLN's domestic policies and actions soon alienated Nicaraguans of many political persuasions, from leaders of the Higher Council of Private Enterprise (COSEP) through peasants to members of the Nicaraguan Communist party, and drove them into opposition, many thousands into armed opposition. And Sandinista international policies caused a breach with major nations abroad, most importantly the United States. But, contrary to the Sandinistas' mythology, the rising resistance of these domestic and international groups was largely a reaction to FSLN policies and not the cause of Nicaragua's economic decline and international problems during the 1980s. As long-time Sandinista spokesman Alejandro Bendaña acknowledged in 1991, peasant discontent with Sandinista policies came "before either the sharpening of the war or the crisis of the economy."[1]

The "Commanding Heights" and All That Jazz

From the time of Carlos Fonseca's trip to the Soviet Union in the 1950s, Sandinista leaders had believed in state-controlled economic development, in Lenin's insistence on party control of the "commanding heights" of a nation's economy. While the Sandinistas publicly advocated a diversified economy, the *72-Hour Document* made it clear that the new economy would "break away from the concept of production for profit" and be part of the general Nicaraguan move to establish its independence from "imperialism." The *72-Hour Document* continued:

We have already lopped off a strategic portion of the economic power of the bourgeoisie, reinforcing the material bases which strengthen the position of the exploited classes. Nevertheless, we can assert without ambiguity that only a change in the relations of production which begins in this area of the social economy of the state administration will really tilt, this time in depth, the balance of power between classes in favor of the oppressed, who already count on—this should not be discounted—the power of the arms of the Sandinista People's Army which assures from now on the irreversible character of the conquests and goals achieved so far.[2]

Thus the Sandinistas argued that central control of the nation's resources, through the regulation of goods, prices, wages, and many other things, would strengthen the nation and greatly benefit the peasants and workers. In labor historian Steve Diamond's words, the Sandinistas sought "to modernize the society and economy of a poorly developed nation through bureaucratic management controlled by a party-state apparatus." The success of its policy depended on many things, ranging from the availability of natural resources to the effective utilization of human resources. The latter, in Diamond's words, depended on "first, the elimination of the private sector as a significant independent economic force; and, second, the anesthetization of the working class."[3]

Prior to the Sandinistas, the total state sector, including the central government, made up only about 15 percent of the national Gross Domestic Product (GDP). There were only nineteen public entities, and some of these had been forced upon the government by foreign donors, particularly the United States. One year after taking power, the Sandinistas had increased the GDP percentage under state control to 41 percent by expanding the traditional areas of state involvement and moving into areas previously dominated by the private sector: banking, insurance, foreign trade, domestic commerce, as well as the purchase, storage, transportation, and distribution of basic foodstuffs. Between early 1978 and 1980, that is the late-Somoza and early-Sandinista years, state control of major sectors of the economy increased as follows: Agriculture, from 0 to 21 percent; manufacturing, from 0 to 33 percent; construction, from 40 to 79 percent; mining from 0 to 95 percent; services, from 31 to 55 percent.[4]

The first step toward state control of the economy was an enormous one, the confiscation of the property of the Somoza family and its supporters, and some others besides. This included some two thousand enterprises and agricultural estates, ranging from hundreds of small farms owned by former guardsmen to half of the nation's large estates, in all about 850,000 hectares of farmland. This totaled about 25 percent of the country's land under cultivation. The state also took most of the agro-industrial complexes and some one hundred thirty industrial and commercial enterprises.[5]

A "Mixed Economy"

The Sandinistas described their economic system as a "mixed economy," but when the term was used abroad it carried with it connotations of far greater freedom than was the case. A textbook written for Nicaraguan university students explained what "mixed economy" meant to the Sandinistas:

> There is an enormous difference between a "mixed economy" where the state is at the service of the capitalists and another "mixed economy" where the state limits the extraction of surplus value that the bourgeoisie obtain and channels the gains toward the most needy sectors. In the first case we find the "neo-capitalist" economies or, more appropriately, "state monopoly capitalism." In the second case we have our economic system.

Private entrepreneurs and managers were servants of the state and, in Agricultural Minister Wheelock's words, "prepare the food" but are kept "hidden away in the kitchen."[6]

In short, the "private sector" would be permitted so long as it served the interests of the state, as those interests were defined by the National Directorate. A high percentage of the economy remained legally in private hands, especially large commercial farms producing cattle, coffee, cotton, and sugar. But state control over markets, pricing, and credit, and making the countryside subsidize the cities, destroyed incentives to produce among marginal peasants in cooperatives as well as in larger private enterprises. Government threats to apply new restrictions on production, or to take over remaining private property altogether, similarly decreased confidence, productivity, investment, and recovery.[7]

The economic result was disastrous. Sandinista policies brought "an abrupt drop in the productivity of laborers, ambiguity about the objectives of economic entities, a slighting of traditional managerial practices and disrespect for economic—in contrast to political—locuses of authority." The acronym APP, which stood for "area of people's property," was cynically said to mean "authorized to be unprofitable." The agrarian APP's had a debt of 1.9 billion cordobas by July 1981, which was some 46 percent of the enterprises' capital. That debt increased by almost five times in the next three years. Inflation increased from about 750 percent in 1986 to an annual rate of at least 20,000 percent at the end of 1988.[8]

Institutionalizing Decline

The most important factors contributing to the economic crisis of the Sandinista decade were the FSLN's freely chosen programs of militarization, state-controlled economic development, and the extraordinary inefficiency of state management. The most crippling attacks on national resources were the building and maintaining of the largest army and interior ministry in the history of Central America. Two years before President Reagan signed the "finding" authorizing military aid to the Contras, more than three years before any U.S. military buildup in the region, and four years before the U.S. economic embargo, Sandinista militarization and centralization were under way. Even before the signing of the 1981–85 Nicaragua/Soviet five-year military aid agreement, the Sandinistas had begun, with Soviet support, to build an army of more than one hundred thousand men and women, a fifth or so regular troops. Even though most of the Sandinista military material and weaponry was donated by governments and groups abroad, the cost of maintaining such a large institution, taken with MINT's bloated structure, regularly consumed at least half of the national budget.

In addition to troop maintenance, the Sandinistas undertook very costly military infrastructure projects, the most expensive of which was the construction of Punta Huete airport. The 10,000-foot airfield, capable of serving the Soviet Union's most advanced aircraft, was under construction for years, consuming enormous amounts of cement. This and other military projects drained the Nicaraguan economy and delayed and/or caused the cancellation of other important development programs.

The legal framework of the attack on the economy, and especially on efficient utilization of private property, began immediately after the FSLN took power in the form of forty-four decrees and statutes promulgated between 1979 and 1981. Typical was that of 21 August 1979, which said that private property would be regulated for the defense and well-being of society generally.[9] On 9 September 1981 the National Director-ate declared a State of Economic Emergency. The communiqué blamed the crisis of the day on a variety of problems inherited from the Somoza period and on reactionary opposition to their policies since July 1979. In reality, the communiqui largely formalized the agenda the National Directorate had been following for two years. The state of emergency laid out the ground rules for the Sandinistas' program to manipulate both the private sector and the worker/peasant sectors while in fact consoli-dating power in their own hands. It and subsequent decrees from the Directorate provided the structure for dismantling the bases of the free enterprise system that increasingly created a climate of investment uncertainty and also an ever more disgruntled and indisciplined work force.

The FSLN divided the business sector into two groups: the patriotic businessmen, who were for the regime, and the reactionary businessmen, who resisted playing by Sandinista rules. Businessmen in the latter group were particularly demoralized because they were subject to having their holdings confiscated at any time, even if they had not had dealings with the Somoza regime or supported antiregime activity. Meanwhile, attacks were made on the freedoms of workers and peasants. Leaders of inde-pendent labor unions, small businessmen and big businessmen were harassed, arrested, and sometimes killed, the most prominent of them being Jorge Salazar, who was murdered by state security forces in September 1980. The FSLN replaced independent unions and other popular groups with its own mass organizations of urban and rural workers and others, in the process generating labor opposition stretching from the right to the Labor Front (FO) on the Marxist-Leninist left.

Finally, the September communique and other decrees formalized the building of a large, enormously costly state bureaucracy that was twice the size of Somoza's and manned by loyal Sandinistas who often lacked the necessary administrative skills for their jobs. Typically, what had once been handled by a single ministry was now given to two. Inefficiency became a major drain on the economy and "bureaucracy" a drag. A laborer in Managua noted at a workers' assembly that "while one works, five people control," alluding to the "supervision" provided by the Sandinista unions, the block committees, the DGSE, and others. Colburn zeros in on the problem from a different perspective, concluding that the government itself stood in the way of making the quick price changes that were needed to deal with serious inflation: revisions in the price of sugar, for example, took as long as six months to complete because the process involved five ministries and required presidential approval.[10] And bureaucracy also provided the channels through which top government officials siphoned off funds for themselves that went into gracious living in Nicaragua and into foreign bank accounts as a hedge against the future, as discussed earlier.

Collectives and Cutting Off Hands

When the Sandinistas took power, the labor situation was something like the following. The national population was approximately 2.5 million, of which about 1 million were economically active. About 40 percent of workers were in agriculture, 40 percent in commerce and services, and 20 percent in industry and miscellaneous activities.

In 1944 the Somoza government had passed a comprehensive labor code that provided an eight-hour day, compensation for injured workers, mandatory rest periods and double pay for overtime. Though the code often was not enforced, one labor historian wrote in 1990, its "provisions have remained to this day a rallying cry for union organizing efforts." Despite obstacles, rural and urban unions—usually at the level of the workplace, not the nation—did organize openly or clandestinely, and sometimes act, against the Somoza dictatorship.[11]

The FSLN rallied support to its anti-Somoza struggle by pointing to the hunger, poverty, and lack of freedom in the city and countryside. Thus the Sandinistas encouraged labor protests against poor living and working conditions before July 1979, undoubtedly in part because the comandantes had a sincere interest in improving the lives of the people. But the main reason the Sandinistas encouraged labor unrest, if one can judge by post-Somoza actions, was to help bring the dictator down and themselves to power, not because they believed in the inherent right of workers to express their opinions and preferences on their lives and working conditions—unless they already agreed with the comandantes.

After taking power, Sandinistas policy was based on several assumptions. Since far more people lived in the Pacific coast cities than in the inland mountains, and the former were stronger supporters of the

Sandinistas than the latter, the urban sector was more equal than the rural. It was critically important for the Sandinistas to keep urban workers as allies so that they would support the revolution when the United States invaded. To this end, prices for goods were set so as to benefit the urban dwellers, meaning that low fixed prices were paid to rural producers even as the cost of goods they needed continued to rise.

Control of rural and urban workers was to be assured by turning the labor movement into an arm of the state. Carlos Carrión, the head of the National Secretariat for Party Organization, said in December 1979 that "the working class is a single class and it must be organized as one," under the leadership of the state.[12] Thus, most of the land confiscated from the Somozas and their followers—that not taken over by the top Sandinista leaders themselves for their personal use—went to agrarian cooperatives or state farms, which the peasants did not want. The comandantes favored cooperatives because they opposed fostering private property on principle, because the cooperatives presumably would be more productive than small private farms, and because in cooperataives the people could be more easily controlled. When rural communities resisted collectivization, necessary measures were adopted to force compliance.

It followed that since the new state was described as the "people's" state, to strike against it would be to strike against or obstruct the interests of the people. The problem was that the living standards of the people got worse and worse under Sandinista rule, especially among the peasantry, making it hard for workers to accept the government's claim to be promoting their interests. The Sandinistas discouraged or outlawed strikes on the grounds that they were an extension of the imperialist attack through the Contra War. Once, in the mid-1980s, Jaime Wheelock even threatened publicly to cut off the hands of any worker who dared to raise his hand in support of a strike. But even the war was not really the point, for as one labor leader said, strikes would not be allowed *after* the war either because "after the war against the contras we have to wage the war against underdevelopment."[13] Instead, the National Directorate insisted upon greater labor discipline and acceptance of increasing austerity, and if this was not forthcoming, harassment and force were used. Again, the bottom line was giving the Directorate the power of coercion.

Thus one of the key failures of the Sandinistas was their agrarian policy from 1979 to the end of 1983, which both sabotaged the economy itself and pushed peasants into the ranks of the Contras. When the original agrarian policy was recognized as counterproductive at the end of 1983, some changes were made, but by then the damage had been done and it was too little too late. For example, in 1984 peasants were given the option of belonging to a cooperative or cultivating their own land, particularly in the territory where the Contras operated, but even then they did not have true title so they could not dispose of the land at will. At the same time other measures were undertaken to improve rural conditions—easier access to loans and technical advice on agricultural matters—in an effort to deny the rebels a social support base. A clear shift in concessions toward the urban private sector occurred in 1985, with the objective of defusing rising unrest in the cities. But by this time much of the harm had been done, and the economy had gotten so out of control that many peasants and increasing numbers of urban workers had no faith in the objectives of the Sandinistas, whatever temporary concessions they might make.

Into the Pit

How was this economic nightmare played out in the lives of the Nicaraguan people? The economic situation after five years of the Sandinista government was chaotic, with wages fixed below the poverty level and widespread unemployment. "At stores and marketplaces," one observer wrote, "nearly every basic product was unavailable or in short supply." By 1984 foreign aid was dropping each year as donors lost confidence in the FSLN. The $1.6 billion national debt the Somoza tyranny had accumulated over a forty year period had already jumped to $3.5 billion.[14]

During 1986 and early 1987, prices increased ten to fifteen times as fast as wages. Unemployment was estimated at about 40 percent. The value of exports fell from $646 million the year before the revolution to $218 million in 1986 while imports over the same period rose from $594 million to $830 million. The national debt now had risen to between $6.7 billion and $9.8 billion, depending on whose figures you used. By mid-1987, Nicaragua was reeling under the simultaneous decline in Soviet-bloc and Western aid. Noncommunist countries—prominent among them Mexico, Venezuela, West Germany, and France—cut or reduced aid and/or trade because Nicaragua couldn't make even partial payments on products and loans. Boris Yeltsin visited Managua as a special envoy of Gorbachev in May 1987, primarily to discuss the economic situation with Daniel Ortega, though he paid a courtesy visit to Humberto as well. Five years later the former Nicaraguan ambassador to the Soviet Union, Adolfo Evertz, revealed that back home Yeltsin had called Nicaragua "a country economically paralyzed and badly administered" by an "incapable and irresponsible government" and concluded that the Soviet Union should not send it resources. A number of representatives from Soviet-bloc countries complained about the gross inefficiency of the Sandinista government.[15]

By 1988 inflation had rocketed to 30,000 percent annually. The average Nicaraguan's living standard was less than half of what it had been in 1948. Whereas when the Sandinistas took over, the average rural daily wage would buy thirty eggs, less than a decade later it would buy only two. "Managua and other cities were swept by waves of violent crime, much of it perpetrated by gangs of hungry youths. At the city's fetid garbage dumps, poor people scavenged like rats for scraps of food." A report by the Health Ministry found that three-quarters of nearly three thousand randomly surveyed schoolchildren were suffering from malnutrition.[16] A study commissioned by the Nicaraguan government and released in mid-1989 found that between 1979 and 1988 the size of the Nicaraguan economy had shrunk by nearly one-third and the per capita GDP had fallen to roughly $300 annually, lower even than that of Haiti. Since 1981 the buying power of salaries, excluding noncash payments, had fallen 92 percent. According to the World Bank, Nicaragua's economy, which for twenty-five years before the revolution had been one of the fastest growing in the hemisphere, had fallen to the level of such African nations as Somalia. Foreign aid and credits, which had peaked at $1.197 billion in 1985 had fallen to $385 million in 1987, with 81 percent of the credits and 51 percent of the aid coming from Communist countries.[17]

What Did It All Mean to the People?

The impact of centralized control and attacks on those who didn't conform was felt daily by the Nicaraguan people. For all their talk of being a people's government, the real representatives of the common people, one of the outstanding characteristics of the Sandinistas was their almost total ignorance of and increasing alienation and isolation from the average Nicaraguan.

The basic assumption underlying Sandinista governance was that the nine comandantes had, or on their own would find, all the answers to Nicaragua's needs. When they lacked an answer, the last place they looked for enlightenment was to the people they claimed to represent. If they had, they would have done a lot of things differently. They considered those who disagreed with them either active counterrevolutionaries or self-destructively ignorant and old-fashioned. While the Contras were to be silenced in whatever way was necessary, from imprisonment to death, the others might be either "educated" or intimidated into line. It was contrary to revolutionary practice to accept the need for evolutionary change of ingrained tradition.

New York Times correspondent Kinzer describes this situation. One day he met a teenage girl who had been searching unsuccessfully for hours for cooking oil in the inland city of Jinotega. He asked the owner of a nearby grocery store if he had any cooking oil. "Cooking oil," he exclaimed. "Why not ask for soap and toilet paper also? Perhaps you would like a chicken or some rice? Well, my friend, you can ask the Sandinistas for those things, because you won't find them here." Kinzer stationed himself for several hours in another small general store. Some fifty customers came in looking for the same necessities. Most were from farm families that had given up growing food or animals because of the straitjacket of government controls. One phrase told the story: "No hay"—there isn't any. Almost all blamed the Sandinistas.[18]

Many shoppers had wanted eggs, so Kinzer told the store owner he had seen eggs a half hour away by car in Matagalpa. Why didn't the owner buy some of those and resell them here? "Oh, no, you don't understand," she replied, pulling out a government price list issued to every store in the country.

In Matagalpa, I would have to pay the official price for eggs, and when I got them back here, I would have to sell them for that same price. I couldn't make back what I would have to spend for gasoline to drive to Matagalpa. If I charged a higher price, they would send a mob against me and paint "House of Thieves" on my wall. That is why there are no eggs in Jinotega.

When Kinzer visited a local Sandinista official and told him how government regulations were affecting the people and what they were doing to the FSLN's reputation, the official replied that it was the people's own fault: they refused to grow what they should, to sell through government agencies, to respect price controls. "The mentality of the market woman," he said, "is one of our most serious problems."[19]

Predictably, the result of this attitude toward the people was alienation and resistance. In frustration over impediments to carrying out their traditional (often subsistence) livelihood, many simply stopped growing products and moved to Managua and other cities where they engaged in other occupations. Many went into "bisnes" as practitioners in the "parallel," illegal market that swelled in Nicaragua during the 1980s. They set up stalls in the Eastern Market, the largest in Managua, or elsewhere, peddled goods that had been grown "illegally," and drove Sandinista leaders crazy, even as they saved the country from utter economic collapse. The police raided their operations and destroyed their goods, but they reappeared. Other Nicaraguans would stand in one of the innumerable and seemingly interminable lines for a fee, or for a fee would scour city and countryside for any of the many necessities that had suddenly become unavailable but often turned up if a bribe were offered or payment was in dollars, a guard against the horrendous inflation.

Conclusions

The 1981 state of emergency ended the FSLN's honeymoon with the people and from then on the economy was on its way down, "even before they [the Sandinistas] were confronted with a U.S.-financed counterrevolution."[20] One of the great deceptions of the decade was the degree to which the Sandinistas and their supporters abroad convinced Americans and many others that the Contra War and the U.S. economic embargo were the main causes of the Haitinization of Nicaragua.

In early 1985 an East German economist in Nicaragua looked at the nation's condition and lamented, "I can't think of any East European economy as messed up as this one," and coming from such a collapsing country as East Germany, that was saying a lot.[21] But the most incisive short critique of Sandinista economic policy for the decade came from the Soviet paper *Izvestiia* of 16 July 1989:

> Ambitious and obviously infeasible long-term projects elaborated in the first years after the revolution, excessive centralization of management, the wave of confiscations which scared off private entrepreneurs, corruption among state functionaries, ineffective use of foreign aid, and poor discipline at state enterprises—all this produced serious disruptions in the economy. The rest was accomplished by the war.

The only positive consequence of the controlled economy was that, in some ways and for a while, it did enhance political control. On the one hand, throughout the country people were far more dependent on the state when earning or receiving their livelihood, and thus they were more easily induced to do as the state told them. If they were not inclined, they could be subtly pressured since, among other things, benefits could be withheld from "troublemakers," such as those who did not participate in defense committees and/or dodged the draft. Or things could get nastier. Outspoken critics of the FSLN could find their property confiscated, as happened to Enrique Bolaños, who lost his cotton farm in 1985; the message was clear, Colburn writes, "engaging in political opposition can lead to the loss of one's assets."[22] Or peasants who sold their produce to private middlemen could have their entire harvest confiscated without compensation.

But in the long term the political losses of the failed economy were enormous. Peasants, workers, and businessmen were frustrated by the web of regulations, incompetence, inefficiency, curtailment of incentives, declining living conditions, limitations on property rights. All contributed to migration to the cities, the expansion of slums in Managua, the growth of a black market, and strong rural support for and involvement in the Contras.

Thus, in the end, the Sandinista determination to circumscribe the potential of the Nicaraguan people guaranteed a failed economy, which in turn made it virtually inevitable that the Sandinistas would be thrown out whenever the opportunity arose to do so. The failing economy was one of the main reasons the FSLN was forced into a relatively free election in 1990, and that was the people's chance. They took it and overwhelmingly rejected the incumbent President Ortega and his movement.

Notes

1. Alejandro Bendaña, *Una Tragedia Campesina* (Managua: Editora de Arte, 1991), 258. We are grateful to Robert Leiken for drawing our attention to Bendaña's book and sending us his extensive notes while we were awaiting the arrival of our own copy.
2. *72-Hour Document*, Falcoff and Royal, *Crisis*, 508, 499.
3. Diamond, "Class and Power in Revolutionary Nicaragua," 391, 395.
4. Colburn, *Managing the Commanding Heights*, 38–41; source of percentages, Sandinista Ministry of Planning.

188   The Civil War in Nicaragua

5. Colburn, *Managing the Commanding Heights*, 1-2, 42.
6. National Autonomous University of Nicaragua, Department of Social Sciences, *Curso sobre la problemática actual*, quoted in Colburn, *Managing the Commanding Heights*, 34-5.
7. See Forrest D. Colburn, *Post-Revolutionary Nicaragua: State, Class, and the Dilemmas of Agrarian Policy* (Berkeley: University of California Press, 1986); and Stephen Diamond, "Class and Power in Revolutionary Nicaragua."
8. The Spanish "Área de propiedad del pueblo" popularly came to mean "autorizado para perder"; Colburn, *Managing the Commanding Heights*, 3, 52-54, 121.
9. See table of decrees in Roberto Cardenal, *Lo que se quiso ocultar*, 238.
10. Forrest D. Colburn, *My Car in Managua* (Austin: University of Texas Press, 1991), 127.
11. Diamond, "Class and Power in Revolutionary Nicaragua," 341-43.
12. Quoted by Diamond, "Class and Power in Revolutionary Nicaragua," 356.
13. Diamond, "Class and Power in Revolutionary Nicaragua," p. 385; also, interview with Luciano Torres, 362.
14. Kinzer, *Blood of Brothers*, 235-36.
15. Evertz' comments were made in an interview with *La Prensa* (17 January 1992, Miami edition), where the date is incorrectly reported as 1984. Also see William Branigin, "Inflation Leaps, Output Falls in Nicaragua," *Washington Post*, 18 August 1987; and Stephen Kinzer, "For Nicaragua, Soviet Frugality Starts to Pinch," *New York Times*, 20 August 1987.
16. Kinzer, *Blood of Brothers*, 377, 380.
17. Mark Uhlig, "Nicaraguan Study Reports Economy in Drastic Decline," *New York Times*, 26 June 1989.
18. Kinzer, *Blood of Brothers*, 121.
19. Kinzer, Ibid., 121.
20. Colburn, *Post-Revolutionary Nicaragua*, 2.
21. David Asman, "Despair and Fear in Managua," *Wall Street Journal*, 25 March 1985.
22. Colburn, *Managing the Commanding Heights*, 120.

14

The Sentinel of the People's Happiness

With the program of deception described above, the FSLN has worn a cloak of virtue that fooled or at least confused people around the world. In essence, the Sandinistas' public position was that their government represented all Nicaraguans except for a few reactionaries who wanted Nicaragua to continue as their personal fiefdom, even if without Somoza, in the service of American imperialism. The Sandinistas claimed that to guarantee the rights of the vast majority sometimes meant terminating the rights of the counterrevolutionary few. But as time passed, the "few" became the vast majority.

The comandantes unhesitatingly relegated to themselves alone the authority to decide what ideas, people, and groups were acceptable in the new Nicaragua. To implement their decisions they needed power, as Arce had said in his 1984 speech on elections. The main institution established to exercise this power, to maintain domestic control and conformity, was the Ministry of the Interior (MINT) under Comandante Tomás Borge, who in true Orwellian terms described the ministry as the Sentinel of the People's Happiness. One writer described Borge as "the little man with the voice of a poet [and] the eyes of a zealot" who "appreciated the nuances, even the beauty of pain."[1]

MINT grew enormously larger and more pervasive under the Sandinistas than its counterpart had been under Somoza. It was the main institution of formal and informal repression, its activities ranging from the legitimate keeping of order through publication of the party paper *Barricada* and censorship of opposition media to manipulation of justice, torture and assassination. MINT never achieved the total power it sought, but its influence was widespread and intimidating.

The major divisions of MINT were the State Security (DGSE), the police, the Directorate V intelligence operatives, patterned on Cuba's General Directorate of Intelligence (DGI), the Tropas Pablo Ubeda (until it was moved from MINT to Defense in the mid-1980s), the monitors of the media and, more informally, the mobs. MINT also manipulated the judicial system. In this chapter we will discuss the widespread repression of rights and freedoms of those who did not agree with the comandantes.

Rights, a Matter of Strategy

In one of his moments of candor, Interior Minister Tomás Borge told a visiting OAS mission in October 1980 that "the most important thing is our strategic, historic decision to be in favor of human rights." That is, the FSLN was not interested in human rights because it supported human rights per se, though in another passage to the OAS, Borge claimed it did, but because the Sandinistas decided that attention to human rights would advance their long-term political objectives. That is what Borge meant by a "strategic" interest.[2]

In the spirit of Marxism-Leninism or almost any arrogant ideology, support for human rights can, with a perfectly clear conscience, be manipulated to serve broader interests. Before July 1979 the Sandinistas, along with many others, rightly condemned the violations of the Somoza government, though sometimes even then they did so deceptively, as when Jesuit Father Fernando Cardenal told a U.S. congressional committee in 1977 that he came only as a churchman "in the name of the barefoot lowly peasants of Nicaragua." He gave no indication that he was a member of the FSLN or that his testimony was based on documentation provided by the Sandinista National Secretariat, a deception he admitted in 1983.[3] And even as strategic interests clearly dictated the condemnation of human rights abuses by their enemies, so they also justified accusing enemies of abuses they did *not* commit and violations by the Sandinistas themselves.

The Guardians of Happiness

The most important institution in terms of control and repression around the country was State Security, strongly influenced and supported by Cuba, which by the mid-1980s had some four thousand members, making it about ten times larger than Somoza's secret police had been. The DGSE chief was Lenín Cerna, who quickly became the personification of Sandinista repression. He was cunning and malicious, vain, prone to overeating—so always on a diet or exercising—and like Humberto a dog-lover who had four dobermans.

The DGSE was divided into several sections, including F-1 (Operations), F-4 (Ideological Orientation), and F-8 (Mass Organizations). DGSE ties went into all aspects of society with a complex web of people and institutions, including informers, interrogators, squads for kidnapping or carrying out the "dirty work" of the government, special jails for holding hostages, the Sandinista Defense Committees, and the like. It used blackmail, lies, harassment, provocation, imprisonment, psychological or physical torture, and execution to achieve its objectives.

However much State Security learned from the Soviets and Cubans, many of its techniques, like those often used by the Sandinista People's Army, were learned from Somoza, though they were more pervasive and at times more sophisticated. Cerna often claimed that "physical torture was a primitive method used by Somoza. We have much more scientific ways to make a prisoner talk," alluding to the de-personalization and psychological torture the Nicaraguans had learned from the Cubans. But EPS chief Humberto Ortega admitted privately, "We have to follow the example of the old Somoza's policy of the three Ps—plata (money), palo (stick), and plomo (bullet): that is, money for friends, a stick for waverers, and a bullet for enemies." And the DGSE itself used a lot of the "primitive" palo and plomo too, as seen in Cerna's personal beating of sixty-year-old Sofonias Cisneros—who was accused of lacking respect for the educational policies of the comandantes—and in many other instances noted in this book.[4]

The most feared jail, in many respects, was El Chipote, an underground detention and interrogation center dug into the hill directly behind the Intercontinental Hotel in what had been downtown Managua. The name was taken from the mountain called that in northern Nicaragua, which in the 1930s had been the headquarters of Sandino. This facility was used mainly for political prisoners, who were usually confined there for a couple of months that were certain to be, at the very least, highly intimidating. One Sandinista official who worked with Borge said, with no little understatement: "People are afraid just of going into El Chipote because it has a somewhat fearsome reputation. That has a psychological impact by itself."[5]

Death and Imprisonment

From the beginning, "exemplary punishment" was considered a "low cost" but effective way to gain and keep order and control in the country. It was used to eliminate and intimidate committed enemies of the regime, but also to warn those who supported the revolution that it would be dangerous to waver or shift sides. Ironically, many of the people whose rights were violated to the point of disappearance or death were precisely the workers and peasants the Sandinistas professed to represent. One extensive, on-the-spot study of labor relations under the Sandinistas concluded that "harassment, intimidation, arrest, and even killing, of workers and peasants who peacefully criticized or protested Nicaraguan government policies was a regular event inside Sandinista Nicaragua."[6]

Some exemplary executions were aimed at individuals in order to intimidate a larger number, while others involved killing more people, playing to a still broader audience. We will give several examples.

Former guardsmen, some of whom had committed serious crimes, and alleged Somoza collaborators, were the first to be made examples by imprisonment and execution. At least thirty prisoners at La Polvora jail in Granada were killed in the months after the revolution and two mass graves were later found outside the city. The Interior Ministry, which had made Granada an unofficial detention center, tried to block investigations by CPDH. But making an example of guardsmen continued. Many hundreds of guardsmen, mostly in their early twenties or younger, were charged with nothing more specific than illicit association and "membership in a criminal organization," but in perfunctory trials they were given ten or more years in prison.[7]

One of the most widely publicized assassinations by State Security forces was of Jorge Salazar, a businessman who had supported the overthrow of Somoza but was considered a threat as early as the *72-Hour Document* because he had very effectively organized small coffee growers. Salazar became involved in a conspiracy against the government and the easiest way to silence him was with death. While unarmed, he was ambushed and murdered in November 1980 by security agents.

It is fairly well known that sixteen prisoners died "trying to escape" from the Zona Franca prison at the end of June 1981. But the details have been hidden. A group of prisoners took several guards hostage. Borge and Walter Ferrety, then chief of the Sandinista police, arrived with some

EPS units prepared to provide support as needed. After some clashes between MINT units and the prisoners, which left several of the latter wounded, Borge said he would spare their lives if they would put down their weapons. When they put their arms down, Ferrety immediately shot several men in front of Borge and the remainder were summarily executed.

The execution of prisoners who caused trouble was particularly important because there were so many prisoners in the country and the Sandinistas wanted to cow them into submission. Thousands of people involved in or suspected of antigovernment activity were killed or arrested and held in inhumane conditions in state security prisons. Some 785 people were reported "disappeared" to CPDH between the fall of Somoza and September 1980, though the rights organization said that the actual number was probably closer to three thousand. While some of these people were later accounted for—reappeared, found dead, etc.— many were not, and more disappeared as time passed. Among the disappearances reported to CPDH in the first five years of the Sandinista government, 342 remained unresolved in 1984: 170 from 1979, 30 from 1980, and 170 from 1981-83. And many of the disappeared, especially peasants, still were unreported. Also, the human rights organization concluded that some 97 people died inadequately explained deaths ("trying to escape," "heart attacks," and the like) between 1981 and 1984 after having been arrested by civil or military authorities.[8]

Some seven thousand people were being held in the Zona Franca, Cárcel Modelo, and other prisons in early 1987, about half of them political prisoners, far greater numbers than were held during the Somoza period. Many prisoners were peasants, some twenty-five hundred of whom were arrested and jailed in 1986 alone, according to CPDH, for refusing to join Sandinista defense organizations, for actually or allegedly supporting the Contras, or for resisting the resettlement programs which involved some hundred fifty thousand peasants between 1982 and early 1987. Some of these prisoners simply disappeared, some "committed suicide," and many were shot "while attempting to escape."[9]

• In many respects the most flagrant and systematic repression by the Sandinista government was the nearly genocidal program launched almost immediately, largely for strategic reasons, against the Miskito, Sumo, Rama, and Creole peoples on the Gulf coast. Traditional organizations and institutions on the eastern coast were forcibly replaced by

Sandinista Defense Committees, the EPS, DGSE, other FSLN entities led and/or accompanied by substantial numbers of Cubans. In February 1981 the heavy-handed repression brought war that continued throughout the decade at varying levels in loose cooperation with Contra forces in Honduras and Costa Rica, interspersed with the "peace negotiations" discussed below. The EPS and Interior Ministry also carried out a program which over several years often brutally resettled some twenty thousand people, while driving fifty thousand into exile in other countries.[10]

• A different kind of "example" occurred in September 1987. Roger Miranda's black phone—the one that carried only calls from Humberto Ortega—rang and the chief, unusually agitated, said only, "Miranda, come to my house immediately," and hung up. In six years with Humberto, Miranda had never received a call like this one. When he arrived, Humberto took him to one of the trees in his private garden where someone had carved "FDN," the acronym for the Honduras-based Contras, into the trunk. Ortega growled, "Miranda, I want you and counterintelligence to investigate this immediately and find out what bastard has the balls to write this in the patio of my house." Miranda met with Lt. Col. Omar Halleslevens, chief of counterintelligence, and within a couple of days the latter concluded it had been done by a gardener who had worked in the house for years. Counterintelligence tortured him to find out if he was part of a broader plot, but concluded he had acted alone and had no contacts with the Contras.

Still, when Ortega was told, he ordered, without pause, "the sonofabitch must be killed." When asked if he didn't think the punishment excessive, he shouted and waved the report in Miranda's face, "What the fuck do you expect me to do when this bastard writes these signs in my own garden!" He would not reconsider. In part he had been personally insulted in his own residence. But also, he felt he had to show the hundreds of servants and security personnel who served and protected him, and had heard of this incident, that any such insult or insubordination meant death. After considering various ways to kill him, Humberto decided that counterintelligence assassins should make him die "accidentally from a falling tree," but gunshot wounds in his back left his family unconvinced by the official story. The gardener's pregnant wife was given some money and told there would be an investigation, but there never was.

Other Exemplary Punishments

Individuals who criticized the government were not always killed or "disappeared." Often they were beaten up instead of, or as a prelude to, being thrown in jail.

• A week after the Esquipulas II peace accord was signed in August 1987, an opposition rally was broken up with unusual force, the police using electric prods. Lino Hernández, the head of CPDH, and bar association president Alberto Saborío, were jailed for three weeks. The calculated brutality of the attack on an opposition event at Nandaime on 10 July 1988 surprised even those who expected the worst from Borge's forces. "They had come to teach the opposition a lesson," wrote Stephen Kinzer. The police fired volley after volley of tear gas into the crowd. Kinzer wrote that just before he too was attacked, and knocked unconscious, he "could see Sandinista police officers kicking and beating people. Never had they broken up a protest with such sustained violence."[11] Thirty-nine protesters, members of opposition political parties who were demonstrating with official authorization, were arrested and held in prison for months after their "trial" by "popular tribunals."

• Sometimes people were blackmailed, as was the case with Bernardo Martínez, known as Bernardo de Cuapa. Martínez was famous because the Virgin had supposedly appeared at his house in the town of Cuapa in Chontales province, causing it to become a pilgrimage site. But Martínez was also a subtle critic of the government. State Security, concerned with his popularity, decided to take action against him, but knew it could not do so openly. So agents gained his confidence and one day, taking advantage of his fondness for drink, lured him to a hotel room where he was drugged. Rendered almost unconscious, he was raped by the state agents. Later he was shown a doctored film of the incident in which he was made to appear a willing participant. Bernardo was told that if he did not stop criticizing the government and halt his claims regarding the apparition of the Virgin of Cuapa, the tape would be made public. He was silent thereafter.

• The Sandinistas made extensive and often very effective use of spies and undercover agents. One former national guardsman, José Efrén Mondragón, had his career as a Contra commander sabotaged by a woman who lured him back to Managua; for a while he campaigned to get other Contras to defect, but in time he was brutally assassinated. One of the most effective undercover agents was Pedro Espinoza Sánchez, known as *El Pez* (the fish), who penetrated and sabotaged several opposition groups in and outside of Nicaragua, bringing many to their deaths. Other Sandinista agents were well known to be spies, among them Marieluz Serrano (Nancy), who spent many months with Edén Pastora, an old friend of her family, while Comandante Cero was on the Southern Front in the early 1980s.[12]

• The relationship between the Church and the Sandinistas in this predominantly Roman Catholic country was very complicated, but it boiled down to this: the cultivation and utilization of highly politicized Christians—the "popular" church—for political purposes, on the one hand, and the manipulation and when necessary the harassment and repression of those who believed the Church should stand above partisan politics, on the other. Increasingly during the decade of the 1980s, the FSLN charged that the traditional church, headed by Cardinal Miguel Obando y Bravo represented only the middle and upper classes, at the expense of the poor. The Sandinistas undertook active measures to discredit the Church and its leaders, one of the most common being the manufactured incident intended to defame a clergyman. For example, Fr. Amado Peña, one of the most important working-class priests in Managua, was set up twice by government agents to make him appear a counterrevolutionary conspirator, preaching peace as a priest but secretly plotting armed insurrection against the people's government.

The Mobs and "Collective Justice"

The common cop-out when a death or atrocity could not be covered up or blamed on the Contras was the same as when evidence was found of military aid to the Salvadoran guerrillas: the government claimed the action had been undertaken by individuals or groups acting on their own, beyond the government's control. There was a logic to this, for many Nicaraguans *did* have very strong and often justifiable resentments against the Somoza regime and the National Guard, but the government systematically used and directed repression rather than trying to reign in these and manufactured resentments, and did so for many years.

Tomás Borge professed government innocence to the OAS in October 1980. He said FSLN leaders had told the police, the security forces, and the army: "'Don't commit abuses; don't be disrespectful to anyone; don't hit prisoners.' Because often they did hit prisoners or kill prisoners." He said that a "tiny minority" of guardsmen had been killed but added, "It was like Fuenteovejuna," alluding to the Lope de Vega drama in which a whole village admits having risen up and killed an oppressive tax collector as an act of spontaneous, collective justice.[13]

The most common instrument of "spontaneous collective justice," which in fact was government planned and often coordinated, was the mob. The "turbas" were gangs that, beginning in early 1981, beat up individuals, broke up political meetings and church services, and ransacked private property. More active in some periods than others, they were unofficial instruments of Sandinista "revolutionary terror" and one of the early signs that the Sandinistas had their roots in the politics of Somoza.

• One of the first major targets of the turbas was Alfonso Robelo, who had been a member of the original government Junta but resigned in early 1980 and subsequently was lambasted as a lackey of the right. Robelo got authorization to hold a rally of his National Democratic Movement (MDN) in Nandaime on 15 March 1981. But on the night of 14 March, EPS trucks transported turbas to the roads leading into the city to prevent MDN demonstrators from getting into town; on the next day the mobs destroyed MDN party headquarters, burned the home of the party's local leader, and vandalized other homes. The government blamed all the trouble on MDN provocateurs. On 15 March, the main headline of the FSLN paper *Barricada* proclaimed: "People's Victory: Provocateurs Turned Back." The next day the National Directorate released a long statement, which said in part: "The Sandinista Front reaffirms it will respect the will of the people, in whatever form the people may express their will." If provoked, it went on, "and its means of expression produces acts that could be classified excessive, the only ones responsible are the provocateurs who have questioned everything about the Revolution and confront a people who have decided they will not go one step backward along their historical road."[14]

• One of the most controversial events in the FSLN's relations with the Church was the visit of Pope John Paul II to Nicaragua in March 1983. The pope stated in advance that his visit was to be pastoral, not political, but the FSLN looked on it as a supremely political act. The FSLN decided to disrupt the pope's visit when it became clear he would not speak out against the Contras, but rather would follow the Nicaraguan church in criticizing the "popular church" and in calling for unity among Nicaraguans. The National Directorate instructed the Regional Committee of the FSLN in Managua to control transportation and access to the 19 July Plaza so as to make it hard for believers to attend the pope's mass, while at the same time making sure there were enough hecklers in strategic positions to disrupt the meeting and create a climate of hostility toward the pope. Predictably, the pope's sermon and communion were broken by amplified heckling and chanting, some of it coming from the comandantes themselves, while the pope's microphone was turned down. In fact, the vast majority on hand loved the pope and popular tensions with the government increased as a result of this manufactured incident. After leaving Nicaragua, the pope condemned the Sandinista regime for its sacrilegious behavior. But Minister of Culture Ernesto Cardenal told *Playboy* magazine (September 1983) that the pope had gotten just what he deserved.

• The Interior Ministry used the turbas many other times, among them: in mid-1983 on the Salesian school in Monimós, which had established its revolutionary bonafides in the war against Somoza, because priests there dared to criticize government repression of the Miskitos and their church; in 1984 on Arturo Cruz and other opposition candidates in the presidential elections that year; and in 1988 after the escalation of atrocities in the wake of the Directorate's above-cited defense of "revolutionary violence," in Nandaime and other parts of the country.

Twisting Justice

But the Sandinistas went beyond saying they were not responsible for violations of human rights. They asserted that human rights and legal norms were scrupulously respected under their government and even claimed that those who were caught deliberately violating norms of proper behavior on their own were punished. But they said this largely to cover their own systematic violations of those very rights and norms.

Between July and October 1979 the National Directorate adopted a vengeful attitude toward former national guardsmen and other supporters of the dictator who were accused—sometimes quite accurately—of crimes against the Nicaraguan people. But many people were blacklisted simply for reasons of personal vengeance. Special Courts were set up as a cover for executions and regional military chiefs were given the names of the condemned. During those months hundreds were executed around the country, often in public, on direct orders from Humberto Ortega, who was acting on behalf of the Directorate. What the tribunals actually did had little to do with justice. A delegation from the United Nations International Commission of Jurists, which made an early inspection of the courts, was openly sympathetic to the Sandinistas. But its secret report to the Sandinista leaders included sixteen "frank" comments, beginning with:

> It is unavoidable that an impartial observer reach the conclusion that the Special Tribunals constitute exceptional tribunals dispensing political justice with only the appearance of legality, abandoning elemental principles of the democratic penal process. These tribunals . . . in reality comply with the old rule of war, according to which the victors punish the losers.[15]

This judgment gave the lie to Borge's often-quoted statement that the Sandinistas are "implacable in battle but merciful in victory." In fact, on orders of the National Directorate, executions of Guardsmen occurred throughout the country: in Masaya, in Managua, León, Estelí, and in several other cities.

Only in Granada, a city that was generally lukewarm in the fight against Somoza, did the executions under the direction of Salvador Bravo draw significant criticism. In August 1979, in response to the negative publicity, Humberto himself assumed the position of a judge imparting justice and made Bravo the scapegoat for what Ortega himself had ordered. The captain was emotionally shaken by the betrayal, and in December 1981, by which time he had been promoted to captain, he committed suicide.

In 1983 the Special Courts were replaced by Anti-Somocista People's Courts (Tribunals), which operated outside the regular court system. This court consisted of three members of the FSLN. According to Stephen Kinzer,

> police and security forces, using the People's Tribunal to legalize their actions, arrested and imprisoned everyone they suspected of ties to the Contras. . . . Human rights advocates were entirely justified in complaining that the People's Tribunal routinely sent defendants to jail on the basis of flimsy evidence or hearsay.[16]

CPDH reported in early 1987 that some two thousand people had already been "tried" in these courts and another two thousand were then awaiting trial.[17]

• In late 1983, when peasants resisted brutal land collectivization in Pantasma, a village in the northern part of Jinotega, a virtual reign of terror, consisting of robbery, rape, and murder, was imposed by the local representatives of the Department of the Interior. When the deaths of dozens could no longer be hidden, the FSLN put accused government representatives, including some members of the EPS, on "trial" and sent them to jail. But the sentences were simply for propaganda purposes: very soon the top perpetrator was sent to study in the Soviet Union and the others were set free. Not surprisingly, Pantasma and Jinotega in general provided many of the unit leaders and fighters in the Contra army.

• Daniel Ortega told the *New York Times* that twenty soldiers were sentenced to prison for abuses committed during the evacuation of Miskito Indians, and that at least five had been executed.[18] In July 1987 Tomás Borge insisted before a large conference of international reporters in Managua that the FSLN did not tolerate violations of human rights. Reacting in part to several recent media articles on Sandinista rights abuses, he acknowledged that "some of our compañeros have committed serious crimes against the people on the Atlantic coast," and added that in Nicaraguan jails over the past eight years "there have been mistreatments and even killings, in isolated form, especially in the theater of war." He then said that these "isolated" incidents had led to the arrest and sentencing of 2,318 members of the EPS and Interior Ministry in the previous *six months* alone.[19]

Notes

1. Christopher Dickey, *With The Contras* (New York: Simon & Schuster, 1985), 64, 65.
2. Tomás Borge, "On Human Rights in Nicaragua," in Borge et al., *Sandinistas Speak* (New York: Pathfinder Press, 1982), 85; Payne, "Human Rights in Nicaragua," 49.
3. See Payne, "Human Rights in Nicaragua," 50.
4. For documents on this incident, including Cisneros statement to CPDH, see *From Revolution to Repression* (Washington: U.S. Department of State, March 1986), 59–67.
5. Kinzer, *Blood of Brothers*, 180–81.
6. Diamond, "Class and Power in Revolutionary Nicaragua," 280.
7. See Christian, *Nicaragua*, 132–34; Kinzer, *Blood of Brothers*, 78–79.

8. CPDH, "Los Desaparecidos: Un abominable crimen Somocista que debemos desterrar de la patria Sandinista," informe oficial, 3 de Octubre de 1980, p. 2; CPDH, "Testimonio Presentado por la CPDH a la Comisión de Derechos Humanos de la OEA," Managua, 12 de Mayo de 1984, pp. 1, 2. On some of the peasant deaths never reported during the Sandinista government but discovered later, see Nina Shea, "Uncovering the Awful Truth of Nicaragua's Killing Fields," *The Wall Street Journal*, 24 August 1990, and Sam Dillon, "A Tireless Crusader Reveals Pattern of Sandinista Abuses," *Miami Herald*, 16 May 1991.

9. CPDH, "The Human Rights Situation in Nicaragua," Special Report, April 1987, 4-5, 10-11.

10. See Nietschmann, *The Unknown War*, 15-42.

11. Kinzer, *Blood of Brothers*, 352, 382-83.

12. See Glenn Garvin, *Everybody Had His Own Gringo* (New York: Brassey's (US), 1992), 182-84; and Ratliff interview with Pastora, 24 March 1992.

13. Borge, "On Human Rights in Nicaragua," in *Sandinistas Speak*, 88, 90.

14. Dirección Nacional, "FSLN siempre respetará la voluntad popular," *Barricada*, 17 March 1981.

15. Comisión Internacional de Juristas, "Tribunales especiales que juzgan a Somocistas y colaboradores del Somocismo," Ginebra, 14. Copy in Hoover Institution Archives.

16. Kinzer, *Blood of Brothers*, 315; also 204.

17. CPDH, "Situación de los Derechos Humanos en Nicaragua: Informe Especial," Managua, April 1987.

18. Kinzer, *Blood of Brothers*, 275.

19. United Press International, "Borge admite torturas y asesinatos," *La Nación*, San José, Costa Rica, 26 de julio de 1987. Among the articles published just before Borge's remarks were William Branigin, "Pattern of Abuses Laid to Sandinistas," *Washington Post*, 18 May 1987, and James LeMoyne, "Peasants Tell of Rights Abuses by Sandinistas," *New York Times*, 28 June 1987.

15

A Giant, Blind and Deaf, Flailing Wildly

Political and other disputes in Nicaragua have traditionally been resolved by violence. Thus it is hardly surprising that from the time they formed their movement, Sandinista leaders conceived the need for a military force to seize power and a permanent army—the EPS—to back up the new government as it carried out its revolutionary changes.

This objective was stated in the 1969 FSLN program, here cited in its revised 1981 version since that version better reflected Sandinista thinking just after Somoza's fall. In the program, the FSLN pledged to abolish the U.S.-created National Guard and replace it with "a patriotic, revolutionary, people's army," which good guardsmen nonetheless would be permitted to join. The FSLN would develop the fighting ability, tactical, and technical levels of the army and cultivate the revolutionary consciousnesses of its members. It concluded that the EPS and the people's militia "will defend the rights won against the inevitable attack by the reactionary forces of the country and Yankee imperialism."[1]

Despite comments on an "inevitable attack by the reactionary forces of the country," no such attack was expected in the immediate future by remnants of the guard or any other domestic armed force. The *72-Hour Document* described the remains of the National Guard thus: "Nothing was left of that army but shame, smoke, and ashes. It was totally routed." The document continued:

> The kind of military victory achieved over the dictatorship makes it impossible for now, from the practical point of view, to organize aggression by the defeated National Guard. . . . At present there are no clear indications of an armed counterrevolution by Somocista forces from abroad which actually threatens our stability.[2]

In 1985, then Sandinista ambassador to the United States, Carlos Túnnermann, openly admitted the insignificance of the Contra forces even up to the time U.S. military aid began, writing that at the end of

204   The Civil War in Nicaragua

1981, when military aid was authorized, "there were only a few hundred ex-National Guard soldiers staging sporadic raids on farms along the border. Their principal occupations were cattle-rustling and extortion."[3]

When the Sandinistas marched into Managua in July 1979 they had a military force of about five thousand, the considerable majority of whom had joined the movement during the final months of the war. At the end of that month, Daniel Ortega proclaimed, "We must organize, organize, organize, to create a great Sandinista People's Army," and progress in that direction came quickly. By the end of 1981—before the U.S. began giving military aid to what became the Contras, and before the United States began its own military expansion in the region—the new EPS had been built into the numerically largest army in the history of Central America. But it was an army with enormous problems, which were zeroed in on by Cuban general Ochoa during an early visit to Nicaragua in 1983 when in a talk with Humberto Ortega he compared the EPS to "a giant, blind and deaf, flailing wildly." By this he meant that though the army was large, its structure and intelligence were not suited to dealing successfully with a peasant uprising. The structure of the army had to be reformed to meet this unexpected challenge. By the end of 1988 the reformed Sandinista army had grown to two hundred fifty thousand, with one hundred fifty thousand of these in the reserves and militia.[4]

For the first few years of the Sandinista government there was no military draft. As the war with the Contras intensified in 1983, more and more specialized troops were needed. But it became increasingly clear that not enough young Nicaraguans were sufficiently dedicated to the revolution to voluntarily join the military to defend it. Humberto went before the National Directorate in late 1983 and argued: "The type of army we have been building wasn't designed to confront this kind of warfare. If we are going to survive and win, we need to restructure the whole army. We need compulsory military service immediately." General Ochoa emphasized the need for military service to develop the BLI (Irregular Warfare Battalions). The National Directorate immediately authorized the military service and by January 1984 young men were being inducted.

The new law specified that men between the ages of eighteen and twenty-five were required to register to serve two years in the army, while those between the ages of twenty-six and forty were required to register for service in the army as reservists. Humberto later realized that the draft should have been for three years, for the following reason: it took six months to recruit and train the young men, another six months for them to become accustomed to and effective in the mountains where they had to serve, after which they had about six months of reasonably effective service. During their last six or so months, most soldiers, anticipating the end of their service, tried to avoid dangerous assignments and were thus less aggressive and effective. The Contras did not have these problems for several reasons, among them the fact that most of the fighters were natives of the mountains in which they were fighting and they were not recruited for a short period of time but were volunteers who often stayed on for years. When in 1985–86 Humberto informally raised the possibility of extending the period of military service, the idea was not well-received because to have extended the time would have given the impression that the Sandinistas felt they were losing the war.

The composition of this military force was quietly debated within the ranks of the FSLN. Humberto believed that military assignments should be made irrespective of family influence, and he often said so publicly. In September 1984, for example, he said in a public interview: "Compliance with the patriotic military service is a citizen's duty, a 'must' independent of the social status of the young person. . . . No one will be exempted except for reasons specified in the law itself. . . . We are going to apply the law accordingly." But Daniel, Sergio Ramírez, and some other top officials thought their own draft-age children should not be exposed to danger. For example, one day Miranda received a phone call from Daniel about the military service of Rafael, his wife's son. "Look, Miranda," Ortega said, "I want you to get Rafael posted here in Managua and assure me that he can go home to visit his girlfriend whenever he wants to." When Miranda informed Humberto about this request, he exploded: "This is the kind of shit I don't like from Daniel." But Rafael and the children of some other top FSLN officials did receive preferential treatment. In reality, almost all the youngsters sent out to fight were the children of poorer families without political clout. The only exception was the son of Miguel Ernesto Vijil, then minister of housing, who was wounded on the front lines.

This buildup was made possible by the close cooperation of Cuba and the Soviet bloc, which provided both the training of personnel and the arms for them to use, as discussed also in the chapters on Cuba and the Soviet Union. Though for a while there were turf wars between Borge

(MINT) and Humberto Ortega (EPS), the military became primarily responsible for fighting the Contra War. As the war expanded, the EPS focused on the Contras and those who might legitimately or opportunistically be construed as Contras. Thus EPS officials and troops were stationed throughout the country to fight the Contras and, as on the Miskito Coast and in provinces on the Honduran border, to "keep order" within the Nicaraguan population.

Inside the Sandinista People's Army

Though he was defense minister, Humberto Ortega devoted most of his time to the internal affairs of the National Directorate, not to the EPS. He turned his attention to the EPS at the beginning of each year, when a strategic military plan and the budget were drawn up and approved, and also once every six months when he had to report to the Directorate on the state of the Contra War. He always took Joaquín Cuadra and other important chiefs to those meetings to make presentations since he did not know enough about the subject to feel comfortable doing it alone.

Humberto rarely presided over meetings of the main officers of the EPS. When he did, he was accompanied by Cuadra, which reinforced the latter's authority with the chiefs. These meetings were not held for discussion; those on hand came to receive instructions. Meetings with Humberto were often particularly boring, because of his inability to communicate publicly. Aside from these occasions, everything was left in the hands of Joaquín Cuadra, the army general chief of staff. Cuadra held weekly meetings with the top chiefs and the chiefs of the Soviet and Cuban military missions. These were called operative meetings. They were intended to evaluate the development of the war and were much more dynamic than the meetings chaired by Ortega, with the Nicaraguan, Cuban, and Soviet military chiefs expressing their points of view and differences of opinion with respect to orders given by the general staff.

But Humberto was always very concerned about and cultivated the loyalty of his officers in a variety of ways. He gave them important sinecures and personal favors and he tried to get them to believe that their promotions were due to his influence on the Directorate. Everyone was indeed indebted in some way to him. The top officers knew the promotions came from the Directorate, but they also knew it was Humberto who put their names before the comandantes.

A Cuban Clone?

From the very beginning, the EPS was a close copy of the Cuban Revolutionary Armed Forces. Nowhere in Sandinista Nicaragua was the Cuban impact greater than on the EPS, for the Cuban military mission, in contrast to the Soviet, was massive and reached down to the level of battalion chief. The central political characteristic of the EPS, like its Cuban model, was its complete subordination to a single political party and its use to promote the objectives of that party. Organizationally, it followed the Cuban pattern, concentrating all power in Humberto Ortega as the military representative of the FSLN National Directorate. The vertical characteristics were:

• All branches of the military—ground troops, the air force, and navy—were subordinated to the Army General Chief of Staff. Within the General Staff was a political directorate charged with conducting the Sandinistas's political work and guaranteeing the loyalty of the officials, classes, and soldiers to the FSLN. For an official to rise to captain or above he had to be a party militant. In the case of chiefs, military promotion was usually decided by the National Directorate more on the basis of political than professional criteria.

The initial subdivisions of the military structure in Nicaragua under the central command were as follows: two military zones and three independent military regions. Zone I included the provinces of León and Chinandega; Zone II included Managua, Masaya, Granada, Rivas, Carazo, Boaco, Rio San Juan, and Zelaya Sur. The military regions included (1) Matagalpa and Jinotega, (2) Zelaya Norte, and (3) Estelí, Nueva Segovia, and Madriz. The zones would have greater forces and means because it was presumed they would be the scene of the first battles against the American army, and of the two zones, the first had the higher priority.

• There was no differentiation between the Ministry of Defense and the armed forces. The minister of defense was the chief of the army and the vice minister of defense was chief of the Army General Staff.

• The rules of the Sandinista army, from the most important to the most trivial, often were a copy of those governing the Cuban army. Sometimes even the wording of regulations was distinctively Cuban.

Before and After Ochoa

Cuban influence on the EPS falls into two general periods: before and during/after the 1984–86 residence in Nicaragua of Division General Arnaldo Ochoa. Ochoa had quietly visited Nicaragua on several occasions during 1983, but relations were truly transformed during the Cuban general's long residence; many of the serious and simply silly but irritating problems of the early years—ranging from military doctrine to daily practice—were overcome with Ochoa's guidance.

Most Cuban advisers could not understand that even though Nicaraguans and Cubans spoke the same language, and their two governments had the same political and ideological causes, Nicaragua was not Cuba and had to be dealt with according to its own customs and problems. The extent and nature of these influences, parallels, and inflexibilities irritated Humberto. Even though he recognized and appreciated the critical Cuban role in building the army, he thought Nicaraguans should not completely lose their own identity in the process. In small gatherings he often criticized the Sovietization of the Cuban army, which he blamed mainly on "the Chinaman," whom he considered much more inflexible than Fidel. He tried to get Cuban advisers to adapt to specific Nicaraguan conditions. In the early years Cuban advisers even treated the Nicaraguans as if they were children; although things improved over time, the problem never disappeared. It proved impossible to consistently and completely reform the practices of the Cuban advisers who were located throughout the military hierarchy and country.

There are many other examples of how the Cuban experience was not adjusted to Nicaraguan conditions, in part reflecting the problem of bureaucratic mentality in general. For example:

• Emmett Lang, chief of the Rearguard office, who followed guidelines used in Cuba, could not understand that soldiers engaged in irregular warfare needed more boots in a year than those on regular duty. The problem dragged on for months until Humberto confronted him:

Lang, I want you to tell me why the regional military chiefs are saying that many of their soldiers don't have enough boots.
But Minister, I have documents to show that I have supplied boots to these units according to regulations.
Look, Lang, I don't know much about regulations, but I don't want soldiers having to fight barefoot.
But Minister, I assure you I am abiding by the regulations of the rear-guard.

Fuck your regulations, Lang. From now on, the troops will get boots every three months.

- According to the rules of conventional warfare, defensive soldiers were supposed to be separated from each other by seven meters, though the chiefs of the troops for irregular warfare said it should be fifteen to twenty meters, depending on the terrain. It took months to modify the regulation.
- The first draft of the military conscription law had to be rejected by the EPS because it was so cluttered with Cuban norms and conceptions it didn't fit Nicaragua's conditions.

The problems of inflexibility quickly declined when General Ochoa became chief of the Cuban military mission in 1984. On his arrival, Ochoa not only had the distinction of having led Cuban troops in the wars in Ethiopia and Angola, and having participated in the Venezuelan guerrilla movement during the 1960s, he also enjoyed the close confidence and personal friendship of the Castro brothers. For the first time Cuba's advisory program became an altogether positive one and the top Cuban adviser in truth became Humberto Ortega's right hand-man. All plans, all decisions, all initiatives were reached through productive consultation between the top Nicaraguan and Cuban leaders.

Ochoa quickly reoriented concepts, types of advisers and institutions to meet the EPS's needs, the most important of which was the capacity to wage an antiguerrilla war while at the same time not overlooking the strategic task of being prepared to repel an eventual direct or indirect invasion by the United States. The structure of the military zones was transformed into regional militaries, with priority on the creation of Irregular Warfare Battalions (BLI). Among the military changes, Ochoa created the Operational Group to centralize the distinct military units fighting the Contras and authorized some artillery designed for conventional warfare to be used under certain circumstances in irregular warfare.

But his reforms went a lot farther. Prior to Ochoa, the Contra War had been considered a strictly military matter. The Cuban general taught that military activities alone would not win the war, that they had to be complemented by political, economic, and social programs. In practical terms this meant that programs and activities not previously considered military were recognized as important, sometimes critical, in waging the war. This involved many parts of the government and made the conflict a truly national effort. On one level Ochoa created the Support Commission for Combatants (CAC), which for the first time recognized that the families of soldiers killed or wounded in combat were the responsibility of the government, not just the EPS. More broadly, there was the Pomares and Fonseca Plan of 1984, the first stage of Ochoa's reforms that subsequently brought programs to finance peasant needs; improve their health, education, and political activism, and a state security program with its own net of informants. In effect, Ochoa's reforms were intended to introduce in Nicaragua what the Cuban leaders were doing at home, developing what the Cubans called "the War of All the People," and what Humberto Ortega called the Patriotic People's National War.

Other Military Ties

The Sandinistas sought military ties to a wide variety of non-Soviet groups and countries before and during their period in office. During half of 1978 and early 1979, prior to the beginning of Cuban aid, financial support of some $27 million for the war against Somoza came in part from: Carlos Andrés Pérez in Venezuela ($150,000-200,000 monthly), Omar Torrijos in Panama ($100,000-150,000 monthly), the ransom from the taking of the national palace ($500,000) and several million from the Salvadoran guerrillas, more specifically Fermán Cienfuegos of the Resistencia Nacional.[5] But there were other ties during the pre-victory years, the most important being with the Palestine Liberation Organization (PLO), which trained Nicaraguans in its Middle East camps beginning in the mid-1960s and incorporated members of the FSLN in some military operations in the 1970s; and with North Korea, which gave military training in the early 1970s to Humberto Ortega and other Sandinistas.

After July 1979 limited military aid was received from Bulgaria, including the aforementioned port, from Poland, and from the German Democratic Republic. East Germany's most important contribution to the EPS by the end of 1985 was some one thousand IFA W-50 trucks, which became the logistical backbone of the Sandinista army. None of the twenty-five or so East German advisers in Nicaragua during the mid-1980s were assigned to the EPS.

Contrary to some reports abroad, there were never military advisers from Korea or Libya. But there were contacts with some of these and other countries. Among them:

Greece—At one point, Greek president Andreas Papandreou gave 5,000 G-3 rifles to the Sandinista government.

North Korea—We have already noted North Korean aid in arms, military training, cement, and some other items.

The PLO—In thanks for its long-term solidarity with the Sandinista cause, Nicaragua in 1979 became one of the few countries in the world to allow the PLO to set up an embassy, not just an office, in its capital. The PLO provided a little aid and training in the early years of the revolutionary government, and Yassir Arafat visited the country in May 1980, but by the end of 1982 the PLO embassy was one of the least important in Managua. In part, this cutting back of relations was in response to President Reagan's campaign to link Nicaragua to the most flagrant international terrorists, including the PLO. The pressure in the National Directorate to cut back on these ties came mainly from the Ortegas.

Libya—In contrast to the PLO, Libya was a new ally at the time of the revolution, but the government quickly recognized that the Libyans might provide significant economic and military aid if properly cultivated. Early trips were made to Libya, in 1981 Moammar Qaddafi approved a gift of $100 million to Nicaragua, and between 1980 and 1982 Qaddafi sent small donations of military equipment as well.

In late-1982 and early-1983, Roger Miranda was assigned to work with the Libyan ambassador in Managua to arrange an important arms transfer, but the Libyans were evasive and probably in the end simply dishonest. Neither the Nicaraguans nor the Cubans could tie them down on a delivery date. Dates were proposed, settled, and changed. The Libyans said this was because they had to keep the Americans, who might suspect something, off guard. A previous air delivery from Libya had stopped at Cape Verde and Havana on the way to Managua. Then suddenly in April 1983 several Libyan planes loaded with arms took off for Managua and touched down in Brazil, where government inspectors quickly discovered the cargo, protested publicly, and refused to let them go on to Nicaragua. Humberto reported to the National Directorate:

I think the time has come to pull back from the Libyans. We are getting burned. I suspect that the capture of the planes in Brazil was premeditated so that the Americans would know they are arming us and will think that Nicaragua is a firm ally of Libya. You know what Libya has given us is negligible compared to what we need for the EPS and what Libya could afford to give. To me the costs of Libyan aid now far

outweigh the benefits. The Libyans are trying to get something for themselves out of
our confrontation with the gringos.

Borge thought Humberto was exaggerating the problem and prejudiced
against the Libyans. Near the end of 1985 Borge made a trip to Libya.
For some time prior to this trip, the Libyan embassy in Managua had
been passing out copies of Qaddafi's *Green Book*—a collection of the
Libyan leader's thoughts—to puzzled Nicaraguans. While Borge was in
Libya, Qaddafi asked if Nicaragua would host an international conference on the *Green Book,* with Libya picking up all the expenses. When
Borge conveyed this request to the Directorate, Humberto was the first
to object. "That guy's nuts if he thinks we are going to turn Managua into
a center for discussion of that book. Once again he is trying take
advantage of the prestige of our revolution and we can't permit it." This
time even Borge agreed and relations with Libya declined further.

• Panama—During the war against Somoza, Humberto, as the archi-
tect of Tercerismo, often through Pastora, had been the contact to
Panama. At first he worked with Omar Torrijos, who had been a great
help to the Sandinistas in 1978–79 but became disillusioned with them
well before he died in mid-1981. After Torrijos' death, Humberto remained the main contact, then with Manuel Antonio Noriega. By and
large, the relationship was superficial since the Sandinistas presumed he
had close ties to the CIA and the Panamanian leader usually did not
respond to FSLN overtures. The most important continuing relationship
was the exchange of intelligence information. The EPS benefited the
most because it got reports on the movement of U.S. military units in the
Canal Zone. The FSLN considered this vital because the Sandinistas
expected any U.S. invasion of Nicaragua would be launched from the
Southern Command headquarters in Panama.

When Humberto realized that Noriega did not want formal ties to the
Sandinistas, he tried to work on the informal side. Noriega responded to
the idea of baseball games between the Panamanian Defense Forces
(PDF) and the EPS, but would not go beyond that except on a couple of
projects, which in fact either didn't get off the ground or were of very
brief duration, as described below and elsewhere in this book. In fact
their contacts came mainly through personal aides—on Noriega's side,
the civilian Didio Souza and PDF Major Pipe Camargo.

In 1986 Humberto sent then Major Ricardo Wheelock to Panama to
meet with Noriega to get his permission to pick up M-79 individual

grenade launchers which the Soviets had not provided though they were needed in the fight against the Contras. The launchers had been secured by General Ochoa through narcotraffic contacts and were available in Panama. Humberto sent $150,000 to Ochoa for the transaction and was prepared to send a Sandinista Air Force plane to Panama immediately to bring the launchers to Nicaragua. But Noriega wouldn't give his authorization and Humberto cursed, "that sonofabitch of a crimeface lets us down when we need him most." At the end of 1986, Noriega invited Humberto to vacation in Panama but Humberto didn't accept; he responded that he had too much work to do but more than anything he didn't trust Noriega, telling Miranda, "That shit just might hand me over to the CIA."

In the middle of 1987, just as Noriega's tie to the United States was being shaken to its roots, the PDF chief agreed to send PDF arms to the FMLN guerrillas in El Salvador through Nicaragua, though details on when this would be done were left open. Roger Miranda left Nicaragua before any action was actually taken. Noriega may have had several motives for this action: (1) cultivating friendships with the region's Marxists so that he would have allies in his burgeoning conflict with the United States; (2) trying to get Washington to cut out its criticism of him by showing the gringos he could cause them a lot of trouble by cozying up to the Sandinistas and the FMLN; and/or (3) gaining the confidence of the FMLN in an effort to turn Panama into a site for peace talks between the guerrillas and the Salvadoran government.

Some overtures—like one to Iraq's Saddam Hussein in the mid-1980s—were turned down, perhaps in this case because Saddam Hussein was then an ally of the United States in the war with Iran.

EPS Military Hospital

During the Somoza period the Military Hospital was the pride of the National Guard; during the Sandinista period the hospital was the pride of the EPS. But throughout the 1980s the excellence of the hospital was more apparent than real. The hospital's director, Dr. Juan Ignacio Gutiérrez, a prestigious Nicaraguan doctor who had taken his medical degree in Mexico and studied as well in the United States, was one of the first to complain about the Cuban doctors and other serious problems at the hospital. The quality of the hospital's doctors, almost all of whom were Cubans or Nicaraguans who had been trained in Bulgaria or Cuba, was uneven and in some respects low. It was assumed that the Cubans sent to Nicaragua were simply incompetent or recent graduates without experience. Gutiérrez himself took care of the members of the National Directorate, none of whom wanted to be treated by a resident Cuban. There were problems even in the heart of the hospital, known as Hall J (Sala J), which was reserved for the use of the most important members of the FSLN, or anyone authorized by one of the nine comandantes, or the principal chiefs of the EPS or the MINT. In the event of a serious emergency, members of the Directorate wanted to be sent abroad. Humberto Ortega instructed Roger Miranda: "If I have an accident and have to receive emergency treatment, under no circumstances take me to the military hospital, but to Mexico or to Cuba."

The reason for their concern was obvious: many who went into the hospital for minor operations died there from medical malpractice. Among the examples: in 1984, Lourdes Bolaños, the sister of a top EPS officer, who died of suffocation due to an error by a Bulgaria-trained doctor; in 1986, an Argentine internationalist who had entered for a minor knee operation died of an overdose of anesthesia; in 1987, a grandson of Col. Santos López—the best known survivor from Sandino's army— who was to be operated on for an ulcer, died after several days from peritonitis. Many deaths were due to infection after an operation, often because operating rooms had window air-conditioners that did not adequately filter the air. Doctors tried to compensate by giving excessive doses of antibiotics. Among those who died as a result of these inadequate conditions was retired EPS lieutenant colonel Ricardo Lugo.

Humberto's Military Shadows

The two EPS officials who were most with Humberto Ortega, had the strongest ongoing influence on him, and the greatest knowledge of his activities, were Major General Joaquín Cuadra Lacayo and Major Roger Miranda Bengoechea.

Humberto Ortega became defense minister shortly after the founding of the FSLN government, but on a daily basis he was more involved with the affairs of the National Directorate than the army. Joaquín Cuadra was vice minister of defense and EPS chief of staff. Although he came from one of Nicaragua's rich families, Cuadra in fact ran and developed the army from the beginning as Humberto's second-in-command. He joined the Sandinistas in the early 1970s, at the age of about twenty, when he was in a Christian movement headed by FSLN collaborator Father Uriel Molina. Prior to July 1979 he was squad leader of the Christmas 1974 attack on the house of Chema Castillo, with its hostage taking and extensive publicity for the Sandinistas. He then became a living legend as an urban warrior in the war against Somoza. Toward the end of the war, he led the insurrection in Managua. Cuadra was very popular with and highly respected by those under his command and he was totally loyal to both the FSLN and the Ortega brothers, as he demonstrated clearly during the FSLN divisions of the mid-1970s. Highly competent, he was nonetheless self-effacing with his subordinates and never spoke for himself, but always on behalf of his chief: he would begin a session of the army chiefs of staff with the words, "as instructed by the Minister of Defense," and he peppered discussions with "as General Ortega says."

Still, Humberto did not trust Cuadra for two reasons. First, like the late Cuban general Ochoa, he lacked a consistent ideological foundation. That is to say, Cuadra was considered a "non-Marxist," though not an "anti-Marxist" like Pastora, and some FSLN hard-liners called him "the EPS's social democrat." Humberto had Cuadra under constant surveillance, having recruited Cuadra's own friends and staff to report on everything he did at home or outside, often in exchange for dollars. What was more, Cuadra had his office next to Miranda, and the latter was in charge of all who had meetings with Ortega. "Look, Miranda," Humberto would say, "if I have learned anything in life it is that confidence is good but control is better. Joaquín is a 'Daddy's boy' who could all too easily sink back to the social status he came from. That worries me." Cuadra's father was Joaquín Cuadra Chamorro, a very wealthy commercial attorney who was converted to Sandinismo and for a while was president of Nicaragua's Central Bank.

But the second and more important reason Humberto didn't trust Cuadra had nothing to do with Marxism, for Humberto himself was ideologically flexible. It was the fact that Cuadra had become a very powerful and popular figure in the EPS, again something of a Nicaraguan Ochoa and, like Castro, who had Ochoa executed on trumped-up charges in mid-1989, Humberto knew that Cuadra was a natural successor to himself. On many occasions, Humberto said to Miranda, "Do you know when Joaquín is going to be chief of the EPS? Never! Never!"

The second major figure aiding Ortega, and the one who spent more time with him than any other EPS officer, was the Nicaraguan coauthor of this book, Roger Miranda. Miranda was born in Granada, and from the beginning generally lived what Humberto called "the life of a hermit." Miranda's grandfather, Bonifacio Miranda, had been brutally killed in 1956 by one group of Somoza's National Guard and Roger Miranda's father, Roberto, gave all of his children a strong anti-Somoza education. In 1969 Miranda joined the FSLN, fired by a loathing of the Somoza dynasty, its allies in Washington, and the increasingly repressive National Guard at home. He was expelled temporarily from the movement in the early 1970s and spent some time in Chile at the end of Salvador Allende's government working with the Castroite Movement of the Revolutionary Left (MIR). After being wounded by the Chilean army, he went to Mexico where he got a degree in economics from the Autonomous University of Puebla. In 1976 he was re-recruited into the FSLN by Tomás Borge with a personal message beginning, "Comrade, the organization has decided to reconsider your case." During Somoza's last year, he was second-in-command of FSLN forces in the key city of Masaya, just south of Managua.

For the first thirty months after the dictator fell, Miranda worked directly with two of the nine comandantes, Humberto Ortega and Carlos Núñez, and with Joaquín Cuadra. For the next six years, from the beginning of 1982 until the end of 1987, he was chief of staff, personal aide to Comandante and Defense Minister Humberto Ortega. In 1985 he was promoted to be a member of the Sandinista Assembly. During those years he participated in all top-level meetings of the EPS, sat in on sessions of the National Directorate that touched on military affairs, and read all minutes of the Directorate meetings. Because of his pivotal position in the ministry, he was often called the Little Minister. Miranda left Nicaragua in October 1987 and publicly criticized the domestic repression and international policies of the FSLN, particularly the Sandinistas' recent agreement with Soviet Union to increase the army to 600,000 by 1995. He now lives in the United States, where he has earned two master's degrees in American universities.

Notes

1. *Programa Histórico del FSLN*, 36–39.
2. See *72-Hour Document*, in Falcoff and Royal, *The Continuing Crisis*, 496, 500.

3. Tunnermann letter to *Washington Post*, 30 March 1985.
4. For details on doctrine and Soviet military aid, see chapters on military doctrine and Soviet Union. Ortega quote from Charles Krause, "Nicaraguans Ask the United States for Military Aid," *Washington Post*, 30 July 1979. For a growth chart of Central American military forces between 1980 and 1985 see *The Challenge to Democracy in Central America* (Washington, DC: U.S. Departments of State and Defense, October 1986), 20; also for comparative figures on Central American militaries, see, International Institute for Strategic Studies, *The Military Balance 1982-83* (London: IISS, 1982), 106; and Stockholm International Peace Research Institute, *World Armaments and Disarmament: SIPRI Yearbook 1986* (Oxford: Oxford University Press, 1986), 528.
5. Ratliff interview with Pastora, 20 March 1992.

PART V
Theory and Practice of War

16

A Military Doctrine to Beat the Gringos

The political views and strategic interests noted above implied a military doctrine that contrasted sharply with that of the Somoza period but that still kept the army the dominating institution in the country as a whole. It was a doctrine built on the expectation of conflict with the United States and the assumption that when the invasion came neither Cuba nor the Soviet Union would send armed forces to help the FSLN stop the Americans. Ironically, the assumptions and actions that followed from this expectation were a major part of broader strategies that in themselves made what would not otherwise have been an inevitable conflict inevitable indeed. It was played out in the heightening of the East-West rivalry in the Americas and by U.S. involvement in the Contra War, with that policy's enormous domestic and international repercussions.

Is Nicaragua Really Europe in the 1940s?

The development of Sandinista military doctrine, and the Sandinista People's Army, fell into two major periods—before and after the U.S. invasion of Grenada, though the post-Grenadian doctrine took almost two years to formulate.[1]

In 1980–81 Humberto Ortega and some other Sandinistas thought the conflict with the Contras would begin with limited frontier encounters with the Honduras-based enemy. This would lead to increasingly bad relations with Honduras and, in time, a conflict between Nicaragua and Honduras, the latter providing the excuse for a U.S. intervention. The most common FSLN slogan into 1982 was "de la frontera no pasaran," meaning that the remains of the National Guard then hiding out in Honduras would never be allowed to cross the border back into Nicaragua.

More formally, prior to the U.S. invasion of Grenada—when the Americans showed they still were prepared to intervene militarily in a Latin American country—Nicaragua's national defense was based on traditional ideas and principles of conventional war as taught in Soviet and Cuban military academies. Soviet ideas had been transplanted mechanically to Cuba and then were passed on to Nicaragua. Thus the needs of the EPS in planning for a confrontation with the United States were governed by plans prepared by the Warsaw Pact for possible conflict in the European theater. With respect to the enemy, the thinking was:

1. The first stage of a U.S. attack on the Sandinistas would be by leftovers from Somoza's National Guard and military units from certain Central American countries allied to Washington, in particular Honduras. The second stage would include units from the U.S. Army.

2. The invasion would come essentially from Honduran territory and from amphibious landing units on the Pacific coast.

3. The main battles would be on the Pacific coast where the political and economic power of the FSLN were concentrated.

On the capacity of the EPS to repel and win in this kind of confrontation, the thinking was:

1. The EPS, in its defensive position on the border and coast, could turn back an American invasion and in a matter of days reestablish the national frontier. If the enemy broke through some defensive positions, the Reserve of the High Command (RAM), with its units of tanks, motorized infantry and artillery, would counterstrike in necessary locations.

2. In order to accomplish this, the EPS was acquiring the armaments needed to repel an invasion. All these arms were in line with the concept of fighting a conventional war against the United States: T-55 tanks; high-powered artillery (122mm, 152mm, and reactive artillery of the type BM-21); a squadron of MiG-21s, etc.

3. The war should be regionalized so as to keep the United States from concentrating all its military power on the EPS. This concept was first elaborated jointly with the Salvadoran FMLN guerrillas in what was known as the Plan Cabuya, named after one of Sandino's generals. The plan foresaw the FMLN joining the EPS on the Honduran coast between El Salvador and Nicaragua, with the participation of small units of the nascent Honduran guerrillas.

4. The EPS was seen as the professional organ charged with repelling the invasion. The EPS consisted of three parts: regular units; the reserves—ci-

vilians who received training twice a month and would form military units when they were needed; and the militias—normally women and older people, whose job in time of war would be to support the EPS but not to engage in combat.

5. Military victory against an invasion was seen following from military blows against the invaders combined with intense international pressure on the United States to pull out.

This doctrine was hammered out in sessions of the National Directorate, with the Ortegas once again arguing heatedly with Borge, the latter insisting that if an invasion occurred, the Sandinistas should retreat into the mountains, a debate that is recalled in the chapter on the Directorate.

In reality, Humberto himself was not convinced by the doctrine he presented to and got adopted by the Directorate, that was the basis for the first Soviet-Nicaraguan military protocol for 1981–85. Though he did not say so publicly, he agreed with Borge that it was madness to meet the gringos in conventional battle, but he thought it was even more foolish to retire to the mountains. In private, Humberto said, "There is something missing here. The Soviets can fight decisive battles against the United States, but are we the same? Can the EPS really militarily defeat the gringos?" Expressions of doubt crossed his face when he heard about using the RAMs "to counterstrike and retake a frontier," or other such triumphalist statements. He repeatedly said to Miranda: "Military plans are nothing more than that, plans, which in the hour of truth are changed to conform to reality." Other military chiefs also had reservations, and would say, only half in jest, "only Mandrake the Magician could stop the gringos."

Meanwhile, all the arms the Sandinistas received during this period conformed to this unrealistic triumphalist strategy to confront a U.S. invasion through conventional warfare. It never occurred to anyone that the EPS might also have to confront a very different kind of enemy—a broadly-based peasant insurgency—because at that time the Contras were considered nothing more than a demolished, discredited band of ex-guardsmen hiding out in Honduras. They harassed the Sandinistas mainly with propaganda; the few who managed to penetrate Nicaraguan territory and survive in the mountains were considered bands of delinquents who were fought by units of the reserves and militias under the command of the recently created irregular forces (LCB) headed by Alvaro Baltodano.

New Thinking after Grenada Invasion

But the conception of national defense strategy changed substantially in the mid-1980s for two reasons: the invasion of Grenada and the successes of the Contras. These two matters led to the assignment of Cuba's most distinguished and experienced military commander, Division General Arnaldo Ochoa, to Nicaragua beginning in mid-1984 as military adviser to the EPS and government.

The National Directorate drew two important lessons from the invasion of Grenada:

1. Before Grenada, talk in the Directorate of an American invasion in the immediate future was more propagandistic than a reflection of real concern. That changed with Grenada, when the FSLN saw that the United States was still willing to invade a Latin American country and that U.S. strategy would be to strike massively in an effort to achieve victory in a matter of days. In these conditions, it would be practically impossible for the Nicaraguans to confront the Americans.

2. Looking at the disintegration of the leadership group in Grenada's New Jewel movement, and the drastic consequences following that fragmentation, Sandinista leaders realized even more clearly than before how serious differences within the Directorate could cause them to fall apart and invite foreign intervention and defeat. Had Fidel himself not said the New Jewel Movement virtually invited the U.S. invasion by its internecine struggles? The Reagan administration might use similar dissension in Nicaragua as a partial pretext for trying to overthrow the Sandinistas. Clearly a return to the kinds of divisions that occurred in the 1970s could bring death to the FSLN and the revolution.

But there was one other factor the National Directorate did not know. Several months before Grenada, Raúl Castro talked with new CPSU general secretary Yuri Andropov in Moscow and was told that the Soviet Union would not provide military support for Cuba in the event of a U.S. invasion. Andropov did pledge to provide whatever military aid the Cubans thought they would need in their effort to deter or repel an invasion. Thus according to Yuri Povlov, a top official in the Soviet Foreign Ministry, even before the U.S. invasion of Grenada Castro knew there was a very big hole in his defensive umbrella. The Sandinistas continued to assume that Cuba's umbrella was in place, however, since the Soviet brigade of several thousand men remained on the island. It was assumed that in the event of a U.S. attack on Cuba, the presence of Soviets there would unavoidably draw Moscow into the conflict.[2]

The experience in Grenada—that is the demonstration that the United States still was prepared under some circumstances to massively invade a small nation—on top of the warning from Andropov, brought a profound rethinking in Cuba that in turn led to important changes in Nicaragua. The new line from Havana seemed to answer, at least in part, Humberto's question: if the arming of the early 1980s would not guarantee the survival of the FSLN, what alternative that the Soviet/Cuban allies would accept might be better? The answer came from Cuba and reflected the lessons Fidel Castro had learned from Andropov and Grenada, though whether it would have actually worked in Cuba or Nicaragua is uncertain. At least it was a vast improvement over the doctrine of the early years.

Cuba suffered a humiliating political and military defeat when it was thrown out of Grenada. With this setback, the Cubans began to doubt whether their military preparations would defend Cuba itself in the event of a U.S. invasion. That is, Castro could for the first time visualize a defeat for Cuba in a conventional war with the United States. When General Ochoa arrived in Nicaragua, he began openly expressing his own doubts about the value of Cuba's defensive strategy and the arming done in Cuba and in Nicaragua during recent years. With his typical frankness, he said to Humberto:

> Look, chief, since Grenada all the defensive strategy implanted in Cuba by the Soviets is being changed. For the first time Fidel has accepted that if a North American invasion comes, they will have the military power to take and control part of the island. What we are trying to do is adjust our plans so that we can make it impossible for them to govern the territory they control and create such active resistance from all the people that they will leave the island. For this reason we have created the territorial militia within the strategic conception of the War of All the People. Imagine what would have happened a couple of years ago if someone had said that if the Americans invaded they might be able to take control of part of the island. He would have been called crazy or a counterrevolutionary.[3]

Such confidences from Ochoa swelled Humberto's pride and in the most intimate circles he said, "I never was convinced by that military strategy of the Soviets. It was pure shit."

But the crisis that hit the Sandinistas in the second part of 1983 wasn't just that they discovered their national defense strategy wouldn't work. The Contras had spread their war to broad sectors in the northern part of

Nicaragua, and what was worse, the training and arming of the EPS left the army quite unprepared to confront the irregular warfare of the insurrection. Thus, beginning in 1984 the EPS tried to adjust its structures and resources to the new situation. Humberto spent many hours talking to Ochoa, with whom he cultivated a very profound personal friendship. More to the point, he gained immense military understanding and experience from Ochoa. Humberto became particularly concerned with the following aspects of national defense:

1. In confronting the United States, the EPS would be up against an enemy that had absolute air superiority, which meant that the chances for the EPS to operate with large units was seriously reduced or nonexistent. The role of RAMs in a future war had to be revised because if original plans were followed, the RAMs would be destroyed either in their bases or while being deployed to the war zone. Humberto's concern was reinforced by the fact that the Soviet MiGs, promised years ago, had not arrived.

2. To carry out a conventional war against U.S. troops would be suicide. The technical and military power of the Americans meant they could quickly penetrate and occupy important parts of the national territory and occupy the country. Looking coldly at these realities, the offensive power of the U.S. Army was so deadly that large quantities of men and arms would be lost trying to avoid the inevitable or trying to evict the gringos from the fatherland. As Humberto put it, "it is not simply a matter of sacrificing, but of sacrificing and winning."

3. Modern technology would enable the gringos to deliver a devastating blow and to do so in a short campaign with few casualties. With the surprise factor, during the first hours of the invasion the main battle units of the EPS could be annihilated and the principal commands of the EPS captured or killed, leaving an EPS seriously mutilated and confused.

In 1984, even prior to the completion of the 1985 plan, the National Directorate had set up the Supreme Council for the Defense of the Fatherland (CSDP) both to assure that the human and material resources were available to consolidate defense against a U.S. military invasion and to direct the war against the Contras. The new council was made up of the two Ortegas, Borge, Wheelock, and Arce. The existence of the CSDP was never announced publicly because to have done so might have given the impression it had been formed exclusively to fight the Contras and that the insurgents had in themselves become a threat to the revolution. Indeed, they *had* become a threat in themselves and the Directorate concluded that the CSDP would serve two tangible functions in the Contra War: it would centralize actions against the Contras and it would resolve the dispute on directing the war that had arisen between Humberto and Borge.

During 1981–82, Borge's Ministry of the Interior had been the primary state body involved in responding to the then still dispersed and weak insurgency. But from the beginning of 1983, when the Contras began to emerge as a considerable military force with a broad base of social support in the countryside, the forces of the MINT were passed over and the EPS took the leading role. Through 1983 Humberto and Borge argued continuously over who was responsible for the war until the Directorate decided to create the CSDP and give the supreme power to the EPS. The MINT role was reduced to responding to whatever urban military force might appear. Humberto said,

> I am charged with the Contras in the mountains, but Tomás must guarantee that no internal military force is formed, because if this happens we are lost. Remember that we have taught our officials to respect and love the people. If focos of armed resistance appear in the cities we are going to have to send our tanks into the streets. The Segovian [José del Carmen Aráuz, chief of the tank brigade in Managua] can go into the streets once or twice, but what is going to happen if he has to go out repeatedly? What explanation are we going to give for why we are repressing our own people?

Ochoa and the Patriotic People's National War

The dilemmas of national defense vis-a-vis both the threats of foreign invasion and domestic insurrection led to a major revision of the concept of military doctrine and all that follows from that concept. This new analysis was detailed in a top-secret document completed by the Ministry of Defense in June 1985: *Principal Plan of the EPS Regarding Doctrine, Strategy, Structure and Equipment for Strengthening, Consolidating and Developing the National Defense for the 1986–90 Period.* In reality, this is the first statement of what can legitimately be called the military doctrine of the Sandinista revolution, though in its basic outlook it reflected much of the Cuban experience as conveyed by Ochoa. It tried to answer the questions of how to respond to a military invasion without falling into the unrealistic alternatives that had previously been propounded by both Humberto and Borge, and for the first time tried to deal realistically with the rapidly expanding Contra War. This plan was more discussed and studied than any analysis produced since the *72-Hour Document.*

The fundamental ideas and strategic concepts of the document that were discussed and approved in mid-1985 were:

1. The EPS had to plan how to defeat a U.S. invasion while also focusing more effectively on militarily defeating the Contras.

2. The defensive strategy fell into two phases: the regular and then the guerrilla strategic defense operations. The first phase referred to the regular units of the EPS—the tanks, artillery, and motorized infantry—that would be the first to confront the U.S. units with the intention of occupying the gringos while the full EPS, reserves, and militias were deployed around the country. This was intended to compensate for the element of surprise and to keep the EPS from being beheaded in the first hours of the invasion. The document said the EPS "must prepare permanent and small units to react quickly to impede the enemy's attaining his initial objectives, while at the same time assuring a vital step in mobilizing the rest of the EPS and country."[4]

The second phase referred to the variety of irregular activities intended to make it impossible for the Americans to govern the territories they occupied. This would be done along with international diplomatic pressure to get the gringos to withdraw. The idea of active resistance was found throughout the document and seen as a key element in defeating the invasion. As Humberto said,

> If the gringos catch us by surprise and decapitate the EPS the international prestige of the revolution won't be worth a thing since by the time our friends begin to move in the international forums, demanding the withdrawal of U.S. troops, it will already be too late. We must resist as long as possible knowing how to attack, but also how to conserve our forces.

The Defense Ministry document continued: "Our tenacious active resistance will obstruct the enemy, extend the crisis into the region and, taken with the international pressures supporting the Sandinista resistance, the interventionist step will be defeated."[5]

3. Managua is defined as the symbol of defense of the country. Earlier plans had not given such importance to taking Managua but now it was believed the Americans would concentrate their forces on capturing the capital to give the impression that they controlled the country and had won the war. In public, Humberto said "we are going to make Managua the Stalingrad of Nicaragua." But in private he said there was no way the

EPS could prevent the Americans from taking Managua and that according to the new strategy, the military chief of the capital, Col. Julio Ramos, had instructions not to die fighting trying to keep the capital out of the hands of the gringos. Rather, Ramos was to retreat to the mountains in the south and from there launch a guerrilla war against the invaders. All the militias and reservists knew, however, was that they were to fight to the death defending Managua in line with Humberto's Stalingrad statements and what they incorrectly believed to be Ramos' instructions.[6]

4. Regionalization of the conflict, though not a new idea, was much more important in the new doctrine. As soon as an invasion was underway, EPS troops with guerrilla forces from neighboring countries would attack targets in their countries to prevent the gringos from concentrating just on Nicaragua. The most important ally here was the FMLN, which had promised to increase its actions at the time of an invasion along with the troops of the EPS and Honduran guerrilla units, the latter with sabotage and irregular attacks on the Honduran army.

But regionalization meant a lot more than drawing in several Central American guerrilla groups. Within this concept, the Sandinista Air Force was prepared to attack specific targets in Costa Rica, such as electric energy centers, bridges and the American embassy in San José. The thinking behind this was to make effective use of Soviet helicopters, which should not be used against the U.S. and Honduran air forces but that could be a destructive force in Costa Rica, which has no anti-air defenses. Also, the Sandinistas could count on the support of armed units in Costa Rica, which had been receiving weapons and training since the late-1970s, particularly militants of the People's Vanguard party. And beyond Central America, some South American guerrillas had pledged to carry out military actions in their countries in the event of a U.S. invasion.

5. There were two high priorities involving American troops: to kill as many as possible in urban combat and to capture many who could then be used in negotiating better conditions for the departure of the rest. As Humberto said, "make each city the gringos capture a Pyrrhic victory for them, both from the political as well as the military points of view."

6. The concept of the Patriotic People's National War reflected in its very name that warfare is more than a military operation, but something that affected society as a whole. The entire population was to play a role in varied ways, from fighting through propaganda and economic reform

to the National Committee for the Support of Combatants (CNAC), which became something of a government ministry to meet the basic needs of families of those fallen in battle. These and other society- wide activities were intended in particular to reduce peasant support for the Contras and to motivate young people in the cities of the Pacific coast to fulfill their compulsory military service, particularly in the new irregular combat units. The military service, which was authorized by the National Directorate in late 1983 was in effect an open admission that not enough Nicaraguans were sufficiently dedicated to the revolution to join the military on their own to defend it.

Notes

1. Published descriptions of Sandinista military doctrine in the two periods, which don't tell the whole story, are *El E.P.S. y la participación de las masas en la defensa de la soberanía* (Managua: Sección de Educación Política, Departamento de Propaganda y Educación Política del FSLN, 1983); and Joaquín Cuadra L., "Doctrina Militar de la Revolución," *Revista Segovia*, no. 40 (September-October 1989): 14–19.
2. Ratliff interview with Yuri Povlov, 17 October 1991.
3. Miranda encountered this interpretation of the Grenada affair in talking with Ochoa and other Cuban military officials in Nicaragua; Ratliff found it hinted or stated in conversations with Fidel Castro and other Cuban officials during a visit to Cuba in December 1983–January 1984, shortly after the invasion of Grenada.
4. Ministerio de Defensa, *Principales Planteamientos del E.P.S., Sobre la Doctrina Estrategia, Estructura y Equipamiento Para el Fortalecimiento, Consolidación y Desarrollo de la Defensa Nacional en el Quinquenio 86–90*, June 1985, marked "muy secreto," 14; in Roger Miranda collection at Hoover Institution.
5. Ibid., 13.
6. For a Sandinista description of how they expected the U.S. invasion, focusing on Managua, to occur, see "Idea Probable de las Acciones del Enemigo en Operación Estrategia de Invasión Contra Nicaragua," in Miranda collection, Hoover Institution.

17

The War That Needn't Have Been

The Sandinista government always claimed that the Contra War was a U.S. terrorist mercenary operation seeking to restore the Somoza dictatorship—with or without Somoza himself—and U.S. domination of Nicaragua. In Bayardo Arce's colorful terms, the Contras were merely the "clowns" in an American circus. The FSLN said the Contras were simply "counterrevolutionaries" who were dominated by former national guardsmen led by Enrique Bermúdez, who had later been joined by a few "traitors" like Edén Pastora, assorted "reactionaries" like Alfonso Robelo and Arturo Cruz, and poor peasant youths kidnapped and forced or deluded into fighting as U.S. mercenaries. For many years most of the top Sandinistas were so convinced of their own mission and propaganda that they actually believed this to be true, as is reflected in the EPS's top secret *Outline History of the Growth of the Counterrevolutionary Organization FDN.* Many foreigners did as well. Incredibly, some still do.[1]

But this Sandinista picture is a jumble of truths, half-truths and lies and in the end presents a basically distorted picture of the civil war and of the opposition that took up arms against the Sandinista government. As explained below, the first significant "Contra" military attacks were carried out by frustrated Sandinistas under the leadership of Pedro Joaquín González, not by or under former guardsmen. And while it is true that former national guardsmen played a major role in founding and leading the Honduras-based FDN, the maximum number of guardsmen in the Contras was only about four hundred, a figure now cited even by long-time Sandinista spokesman Alejandro Bendaña, and this four hundred included far more soldiers than officers. What is more, peasants, who soon were the overwhelming majority of the Contras, began joining very early, particularly under the influence of former Sandinista peasant Encarnación Baldivia (Tigrillo). On the more negative side, some of the early Contra fighters were criminals before and after they joined the guerrillas, and some Contra leaders were guilty of gross human rights abuses against civilians and even their own forces, among the most notorious being Chino Lau, Renato, Suicida, and Krill.[2] Finally, the United States provided aid, in a variety of ways at different times, to the Contra movement, but only a small fraction of the amount of aid the Soviet bloc sent to the Sandinistas.

What so many top Sandinistas, their domestic followers and their foreign admirers could so seldom see or admit during the 1980s was that the Sandinistas' own policies were what sparked the Contra uprising and gave the struggle its surging vitality, particularly among Nicaragua's peasants. By 1983 the Contra War had become a far-ranging peasant insurrection, in scope second only in Latin Americana history to the Mexican revolution at the beginning of the century. The enemy was a Sandinista movement that had not just failed to live up to unrealistic expectations of peasants and others, but was actively carrying out policies an increasing majority of Nicaraguans felt were repressive and contrary to their beliefs and interests. In his *Comandos*, Sam Dillon focused on one Contra leader, Luis Fley (Jhonson) and correctly generalized from there: "He wasn't a thug or a thief; he was neither a mercenary nor a murderer. Like the vast majority of the rural men who'd joined the contras, he was fighting for a simple vision of good government."[3]

How to Provoke a Peasant Insurrection

Underlying the conflict was the Sandinistas' failure to do what the majority of Nicaraguans wanted, or what neighboring countries, who had their own interests to watch out for, had been led to expect. That is, the Sandinistas reneged on their promises of political pluralism, a truly mixed economy, and international nonalignment, and pursued contradictory political and economic routes, with predictable results: an increasing majority of Nicaraguans rejected the FSLN's legitimacy and conflict emerged both within Nicaraguan society and between Nicaragua, its neighbors, and the United States.

Of course throughout the 1980s the Sandinistas and their supporters at home and abroad steadfastly maintained that they *had* lived up to their promises, or if they had fallen short it was because of the opposition of domestic and foreign reactionaries. They argued they had established a democracy without precedent, an economy that took the best of various options, and an international alignment that for the first time freed the country of U.S. domination.

But viewed objectively, the Sandinistas' political positions and policies from July 1979 on were not what most Nicaraguans (or foreigners) wanted and made a new civil war with foreign involvement indeed unavoidable. Following the Sandinistas' original decisions were such corollaries as the development of the largest and most sophisticated army in the history of Central America, which drained the national treasury, and support for guerrillas in El Salvador and other countries, which promoted the decline of neighboring economies and guaranteed international tensions and involvement, not least because hundreds of thousands of Nicaraguans became refugees, especially in Costa Rica.

The expanding FSLN domination of the power structure—including the news media, where nonviolent discussion of alternatives could have been carried out—meant there were only increasingly ineffective vehicles for expressing popular discontent within the system. The most decisive option, many calculated, appeared to be armed conflict, as had so often been the case for Nicaraguans in the past.

Although there had been some rural support for the Sandinistas during their fight to overthrow Somoza, the dictator had been defeated mainly by urban workers and most of the middle and upper classes who had little sense of, or indeed true interest in, what the peasants thought and wanted. Somoza had kept the rural population poor mainly by denying them access to vast land holdings, but he allowed a largely free agricultural market economy in the countryside, which at least permitted subsistence living. The Contra War was fueled by peasant disaffection with the Sandinista government's step backward toward collectivization. The Sandinista leadership, influenced by the Cuban experience, didn't understand that what the peasants wanted was a piece of land and the resources to cultivate it. They did not want cooperatives, production units in which peasant families worked together and shared the produce of the land. The collectivization and other programs assured the alienation of the peasants, declining production, and in an agricultural country, a failed economy. These programs and the brutalities that often accompanied them drove many peasants to join the Contra armies.

Over the years, the Contra War remained a predominantly rural uprising, although by 1987 Contra forces operated with considerable impunity in well over half the country. To a considerable extent the fact that the war remained in the countryside made it easier for the Sandinistas to deny even to themselves the basis of the problem and the seriousness of the situation.

After the overwhelming rejection of the Sandinistas in the 1990 election, many members of the FSLN tried to figure out what had happened and some even concluded that the Sandinistas themselves had been at least partly responsible for starting the stampede of peasants into the Contra army. One longtime spokesman for the FSLN, Alejandro Bendaña, wrote in 1991 that "the contra army grew beyond the North Americans' own expectations, not because of sophisticated recruitment campaigns in the countryside, but at first mainly from the impact on the peasant landholder of the policies, limitations and errors of Sandinismo." And again, "It was Sandinismo [that] fertilized the ground for the integration of thousands of peasants into the counterrevolutionary army."[4]

The Contras

Between 1980 and 1982 opposition to the Sandinistas emerged in a variety of forms. An early but isolated military incident that pointed clearly to the future was the uprising against collectivization launched on the first anniversary of the revolution in July 1980 in the town of Quilalí near the Honduran border. The leader was Pedro Joaquín González, known as "Dimas," one of the few Sandinista military leaders who had been a small farmer. Dimas and his forces called themselves MILPAS, originally the Anti-Somoza Popular Militias—which became the Anti-Sandinista Popular Militias—though the term also pointed to their peasant origin since *milpa* is Spanish for cornfield. They recognized very early the direction of the FSLN's agrarian policy, and the repression being used to accomplish it, and turned against the new government. His uprising signaled the spark of social unrest among peasants that in time flared up out of control in the countryside. Dimas did not immediately set off uprisings or rebellions on behalf of the peasants by other Sandinistas, but he pointed a finger at the comandantes and warned them of what was in store. After taking Quilalí, Dimas retreated to the El Chipote area, where revolutionary idol Sandino had gone a half century before. But like coffee grower Jorge Salazar, Dimas was soon betrayed by a man he thought was a friend and killed.[5] Both the Dimas and Salazar incidents were used by the Sandinistas to justify attacks on and repression of Alfonso Robelo's MDN and others. The names of Dimas and Salazar soon were given to "regional commands" of the Contra forces.

At the end of 1981 most of the limited armed opposition, which became the Nicaraguan Democratic Force (FDN), consisted of former members of Somoza's guard. During 1982 and 1983 things changed completely. Besides the rapidly growing Honduras-based peasant FDN, two other groups emerged: the Democratic Revolutionary Alliance (ARDE) in the south, headed by Edén Pastora, and the still smaller MISURA alliance of dissident indigenous peoples of the Atlantic coast.

The Nicaraguan Democratic Force

The FDN was concentrated in the mountainous regions of the north. During 1983–84 it became a peasant army and the war it waged was a virtual peasant insurrection. Although it is difficult to estimate the size of a guerrilla force, the FSLN estimated the maximum strength of the FDN at about twelve thousand fighters, several dozen times larger than the FSLN only six months before it took power and more than twice as large as the Sandinistas on the day Somoza fell, if FSLN forces are taken to mean militants and hangers-on. But the FSLN's estimate was low, for according to a United Nations report on the disarming process in 1990, some 21,863 Contras were disarmed.[6]

In 1984, the FDN was reorganized from a task force structure, with 120 men divided up into small units, to one employing fourteen regional commanders. Whereas previously there had been tactical unity only for operations, now there was a greater level of cohesiveness. At the end of 1985, three of the regional commanders were former guardsmen, six were ex-Sandinistas, and five were men with no previous military experience. The top man was still former national guard officer Enrique Bermúdez, with some two hundred other former guardsmen as well. Until 1985, when Ochoa's reforms began to take tangible effect, the Contras had the strategic and tactical initiative: they generally decided when, where, and how to fight. While they retained the tactical initiative in 1985, they lost the strategic, and from that time on their long-term military prospects declined despite the significant resurgence in 1987.

The EPS always considered the FDN by far the best trained and most dangerous of the armed opposition. By 1984 the group was made up of battle-hardened and skillful fighters. Their operational capacity continued to grow: they obtained good information on the movements of EPS troops, in part from U.S. intelligence, and they had an impressive capacity to operate in large groups and then suddenly break into small units and disappear. Although they lacked motor transport, their units were quite mobile and often attacked the EPS without warning. Their ambushes were better organized and executed than any carried out by the Sandinistas in the war against Somoza.

The FDN guerrillas could pull this off for two reasons: (1) they knew the mountains they were fighting in since they had been raised in them, while most of the EPS troops, particularly in the early years, were from the Pacific coast; and (2) contrary to the assertions of Sandinista propaganda, they had a very broad base of popular support in the local population, which made possible both the easy flow of information on EPS movements and the quick replacement of resources when they suffered heavy losses.

ARDE and MISURA

The second faction of the armed opposition was ARDE which, unlike the FDN, did not include former Guardsmen. Rather it was founded, originally led and to a certain extent manned by former non-communist Sandinistas. ARDE was founded in Costa Rica in 1982 by Alfonso Robelo, Brooklyn Rivera and Edén Pastora, the latter the foremost hero of the anti-Somoza revolution. From the beginning its motto was "Without Totalitarianism or a Return to the Somocista Past."[7] ARDE's scope of operations was in the southern part of the country across the border from Costa Rica. ARDE, like the FDN, enjoyed a large degree of peasant support, for the same reasons, and soon scared the Sandinistas into implementing agrarian policies that were more attractive to peasants, in particular into turning away from the strong move toward collectivization.

The defection to the armed opposition of the popular Comandante Cero was a serious blow to the Sandinistas. ARDE was not vulnerable to charges that it merely wanted to return the country to Somoza, though that didn't keep the Sandinistas and some of their foreign supporters from trying to peddle this line. ARDE's prominent leaders had been Sandinistas, had served in the FSLN government, or at least had supported the overthrow of Somoza. Despite its greater political credibility, however, ARDE suffered from problems of objectives, and internal divisions, as well as Pastora's unwillingness to accept the dictates of the U.S. government. Pastora's defection from Nicaragua would have been a great deal more harmful to the Sandinistas if in his own dramatic way he had immediately articulated his deep concerns about the FSLN's political orientation, which he was one of the first to recognize. Instead he waited for almost a year, spending much of the time under house arrest in Cuba, in what he describes as an effort to persuade the nine comandantes to change their ways. Pastora alienated Washington by his flamboyant independence and his refusal to join forces with the Honduras-based FDN because of its origins in the Somoza's National Guard. Even when the FDN forces became overwhelmingly peasant, he believed the National Guard leaders converted them into "neo-guardias." Seen from the other side, many in the FDN, and in the U.S. government, were suspicious of ARDE's leaders because of their former ties to the FSLN, unimpressed by Pastora's military activities, some even believing that Pastora still had formal or informal ties to the Sandinistas.[8]

The bottom line was a lack of agreed upon objectives and coordination among the anti-Sandinista armed forces and this both weakened morale and military operations. Cohesion and discipline problems within ARDE came to a head in 1984 when Alfonso Robelo broke away. One faction of ARDE remained with Pastora while the other joined forces with the FDN. In 1986 Pastora himself, utterly frustrated with problems of leadership and support—especially the U.S. blockade of all supplies of whatever origin—retired to his life as a fisherman in Costa Rica.

Finally, the third military force was made up of the indigenous peoples of eastern Nicaragua who rose up against Sandinista suppression of their traditional life. The FSLN was determined to consolidate its control on the east coast for several reasons: (1) national defense, for it bordered on Honduras on the North, the Caribbean on the east, where the United States maintained a naval presence; and had the ports of El Bluff and Puerto Cabezas, which were the shortest sea routes to Cuba and the Soviet bloc countries; (2) economic development, because it had abundant natural resources and the aforementioned ports; and (3) ideological unity, the determination to integrate all areas of the country into a single

Sandinista unit. Serious clashes with the government began in 1981; war exploded later that year and in early 1982 after the Sandinistas burned 65 Miskito Indian villages on the Coco River. Conflict persisted throughout the decade though "peace" negotiations began in 1984, as discussed below. There were some excellent individual fighters here, but these forces too were uneven and beset by internal divisions and differing objectives which diminished their impact.[9]

The FSLN Responds

By the beginning of 1983 the Contra conflict had extended from the north into six of the country's sixteen provinces and raised questions Sandinista leaders still did not honestly ask or answer: was the FSLN really facing simple aggression by Somocista bands based in Honduras, which could be handled by existing military doctrine, supplies, and training? Or did the conflict represent rapidly expanding national opposition to the government and its policies, which in itself raised two questions? Did the FSLN program actually have the support of the Nicaraguan people, and were the people prepared to defend the Sandinista program militarily against a higher level of domestic armed opposition than they had thought would emerge? Or was the FSLN prepared to reform itself so as to respond to the interests of a broader cross section of the people?

At the beginning of the war, fighting incursions from Honduras had been the responsibility of the Frontier Guard Troops, who lacked anything like the training they needed for the job. The FSLN also mobilized equally unprepared militia and reserve troops, mainly from the Pacific coast area, to send to the combat zones. But what they had thought would be a military pushover became a swirling nightmare. The militia and reserve units had no links to the local peasantry, social support from the mountain people, or familiarity with the terrain. What is more, their political motivation was anti-Guard and they were not prepared for anti-Sandinista peasant rebels. Thus, despite their commitment, the militia and reserve units failed to overpower the rebels, and were easily ambushed; casualties mounted. Morale began to fail both as a result of the high death tolls and the negative economic impact on families whose members had been mobilized. Also, "criminals were among those who mobilized themselves," Comandante Luis Carrión told Roy Gutman:

"These people would many times [cut off] the hands of the peasants, treat them badly."[10]

By late 1983 Sandinista schizophrenia was almost complete. On the one hand, FSLN leaders still could not grasp the extent of peasant support for the war, thus Bayardo Arce's disparaging remark, "If negotiations are ever to bring an end to conflict, the FSLN will negotiate only with the owners of the circus, not the clowns." The Sandinistas still could not see that this was becoming the most far-reaching insurrection in Nicaraguan history. Entire villages of peasants had taken up arms and freely supported the war against the Sandinistas in the provinces of Nueva Segovia, Madriz, Matagalpa, and Jinotega in the north, on the Atlantic coast, and in Zelaya Sur and the province of Rio San Juan. With rebels so freely roaming the mountainous areas of the country, the FSLN could no longer fight as if the war were nothing more than irksome border incursions. Militia and reserve units clearly suffered from inappropriate and inadequate weapons and training, and they could not come close to containing, much less eliminating, the enemy.

Both the growing war and the heavy Sandinista losses forced the FSLN in late 1983 to issue the decree mandating compulsory military service. In many areas and groups, including the Church, the decree provoked strong negative reactions and police and state security officials had to be sent out to deal with the protests. While the EPS's numbers were expanded by turning from volunteer to compulsory service, numbers increasingly took precedence over commitment to the Sandinista cause. And despite claims that no one would be exempt, some leaders of the FSLN could and did ensure that their offspring were posted away from all the fighting.

Roger Miranda accompanied Humberto Ortega on a trip to Havana at the end of June 1983, the latter asking the Castros to send a brigade of 3,000 Cubans trained in irregular combat to Nicaragua until the EPS could deploy its new battalions. Ortega even promised to send some of the region's lumber, which Cuba desperately needed. The Cuban leaders refused, however, pointing out that they were very heavily committed in Africa. But the Castros also were concerned that the presence of Cuban combat forces in Nicaragua might give the United States an excuse to invade the country, almost as if Castro had foreseen the events of Grenada several months later. Fidel did agree to increase the number of instructors, however, sending personnel experienced in irregular combat. And most important of all, he agreed to station Gen. Arnaldo Ochoa in Nicaragua for several years as head of the Cuban military mission.

The Tide Turns

Several things happened in 1984, just as the Contras were becoming a serious challenge to the Sandinistas, to turn the tide of the war toward the other direction: the mistakes and waffling of U.S. policy; the Sandinista reforms, which finally put a counterinsurgency program in order; and the Contras' failure to take advantage of their 1984 strategic opening.

With respect to U.S. Contra policy, in January and February 1984 the CIA mined Nicaraguan harbors while the Contras themselves watched impotently from the sidelines. Glenn Garvin has correctly called this "one of the most catastrophic covert actions in the history of U.S. intelligence."[11] The mining was seized upon by opponents of Contra aid in the U.S. Congress and used to kill legal military aid at a critical juncture. In April 1984 the U.S. Congress adopted a nonbinding resolution prohibiting the U.S. government from mining Nicaraguan ports and in May of that same year, the U.S. Congress voted down the $21 million in aid requested for the Contras by the Reagan administration. At the same time, the mining was skillfully manipulated by the Sandinistas, who took the incident to the World Court. In a fit of legalistic foolishness, the Reagan administration refused to argue the case, demonstrating yet again its failure to understand the political nature of the war and respond creatively to unfolding events. Consequently, the Americans took a political plastering with their mouths self-righteously closed and, in time, a legal scolding as well.

In Nicaragua, the 1984 mining of the harbors brought problems between the FSLN and the Church to a head. In a pastoral letter, the Church refused to join in the government's condemnations of the United States but sought instead to remain neutral in what it openly recognized as a civil war between two large groups of Nicaraguans. The Church called for dialogue between the two sides and for a general amnesty as a step toward national reconciliation. Daniel Ortega reacted violently, saying the letter supported the U.S. government and indeed had been written with the direct cooperation of the U.S. embassy in Managua. The FSLN paper *Barricada* then expanded its defamation campaign against the Church and individual leaders, particularly Obando, who was now depicted as a loyal friend of the Somoza regime and the National Guard. A less publicized CIA ordered operation at about the same time brought another serious setback for the Contras. In late 1983 and early 1984 the Agency required the Contras to attack Sandinista bases on the Cosigüina Peninsula in northwest Nicaragua. The peninsula jutted into the Gulf of Fonseca and was an important supply route for Sandinista arms shipments to the FMLN guerrillas in El Salvador, thus the attacks were in line with the then-stated U.S. objective of supporting the Contras in order to interdict arms supplies to El Salvador. But while the attacks did not stop the shipping of arms to the FMLN, they caused such tensions that the Honduran government closed down Contra camps in Choluteca and elsewhere on that side of the country. This in turn made it almost unnecessary for the Sandinistas to station troops in that region and, in the words of Glenn Garvin, "cost Bermúdez half his theater of operations." Thereafter, the Sandinistas could afford to concentrate more troops in a smaller area and make Contra infiltration into Nicaragua and supplying other troops all the more difficult and costly.[12]

Perhaps most important of all, the 1984 setbacks in U.S. policy sparked the search for outside funds that resulted in the Iran-Contra affair.

The Sandinistas were catching on that the Contras were a serious threat; in the words of the ancient Chinese strategist Sun Tzu, they were operating like fish in water. Thus the EPS looked for a way to "drain the water from the fish," as Humberto Ortega put it. This was attempted in a variety of ways, including the forced resettlement of nearly two hundred thousand people into at least 145 settlements around the country, paralleling the resettlements at that time of the indigenous peoples on the Atlantic coast. While the government claimed it was moving the peasants to protect them from being raped and kidnapped by the Contras, in fact the program was intended to get the peasants where they could be controlled more easily and turn much of the border region of Nueva Segovia and Jinotega, and the northeastern corner, into free-fire zones.[13]

With its 1984–85 reforms, the National Directorate acknowledged that the war could not be treated simply as a minor incursion or a strictly military problem. This led to a plan to integrate the military efforts of the EPS and MINT, civic action programs of the government, and FSLN policies into a single, national strategy, as noted above. Sandinista fortunes also turned for the moment in 1985 when the Sandinistas first

242					The Civil War in Nicaragua

introduced the Soviet MI-24 "flying tank" helicopters against the Contras in the latter's July-August "La Trinidad" operation, its most ambitious offensive in several years.

Important developments during 1985 once again demonstrated the shallow and often ineffective nature of U.S. policy toward the Contras and the Sandinistas. On 24 April, Congress rejected the administration's Contra aid bill. In less than a week Nicaraguan president Ortega made a trip to the Soviet bloc and Congress reversed itself, voting $27 million in humanitarian aid on 12 June, an action examined in an earlier chapter. On 1 May the Reagan administration imposed an embargo on U.S. trade with Nicaragua, an action of moderate economic impact—except on Nicaragua's private sector—but of immense propaganda value for the FSLN.

The Contras's Final Offensive

The Contras had another—their final—spurt of activity after the U.S. Congress voted in June 1986 to provide $100 million in aid, including the first $70 million intended just for arms. By mid-1987 at least ten thousand newly trained and equipped troops were fighting in Nicaragua, moving quite freely around much of the country and utilizing U.S. intelligence information and technology. Their most important new weapon was the Redeye antiaircraft missile, which during the year brought down more than twenty Sandinista helicopters and suddenly took away the enormous tactical/psychological advantage those aircraft had given the FSLN over the previous two years. Air supply lines were operating much more efficiently than ever before, enabling the Contras in Nicaragua to operate more freely in much of the hinterland and keeping them in touch with outside sources of supplies. Hundreds of minor attacks on military convoys, electrical towers, and other facilities, mostly planned by individual Contra leaders, and a few major operations, stretched the Sandinista capacity to respond and had serious military, economic, and psychological repercussions. Several major attacks on power stations were launched with the destruction of the La Trinidad station in February and the Rama road was finally closed in October. In December the Contras launched Operation Olivero, their most complex offensive ever against a variety of economic and military targets, including a Soviet radar station, in north-central Zelaya department.[14]

Roger Miranda got a very clear impression of peasant dissatisfaction with the government in 1987 when he conducted an official inspection tour of the war areas for Defense Minister Ortega. Visiting remote villages, he found he was looked on with mixed suspicion, fear, and hatred. Even in the inland province of Boaco, he and Brigade Chief Major Patricio Lorente felt such hostility they hardly dared stop to eat lunch. The possibility of being ambushed was very real and Miranda left the region with the terrible feeling that he was regarded as the chief of an occupying military force in his own country. When Miranda remarked on this hostility, Lorente responded, "Look, chief, all these peasants you have seen, all these little villages we have passed through, all these sons of bitches are Contras. All of them." Brigade chiefs in other areas said much the same thing. These EPS officials advanced the standard FSLN explanation of this situation to Miranda, that the peasants were politically backward and manipulated by the reactionaries and imperialists, though the officers may just have hidden their true thoughts for fear their names and views would be passed on to Humberto Ortega.

But increased operations within Nicaragua posed their own problems for the Contras and the Americans, among them getting supplies to the guerrillas, for deliveries by air—the preferred method for many kinds of supplies—required a high degree of organization and precision. Contra leaders claimed that nearly five hundred airdrops of supplies reached them during 1986. Oliver North, who oversaw the Contra War at that time for the United States from his position in the National Security Council, has commented that

> the hardest part of supplying the contras wasn't buying the weapons, but delivering them to the resistance forces inside Nicaragua. After the CIA pulled out [in 1984, until 1986], the entire contra 'air force' consisted of half a dozen aging, rundown transport plans flown by former National Guard pilots. They had neither the training nor the equipment to make nighttime drops, which are absolutely essential in this kind of war.[15]

The inadequate air supply operation ran into a major problem in October 1986 when a plane flying out of El Salvador's Ilopango Air Base was shot down with a SAM-7 ground-to-air missile just north of the Costa Rican border. One of the four crew members, an American named Eugene Hasenfus, parachuted to the ground and turned himself in to the Sandinistas. This event was important because Hasenfus was the first American captured on Nicaraguan territory helping the Contras and because the plane, and more importantly the program it was a part of, offered dramatic proof that the U.S. had been supplying arms to the Contras at a time when such aid had been prohibited by Congress. For Sandinista supporters, one widely circulated photograph seemed to tell the whole story of the war: a scruffy Hasenfus, with has hands bound, being led through the countryside at the end of a short rope by an EPS soldier, just as triumphantly as Peter led the wolf to the zoo in the Prokofiev story.[16] The bedraggled captive was paraded through the streets of Managua and across the media of the world, resulting in much mud on the faces of the Contras and the Americans. At the end of the year, Hasenfus was tried, convicted, and given a thirty-year sentence. But just before Christmas, in an act of "charity and good-will," Daniel Ortega released him to visiting Senator Christopher Dodd, a strong congressional critic of Contra aid. Humberto summed up the National Directorate's position when he said privately, "We get a lot more good out of this war criminal by turning him over to Dodd than we would have by letting him rot for years in jail."

But even as the Contra guerrillas operated more effectively during much of 1987, a combination of factors was about to leave them dead in the water. These were the Iran/Contra scandal, which like the mining of the harbors was far more deadly to the Contras than any military actions by the EPS, and the emerging Arias peace plan. In late 1987 the Sandinistas estimated, very accurately, that by 1990 the Contras would be history.

Ploys to Defeat the Contras

The Sandinistas conducted a variety of military and political actions in their efforts to destroy or discredit the Contras. Among the actions were military incursions into Honduran territory. During the mid-1980s, the Sandinistas sometimes stationed up to tens of thousands of troops along the border to block Contra infiltration into Nicaragua from base camps in Honduras. Periodically the Sandinistas attacked Contra camps without much international fuss, both sides maintaining the fiction that nothing happened: the Sandinistas not wanting to admit they had violated the Honduran border and the Nicaraguan resistance not wishing to officially admit its presence in the neighboring country. By early 1985 the Sandinistas were moving their BM-21 rocket launchers up near the frontier and shooting into the Las Vegas camp just into Honduran territory. Contra counterattacks were repulsed by Sandinista infantry battalions that protected the rockets' positions. When several Hondurans were killed, the military in Tegucigalpa ordered the Contras to retreat farther north to Yamales.[17] A major incursion in March 1986 became a critical issue in part because the Reagan administration drew attention to it in an effort to swing Congressional votes in favor of renewed aid to the Contras. A vote against aid just before the incursion was reversed in June, though opponents of aid managed to block delivery for several months. Another attack on Honduran territory, discussed above, came in November-December as substantial military aid began arriving in Contra base camps.

Many other clashes between the Contras and Sandinistas during the mid-1980s occurred in the northwestern provinces of Nueva Segovia and Madriz. The broad social support the Contras enjoyed there, which along with Honduran noninvolvement enabled the rebels to move freely across the border, angered the Sandinista leadership. One of the critical supply routes was the narrow, rolling, curving dirt road that ran for about ten miles through scruffy underbrush and spindly trees between the small towns of Las Trojes and Cifuentes only about 100 yards into Honduran territory. The Nicaraguan side swarmed with heavily armed Sandinistas who destroyed Contra supply trucks and killed many guerrillas—among them the bloodthirsty Suicida's girlfriend, La Negra—as well as Hondurans and others. No one who knew the road traveled it in the daylight.

One notable incident occurred in June 1983 when Humberto Ortega, with the approval of the National Directorate, ordered the chief of Military Zone I to mine the road between Trojes and Cifuentes on the Honduran side of the Nicaragua/Honduras border. When the mine exploded at midday it did not kill the targeted FDN but rather two American journalists—Dial Torgerson, a reporter for the *Los Angeles Times*, and Richard Cross, a free-lance photographer on assignment for the *Times*— who were exploring the border that day in their tiny white Toyota. Ironically, the Sandinistas considered these two sympathetic to their cause. *Barricada* described Torgerson as "a responsible journalist who did not cave in to the manipulations of the Reagan administration intended to deceive the American people and lay the groundwork for a large scale aggression." Cross was hailed for having provided the photographs to accompany Ernesto Cardenal's poems in *Nicaragua: The*

War of Liberation, a book on the overthrow of Somoza. When the Honduran government said the Sandinistas were responsible, Foreign Minister D'Escoto retorted that that was "unspeakable cynicism," adding that everyone knows "the United States is looking for a pretext to begin a war in the region." Daniel Ortega said that the United States alone was responsible. The incident resulted in the exchange of a series of diplomatic notes between Managua and Tegucigalpa and a Sandinista letter to the United Nations Security Council charging that the whole incident was a U.S. provocation. The bombing ended EPS mining on the Honduran side of the border, however, at least for a while, though cross border incursions continued to be an issue that strained Nicaragua's relations with both Honduras and Costa Rica.[18]

The FSLN attempted in other ways to damage relations between the FDN and ARDE and their respective "host" governments of Honduras and Costa Rica. In October 1983, for example, the EPS blew up two electric towers in the Chinandega region of Nicaragua. These towers formed part of a Central American switching system through which Costa Rica sold electricity to Honduras and Nicaragua. The destruction of these towers caused serious shortages of electricity in Honduras and cost Costa Rica hundreds of thousands in lost revenue. The Sandinistas had taken preventive measures in advance so Nicaragua was not affected. Daniel Ortega personally ordered that the repair work on these towers be dragged out as long as possible. Meanwhile, the day after the towers were destroyed, the Sandinista government gave statements to the regional and international press blaming rebel organizations for their destruction, an act Daniel Ortega referred to as "terrorism by the puppets of American imperialism." The EPS continued to use this tactic throughout the war. In 1986, infantry units responded to an attack by ARDE on the Peñas Blancas custom post by blowing up two electrical switching towers in the Rivas region, again blaming the rebels. In this case, however, Costa Rica and Panama were affected and General Noriega, who suspected what was going on, sent an emissary to Managua who requested that repairs not be delayed unnecessarily. They were made quickly.

Another far from isolated type of Sandinista anti-Contra propaganda—the "making the most of a bad situation" ploy—is illustrated by a frame-up that occurred in northern Matagalpa in June 1986. While driving his car in the countryside, Paul Dessers, a volunteer civil engineer or "internationalist" from Belgium, was challenged to stop by a drunk

EPS soldier. When he did not stop, the soldier shot him dead. But the Sandinistas were experienced in handling such matters: the military's judge advocate's office and counterintelligence, with the participation of Roger Miranda, were ordered to fabricate a file on the soldier, Francisco Pérez, to "prove" that he had been in touch with the Contras. This done, the murder of the "internationalist" was blamed on the FDN.[19] The Belgian government never bought the story, but the anti-Contra lobby abroad did, and Dessers, among others—some of whom were indeed killed by the Contras—became an international martyr for the Sandinista cause though he had been killed by the EPS.[20] The EPS soldier, on Humberto Ortega's orders, was killed.

Similarly, in the early 1980s an MI-8 helicopter crashed while forcibly relocating east coast residents. The helicopter, which normally carried thirty-two people, was stuffed to twice its capacity with women and children. When it crashed and almost all were killed, the Sandinistas blamed all those civilian deaths on the Contras.

The Sandinistas benefited also by their unilateral and arbitrary announcements of cease-fires. These cease-fires were meaningless because the EPS continued to seek out and attack rebel units. The only difference was that the attacks were lower profile to avoid notice. If a big clash occurred, the Sandinistas claimed that the rebels had broken the cease fire and the EPS units were merely responding in self defense. And the existence of the cease-fires made it more difficult for the Contras to convince the U.S. Congress that they needed a consistent source of military supplies.

Tens of thousands of Nicaraguans died during the decade of warfare. The Sandinistas lost more than two thousand troops in 1987 alone, by their own statistics. Some Sandinista bodies could not be retrieved from Honduras or isolated parts of Nicaragua. When retrieval was impossible, the EPS sometimes told the families the bodies were in sealed metal coffins, when in fact they were not. One of these was Lt. Hernán Serrano, the son of a family Humberto knew well and brother of Nancy (Marieluz Serrano), the aforementioned Sandinista spy. Serrano was killed in July 1982 in a battle at Los Llanos de Butko some thirty kilometers northeast of Puerto Cabezas on the Atlantic coast. As in several other cases, his parents received a sealed coffin that contained nothing but stones.

Conclusions on the Contras

At times the Contras were a much more serious military force than their critics cared to recognize or admit. The FSLN did not grasp this for several years. Why, then, did the Contras fail to seize power, even though their pressures did contribute to the decline of the economy and the holding of the 1990 elections, in which the Sandinistas were soundly beaten?

The one time the Contras might have moved ahead to a military victory was in 1984, when the EPS did not yet have the military units it needed to stand up to the rapidly expanding peasant insurgency. Also, during 1984 the Sandinistas were forced to be somewhat more open, to reduce their repression to some degree, in order to make the election of that year seem a legitimate one. The major battles were in the departments of Jinotega and Matagalpa. But the Contras didn't make the stab. It is not altogether clear why they didn't. Was it a failure of leadership among the eternally divided Contras, where some sought military victory, some wanted to force elections from the Sandinistas, and some had other agendas? Was it the hope or expectation that the United States, after its success in Grenada, would in time do the job for them? (During the debates over renewal of congressional Contra aid in February 1985, both President Reagan and Secretary Shultz said the administration sought the "removal" of the Sandinista government in its present form.) Whatever it was, the Contras lost their chance, and while Sandinista leaders breathed a deep sigh of relief, they launched reforms to assure that they would be better prepared for such a military challenge in the future.[21]

Between 1985 and 1987 the Contras usually maintained the tactical initiative, and the focus of much of the fighting was in Boaco, Chontales, and Nueva Guinea in addition to Matagalpa and Jinotega. But the tide had turned strategically. For one thing, the EPS counterinsurgency units, the BLIs, were coming on line. These elite units were offensive forces, sent out to take positions from the Contras. At the same time, Soviet MI-25 helicopter gunships began arriving in late 1984 and were first employed in August 1985, bringing both firepower and terror to the attacks on Contra positions. Finally, Sandinista agrarian policy was undermining to some degree the Contra social base in the countryside. During the same period, the Contras lost much of their support in the United States because of continuing charges of human rights abuses, escalating efforts to find a peaceful solution to the crisis, and the Iran-Contra scandal.

The principal failures of the armed opposition and their allies were:

1. The Contras never fully established themselves among Nicaraguans as a legitimate nationalistic force with a program of their own and a clear and appealing idea of what kind of government they would bring in. The problem was not so much that the Contras had the United States as a strong ally, though that alone could be used for propaganda purposes for some audiences in some places, as that they seemed to have so little concrete to offer for the future that they seemed to be puppets for U.S. interests in the region and could more easily be branded agents of the Somocista past.

2. The Contras could never form a strong and cohesive political leadership. This made it impossible for the resistance to clearly represent the peasant fighters or other Nicaraguans and fed the Sandinista-promoted image that the Contras were standing in above all for the U.S. imperialists.

3. The fact that former National Guard officer Bermúdez was military chief of the Contras had military advantages but was often a political liability that the Sandinistas used very effectively, and often dishonestly, in many quarters, to paint a picture of the FDN as nothing but a band of bloodthirsty Somocistas doing the bidding of the United States. Out-and-out Sandinista supporters, and many others who were simply ignorant, bought this line for years. Some still do.

4. The priorities of the Contras did not include serious military and other actions in urban areas where Sandinista power was based, though there was burgeoning discontent there. A senior staff member of the U.S. Senate Select Committee on Intelligence during the mid-1980s says many in the U.S. government believed the presence of so many T-55 tanks was one of the main reasons the Contras did not undertake major operations in the populated areas of the Pacific coast, and a senior Soviet diplomat agreed that this was probably so.[22] The presence of the tanks undoubtedly had a psychological impact on the Nicaraguan people, but the primary reason the Contras stayed away from the cities was probably because of the general concentration of Sandinista power there, particularly in such institutions as the state security, the police, and the Sandinista Defense Committees. Isolated actions in Matagalpa, Jinotega, and even Managua in 1987 surprised and worried the National Director-

ate, and anyone suspected of involvement in these activities was executed. The National Directorate was always afraid that the Contras would make a move in the cities, which is where the challenge to the FSLN ultimately had to be made, and that this would have forced the FSLN to take tough measures that would have further alienated much of the urban population. But the Contras largely limited their actions to the mountains.

5. Finally, the Contras' high-profile ally, the United States government as a whole, couldn't decide what was in its own best interests, much less the interests of Nicaraguans. Over and over again the Americans shot themselves—and thus the Contras and the Nicaraguan people—in the foot or worse. On the one hand, the Reagan administration was very outspoken in its support for the Contras, which opened it up to Sandinista charges of U.S. imperialism once again meddling in the affairs of small nations. The price would have been more obviously worth it if the U.S. had then consistently followed a policy of support for the armed opposition along with a serious but forceful second track on the diplomatic front. But actual U.S. military aid was very limited—almost nothing in comparison to Soviet bloc military aid to the Sandinistas—and it could never be depended upon. Also, the CIA and other branches of the U.S. government were often too heavy-handed, too closely involved in Contra affairs, a consequence of not trusting the Nicaraguans to handle things effectively themselves, and often with very negative results. Two of the most counterproductive actions of the war for the Contras were the mining of the harbors in 1984 and the Iran-Contra scandal beginning at the end of 1986, neither of which had Contra participation but both of which did far more damage to the Contras than the EPS had ever been able to do.

In contrast to the Sandinistas, Washington never understood to what extent this was a political conflict, only in part because democracies often fail to be able to act consistently in their own interests in foreign affairs. The Sandinista leaders, not bothered by legislative or media involvement or criticism, carefully used Washington's hesitations, failures and inconsistencies to tarnish the image of the United States.

And yet in the end the Contra War was a success in that it represented a potent outlet for Nicaraguan opposition to the FSLN. Without the pressures of the Contras there never would have been an election in 1990, a fact Ortega implicitly acknowledged in his remarks to the National Directorate after signing the Arias peace plan. U.S. assistant secretary of state for inter-American affairs Bernard Aronson called Contra military leader Enrique Bermúdez after the election to tell him just that.[23] But the Contras' contributions to that end could have been achieved at far less cost to all concerned if the United States and they themselves had had consistent and better coordinated policies to deal more effectively with the FSLN challenge and take advantage of the Sandinistas' own weaknesses.

Notes

1. *Reseña Histórica del Surgimiento de la Organización C/R. F.D.N.*, in Roger Miranda collection in Hoover Institution Archives.
2. On the number of guardsmen, see Alejandro Bendaña, *Una Tragedia Campesina*, 31, which cites Morales Carazo. On Tigrillo, see Garvin, *Everybody Had His Own Gringo*, 66ff. On the real and alleged activities of these and other brutal Contras see the Garvin volume cited above, Sam Dillon, *Comandos*, and Christopher Dickey, *With the Contras*.
3. Dillon, *Comandos*, xiii.
4. Bendaña, *Una Tragedia Campesina*, 13, 38, 258.
5. On González and MILPAS, see Garvin, *Everybody Had His Own Gringo*, 18–20.
6. UN figures cited in Ibid., 261.
7. See Alfonso Robelo papers in Hoover Institution Archives, Stanford University.
8. Ratliff interviews with Pastora, 19 and 20 March 1992. On U.S. attitudes toward Pastora, see McNeil, *War and Peace*, 157–61, 233–35.
9. Nietschmann, *The Unknown War*, 76.
10. Roy Gutman, *Banana Diplomacy*, 299 11. Garvin, *Everybody Had His Own Gringo*, 128.
12. Ibid., 123.
13. Dillon, *Comandos*, 159.
14. For more detail see Dillon, *Comandos*, 180–84, and Garvin, *Everybody Had His Own Gringo*, chap. 14.
15. North, *Under Fire*, 256, 307.
16. The Hasenfus incident also dramatically increased Democratic criticism of aid to the Contras and tied Contra supply programs to both Washington and El Salvador. The photo of Hasenfus is on the front cover of the Nicaraguan magazine *Soberanía*, no. 19.
17. Dillon, *Comandos*, 157–58.
18. *Barricada*, 22, 23, and 25 June 1983.
19. The heads of these two offices did not change under the Chamorro government (as of the end of 1991) and thus the murder of FDN military leader Enrique Bermúdez in early 1991—which a Nicaraguan Assembly investigating committee traced to the Sandinistas—is likely to remain "unsolved."
20. For example, see Dessers's inclusion as a victim of Contra terror in the large paid advertisement, "They Died Because They Were Working with the Poor in Nicaragua," *New York Times*, 24 August 1986.

21. See *New York Times*, 22 February 1985. On the internal problems of the Contras, see Garvin, *Everybody Had His Own Gringo*; Dillon, *Comandos*; R. Pardo-Maurer, *The Contras, 1980–1989: A Special Kind of Politics* (Washington: Praeger, 1990); and Ratliff interviews with Pastora, 19 and 20 March 1992.

22. Ratliff conversation with Angelo Codevilla and Yuri Povlov, Hoover Institution, 17 October 1991.

23. Ratliff interview with Elsa Bermúdez, Enrique Bermúdez's widow, on 28 October 1991 in Miami, Florida.

18

Peace as a Strategy in War

From July 1979 on Sandinista domestic and international policies were in large part determined by the comandantes' conviction that their objectives had to be won through conflict. And yet, the nine comandantes repeatedly said all they wanted was peace. In this chapter we will examine the Sandinistas's manipulation of "peace" in domestic and international policies and forums.

Fighting and Talking on the Atlantic Coast

Somoza had few problems with the indigenous peoples on the Atlantic coast because he left them alone to live in their poverty. The Sandinistas, however, for ideological and geostrategic reasons, felt it necessary to draw the Miskito, Sumo, Rama, and Creole peoples fully into the Sandinista nation. They resolved to use whatever force was needed, but found the endeavor far more difficult than they had anticipated and the only serious blemish on their international image during the early years of the revolution. Thus by the end of 1984 they began talking about negotiations, while the war continued. The decision to begin negotiations came in an October 1984 meeting in New York involving Daniel Ortega, Misurasata coordinator Brooklyn Rivera, and U.S. senator Ted Kennedy.[1]

Bernard Nietschmann, almost the only American who knew the Miskitos existed a decade before the Sandinistas attacked them, summarized early FSLN efforts to forcefully suppress Indian and Creole peoples before they turned to a fight/talk policy. The Sandinistas

burned to the ground sixty-five Miskito and thirty Sumo communities; forcibly displaced 70,000 Miskitos and Sumos (one half of the population) into state camps and external refugee camps; carried out arbitrary mass arrests, jailings and torture; sent Soviet helicopter gunships and elite army and security forces to attack Indian

254 The Civil War in Nicaragua

communities because they opposed the occupation; imposed hunger and food dependency by destroying crops, fruit trees and fishing canoes, and restricting access to staples such as rice and beans; outlawed any independent Indian government or organizations and replaced them with an FSLN occupation government and Sandinista organizations; conscripted—often forcibly—Indian and Creole youths into the invaders' army and security forces; and then used Soviet-style autonomy laws in an effort to stamp out the peoples' wishes for self-determination.

One Miskito leader described the Sandinista policy as "ethnocide and genocide" and quoted Tomás Borge as saying in February 1981: "We're ready to eliminate the last Miskito Indian to take Sandinism to the Atlantic Coast."[2]

When these counterinsurgency tactics didn't subdue the coastal peoples, but instead drew a storm of criticism from abroad, the Sandinistas decided to put a better face on their repression by professing their willingness to resolve peacefully the problems they had just created.

Nietschmann, who was an adviser to the Miskito negotiators during the 1980s, notes correctly that the FSLN reasons for supporting peace negotiations were to

1. wind down or end Indian guerrilla resistance, thus reducing the "Contra" fronts fighting the Sandinistas from three to two;

2. wind down or end Indian and Creole agitation for self-determination by incorporating some of their leaders into the occupying Sandinista government and seeming to concede to some of their demands;

3. reverse the tenor of world opinion, which in the early 1980s had become highly critical of Sandinista repression of the Indians.[3]

Misurasata/Yatama peace terms changed little over the decade, though certain leaders were more receptive to a deal than others. Among their demands were: the withdrawal of FSLN military forces and institutions and a formal bilateral peace treaty between the Sandinistas and the Indian/Creole nations; the release of Indian and Creole people in relocation camps and prisons, an investigation into the disappearance of people, and FSLN indemnification for Sandinista-destroyed communities, stolen goods, and confiscated property; Sandinista recognition of the territorial boundaries of the Indian and Creole nations, of the latter's inalienable control of resources therein, or their rights to self-government and self-determination.[4]

The Sandinistas, for their part, considered the Atlantic coast forces more receptive to a "deal" than other Contra forces for several reasons. Most importantly, their demands were not for power in Managua or most of the country, but simply to be left alone on the coast, and thus a concession or seeming concession was less of a challenge to FSLN power in the country. Also, there were splits within the Indian and Creole forces themselves, which could be manipulated. One group, Misurasata (later called Yatama), was allied to Edén Pastora's forces in Costa Rica/southern Nicaragua, while another group, Misura, had its ties to FDN forces in Honduras/northern Nicaragua. And there were varied tensions between the coastal forces and their Contra allies. For example, after the U.S. mining of the Nicaraguan harbors in early 1984, and the subsequent Boland amendment, formal U.S. aid to the Contras ended and both formal and informal supplying of the Indian and Creole forces by the other two Contra armies was cut back drastically; in part this was due to lack of supplies, but it also reflected many Contra leaders' concern over heavily arming groups with clear-cut territorial objectives.

The four rounds of Atlantic coast negotiations in 1984–85 were conducted under the sponsorship of the Colombian and Mexican governments. The Sandinista delegation was headed by Luis Carrión, second in command at the Ministry of the Interior, and Omar Cabezas. After two years of break, negotiations resumed in 1988, when they were mediated by a commission of church groups; the FSLN delegation was headed by Interior Minister Borge. Borge was particularly interested in being involved in the coastal war because it gave him a field of military operations not dominated by his rival, Humberto Ortega. Also, he had a more rural-oriented vision of military doctrine than the Ortegas and believed that if the inland people could not be subdued, they should in some degree be placated since it was possible that the Sandinistas might one day have to retreat again to the hinterland.

In Nietschmann's words, "if there was an impending vote on contra aid in Washington, the Sandinistas would make concessions in the negotiations, publicize them, and then forget about them after the vote," as on 23 April 1985 and 3 February 1988. "If there was no impending vote . . . , the Sandinistas would make no concessions, promote a signed promise to continue the negotiations, publicize that, and then launch attacks on Indian communities," as they did in January 1985, May 1985, and February 1988. Nietschmann correctly concluded that the

Sandinistas "used the negotiations as propaganda to cut off outside military assistance to the Indian and Creole fighters, to promote a false international image of conciliation, and to strengthen their military and institutional grip on the occupied nations."[5]

First Regional Peace Proposals

The first effort by a Latin American government to reduce tensions and avoid war between Nicaragua and the United States was made by Mexican president José López Portillo. In the third week of February 1982 López Portillo visited Nicaragua at the invitation of the National Directorate to receive the prestigious Sandino Award. In his acceptance speech he set forth his government's three-point proposal to reduce tensions. He called on the United States to renounce all threat or use of force against Nicaragua; for the disarming of fledgling Contra groups in Honduras and a reduction in the size of the Sandinista military; and for Nicaragua to sign a nonaggression pact with its neighbors and the United States.

The United States and other Central American governments could hardly have been pleased with the Mexican proposal since it failed to deal with major factors that were already escalating the regional conflict: Sandinista support for regional guerrilla movements, Sandinista ties to Cuba and the Soviet bloc generally, and the increasingly antidemocratic nature of the regime in Managua. For precisely those reasons, the bulk of the proposal was well received by the Sandinista Directorate, which however rejected the phrase on the reduction in the size of the armed forces.

Daniel Ortega responded to the Mexican proposal with a counteroffer from the Directorate. Nicaragua would

1. maintain a nonaligned foreign policy—expressed by having ties to all countries of the world irrespective of their social and economic systems—as well as a diversified economy and political pluralism (general elections would be held in 1985);

2. support treaties of nonaggression and mutual security with Central American neighbors based on nonintervention and mutual respect;

3. support joint patrols at its borders with Honduras and Costa Rica;

4. develop friendly relations with the United States.

In March 1982, in the Organization of American States, Honduras proposed a reduction in arms and military advisers, respect for nonintervention, and international verification of agreements. This plan omitted matters each side felt vital to an agreement and thus was stillborn.

The first serious multinational effort to find a regional solution to the Central American crisis came in October 1982 at an Inter-American conference of democratic and semidemocratic governments hosted in Costa Rica by that country's newly elected president, Luis Alberto Monge. In the words of one of the U.S. delegates to the conference, the proposals were for "*negotiations* within and among countries, *reduction* of armaments and military establishments, *elimination* of military and security advisors, *cessation* of support for insurgents, and *democratization*." The Sandinistas, who had not been invited to San José, blasted the session. Tomás Borge made belligerent noises toward Costa Rica and hinted that the Soviet Union might build an interoceanic canal along the disputed San Juan River frontier. Mexico had refused to go to the conference because Nicaragua had not been invited and the Mexican press dumped on Monge as a tool of the gringos.[6]

Climbing Aboard Contadora

The Contadora peace process, which was launched in January 1983 by Colombia, Mexico, Panama, and Venezuela, is usually considered the first serious regional effort to resolve the crisis, though the basic principles of the 1982 Costa Rican meeting "are identical in substance to the more repetitive twenty-one principles" turned out by Contadora eleven months later.[7] The Contadora group looked on the problem as a regional one on the economic, social, and political levels. At first the Sandinistas opposed Contadora because the FSLN did not want a "solution" based on criteria that went beyond the Managua-Washington confrontation. To the FSLN it was a question of U.S. sponsored aggression and unthinkable to draw a parallel between what was happening in Nicaragua and El Salvador. The Salvadoran war, in the view of the FSLN, was a civil war caused by internal problems, while the war in Nicaragua was essentially the creation of the United States and other hostile external forces. Sandinista leaders also feared that accepting a multilateral resolution of the regional problem would at least tacitly recognize the U.S. contention that Managua was involved in arming guerrillas and stirring up the crisis in El Salvador.

The Sandinistas finally agreed to participate in the Contadora process only because they feared isolation and did not want international public opinion to conclude that they were boycotting the peace effort. Before long they realized they could manipulate Contadora and twist its goals to their own purposes. The Sandinista response to Contadora in July 1983 was a proposal for regional peace—its first within the Contadora context—which included the following points:

1. The commitment to end any prevailing belligerent situation through the immediate signing of a nonaggression pact between Nicaragua and Honduras.

2. The absolute cessation of all arms supplying on the part of any country to the forces in conflict in El Salvador, thus allowing the people of that country to solve their own problems without any foreign interference.

3. The absolute cessation of any military aid, whether it be arms, training, using territory to launch attacks, or any other form of aggression against any of the Central American governments.

4. Commitment to guarantee absolute respect for self-determination of the Central American peoples and noninterference in the internal affairs of each country.

5. The cessation of aggression and economic discrimination against any Central American country.

6. The outlawing of any foreign military bases in Central America, as well as the suspension of military exercises with the participation of foreign armies in the region.

Why did the National Directorate make these particular points?

• The Directorate had great trouble with the second point on El Salvador; it was discussed in detail with FMLN leaders and received their approval before it was released. In this point, the Directorate implicitly admitted that the Sandinistas had been supplying arms and munitions to the FMLN and they knew that the admission might to some degree hurt them politically. But they concluded that there was more to gain than lose because (1) it allowed the Directorate to respond to a point repeatedly raised by the United States, but in such a way as to focus attention on critical U.S. military support for the Salvadoran government. What is

Peace as a Strategy in War

more, the Directorate knew its aid to the FMLN was difficult to prove and would be continued in any event.

- To some, points two and three may seem to say the same thing, but they don't. Point (2) is intended to present the FMLN as a legitimate belligerent force in the country and an alternative to the existing government while point (3) is intended to suggest that Nicaragua was a victim of a war of aggression and that the armed opposition appeared neither as a legitimate force nor as an alternative to the Sandinista government. If point (2) had not been presented as it was and separated from point (3), the FMLN would have felt betrayed by the Sandinista government.

- Point (6) is a clear allusion to the joint military maneuvers carried out by the United States and Honduran armies as well as the increasing U.S. military presence in that country. In February of 1983, the Big Pine I exercises were completed and the FSLN had information that such exercises would continue throughout 1983 and 1984. U.S. exercises on the Nicaraguan border always worried Sandinista leaders because from a strictly military standpoint armies undertake exercises so as to be prepared to fight. And there was always the possibility that the exercises might in fact turn into attacks into Nicaragua. Finally, the point in no way hurt the Sandinistas because the FSLN had no plans in the short, medium, or long term to conduct exercises with the armies of any other country.

Increasingly the Sandinistas realized that the Contadora effort could be used to strike at the credibility of the United States. In fact, by early 1984 the Sandinistas took it so seriously that a highly specialized body, presided over by Daniel Ortega, was set up to draft judgments and recommendations on Contadora to the National Directorate.[8] This did not mean that the FSLN set aside other forums for making its case against the United States, such as the UN Security Council, of which Nicaragua was a member, and the International Court of Justice at the Hague.

In September the five Central American foreign ministers signed a twenty-one-point document of objectives to achieve regional peace. The document called for the observance of the principles of international law, national reconciliation and pluralism, social justice, national integrity, regional economic integration, an end to the arms race, the prohibition of foreign military bases and support for paramilitary forces across borders, and the reduction of foreign military advisers and security actions. These ideas were incorporated into the draft treaty, the Acta, of 7 September.

Suddenly, on 21 September, the Sandinistas caught the other countries by surprise when Daniel Ortega, on behalf of the Directorate, accepted the Contadora draft treaty as a final document. The United States, which had supported the twenty-one points, did not accept the draft as it was, nor did the other Central American countries, though Guatemala was less outspokenly critical. When they refused to sign they argued that the draft was a talking paper, as the Contadora countries had intended it to be. But the impression given to many, and assiduously cultivated by the FSLN, was that the Sandinistas were the only party that really wanted peace and wished to cooperate with Contadora. Many around the world bought the Sandinista line.

Why the Sandinistas Signed the Contadora Draft Treaty

The Sandinistas signed the Contadora draft treaty for one reason only—propaganda. Political warfare is a game the Sandinistas often handled much more effectively than the United States, in part because the FSLN often played to a more credulous audience but also because the United States often acted much more defensively than creatively. In some cases, the vagueness of the formulations made Sandinista evasion of points they did not like relatively easy, which was precisely what the critics of the draft treaty argued. In other cases, where the wording was sufficiently specific, the FSLN simply had no intention of complying if they thought doing so would weaken them vis á vis the other countries or act against their perceived interests.

For example, one portion of the draft dealt with moves to achieve national reconciliation in the various countries. It called on each country to improve representative democracy and popular participation in government through regular elections and other means as a way to bring about and maintain domestic and regional peace. This was a crucial point in Nicaragua because the fundamental causes of the civil war, which by then had deeply divided Nicaraguan society, were the broken promises of democracy, freedom, and pluralism the Sandinistas had made on the eve of the July 1979 revolution. Of course the Sandinistas argued they were already the most genuinely democratic government in Central America. Other sections dealt with military and security matters. The call to slow down the arms race and start negotiations to control weapons and troops would have stalled in endless negotiations. The Sandinistas would argue that their situation was different from those of other countries because they had to be prepared for direct confrontation with the United States. In fact, the FSLN had no intention whatsoever of reducing either its number of weapons or its troops on active duty. Indeed, it was in September, the month the FSLN signed the draft, that Humberto Ortega set up the tripartite committee to begin working on the second Nicaraguan-Soviet five-year military protocol discussed above. This treaty covered the five-year period 1986 to 1990 and was designed to accomplish precisely the opposite of what was sought by the Contadora document.

The draft treaty also included specific commitments on arms trafficking, banning the support of irregular forces, and ceasing the support for subversive activities or sabotage aimed at destabilizing the governments of the region. The Sandinista government was not prepared to comply with any of these points either, on the grounds of principle and strategic necessity, as explained in the chapter on the FMLN. But they knew it would be hard to pinpoint violations due to their operational methods and secrecy.

It should be noted that from April 1983 on, the Sandinistas shifted their response to charges that they were supporting subversive activities, though they never had any intention of ending their support, especially for the FMLN. They seldom answered with a categorical no, but indicated a willingness to discuss the matter if evidence of involvement were put on the table. Thus on 25 April Daniel Ortega said:

> We have rejected the accusations that we have been supplying the Salvadoran guerrillas with weapons; however, we reiterate once more that if the United States alleges, as its primary concern, a supposed arms trafficking to El Salvador, we are prepared to address its concerns if it can furnish us with proof or concrete information so that we can take the relevant measures or include these concerns in bilateral negotiations.[9]

So why did the Sandinistas sign the draft treaty?

1. The FSLN based its decision on the assumption that the United States and the other Central American countries would *not* sign this draft version. Their assumption proved to be correct.

2. In its draft form, the treaty had many more advantages for the Sandinistas than for other parties. Simply by signing, the FSLN won major propaganda and diplomatic victories and proved it had learned how to exploit Contadora and the desire for peace to its own advantage. Had

the other parties signed, the Sandinistas knew they would have won short-term advantages but that these would have been more than offset in the medium term by evidence of their violations and the discrediting of their compliance. Indeed, the Sandinistas long feared that the United States might become more innovative and really put them on the spot by signing.

3. If the other governments had signed, the Sandinistas would have won the following short-term gains:

A. The immediate proscription and suspension within thirty days of military maneuvers in Central America by extraregional military forces, a clear reference to U.S. army maneuvers. This would have removed an enormous source of tension and pressure on the Sandinistas, for the FSLN feared, with varying levels of intensity, that an invasion might begin at any time.

B. The bulk of critical aid for the resistance came from the United States through Honduras and this would have ended with the treaty, dooming the opposition to stagnation and eventual failure. At the same time, since Sandinista support for the FMLN was truly covert, though all informed observers knew it was happening, including the governments of the region, the treaty provided no effective way to document and stop it, and the Sandinistas had no intention of stopping voluntarily.

C. After six months the Central American governments would have had to get rid of the foreign military bases and schools on their soil. The Cubans and the Soviets had refused to provide this kind of support for the Sandinistas, who had asked for it, so they had nothing to lose and much to gain from this clause.

D. The Sandinistas would have benefited in relative terms by the withdrawal of foreign military advisers. Anticipating the inclusion of a foreign adviser clause in any peace agreement, the DN had instructed Humberto Ortega to carry out a study of the relative impact of the removal of foreign advisers from Nicaragua and from other Central American countries. In April 1984 the study was completed, with the conclusion that this point was negotiable because at this point other countries, particularly the Salvadorans, were relatively more dependent on outside advisers than the Sandinistas.

As time passed, Contadora refined its documents but in terms of achieving peace, it was mainly spinning its wheels.

The Crimeface Caper

In August 1985 Manuel Noriega went to Managua for a private meeting with the two Ortegas. He proposed a peace plan for Central America promoted by the military chiefs of the region. According to Noriega, he had already talked with the other military chiefs and they were in agreement in principle with the idea. The first step was to be a meeting of military leaders in Panama in order to discuss and then set the basics for the peace plan. Noriega said, "the military forces should play a much more active role in the political lives of the nations. We have to get out of the barracks." The idea of Noriega acting as prime mover in a Central American peace plan wasn't to the liking of the Directorate, considering his ties to the CIA, his known criminal activities, and his lack of interest in compromise. The Directorate decided to go along nonetheless in order to get what it could from any talks that might be held. If Humberto were able to meet with the military leaders of the other countries, that in itself would be a political victory for the Sandinistas. But nothing further came of the proposal and it was assumed that Noriega had lost or never really received the support of the other military chiefs.

Arias and Esquipulas II

The next big step in the peace process came in early 1987 with the peace plan launched by Costa Rican President Oscar Arias. It bore signs of frustration with past efforts, both Contadora and bilateral. The Arias plan differed from earlier efforts in a number of ways, but above all it narrowed the scope of negotiations to focus on just a few essentials: democratization, which Arias felt was the *sine qua non* of a peaceful region; and ending support for insurgencies abroad—whether the Contras or the FMLN. From the beginning, Arias had stressed that the main obstacle to peace in Central America was the government in Managua. On 6 February he said on Mexico City television that "with or without Contras and with or without military aid, I continue to think there will be violence in Nicaragua if the Nicaraguan people cannot elect their leaders freely."

Thus it was not altogether surprising that when Arias called for a preliminary meeting of Central American presidents in San Jose on 15 February, he did not invite the Sandinistas. The FSLN blasted Arias and said he was simply a tool of the U.S. State Department. But, as in the case of Contadora, the Sandinista position shifted when Nicaragua was invited to later meetings and it was clear other countries were taking Arias seriously. As before, the Sandinistas could not afford to be left out.

In the case of the Esquipulas peace accord, it was the United States that was left out, for from the beginning it was the Reagan administration that tried to throw up barriers to its success. And how ironic it was, for Arias's proposal was very close to the policy proposed by President Reagan in February 1985 in his famous "say uncle" press conference. At that time, he explained that the U.S. objective was to remove the "present structure" of the Nicaraguan government, something the Sandinistas themselves could do if they would simply permit "a government chosen by the people." At the time, the Reagan administration was belittled and maligned for being "seized by its own kind of 'liberation theology.'" According to an editorial in the *Washington Post*, Mr. Reagan "seems all but ready to swing into the saddle and charge up the Nicaraguan equivalent of San Juan Hill."[10] At the beginning of 1987 President Arias proposed essentially the same thing, won the Nobel Peace Prize and brought a virtual end to the fighting in Nicaragua.

The U.S. administration raised legitimate questions about the comprehensiveness of the Arias plan, but in doing so missed the very simple point that Reagan himself had made earlier and Arias had picked up on now: if Nicaragua were truly democratic it would not have an aggressive foreign policy toward its neighbors and it would no longer be closely allied to aggressive totalitarian countries around the world. By 1987 the Sandinistas were far more receptive to this kind of settlement than they had been before, even if one could expect them to manipulate it in any way possible: the war had dragged on far longer than they had expected and frustration with it had deepened; economic pressures and the renewed Contra offensive had effectively forced the Sandinistas to the point of national desperation; and while the Contras still had significant arms on hand and coming their way for a while, the Iran/Contra scandal had greatly reduced prospects of Congress's voting more military aid in the foreseeable future.

Thus when the Reagan administration persisted in demanding more arms for the Contras it made the U.S. president look like he was the only remaining warrior and his intransigence seemed to make him a plausible scapegoat for the Sandinista's own intransigence. The Sandinistas quickly took advantage of Washington's positions to justify their own foot-dragging and even renewed repression. What else could the endangered nation do, they argued, if even as peace talks were underway the United States insisted on talking about more arms and war?

When Ortega left for the 6–7 August 1987 meeting of Central American presidents in Guatemala, Sandinista leaders didn't expect an agreement to be reached and thus the president had no specific authorization to sign one. At the same time, the Directorate had given him a free hand to respond to what happened in Guatemala. But Ortega and the other presidents did sign an agreement, and a major factor in getting them to do so, ironically, was President Reagan. The day before the meeting opened in Guatemala, Reagan joined House Speaker Jim Wright in releasing the Reagan-Wright peace plan. Wright evidently thought this might prompt the Central American presidents to sign their own more flexible agreement while the president evidently believed the Sandinistas would sign neither, thus improving the prospects for renewed Contra aid. Wright was right, and Reagan was wrong.[11]

On returning to Managua after signing Esquipulas II, Daniel immediately visited Humberto and told him what had happened:

> Reagan's announcement of his proposal just before we met had a lot to do with our reaching an agreement. When he put out a proposal without even consulting the presidents of the area, he stung everyone's pride. Before we began our discussions, I proposed that we reject Reagan's plan out of hand, and it was accepted unanimously. . . . What we have to do now is turn these agreements into another arm to eliminate the Contras.

The agreement had helped consolidate the revolution and laid the groundwork for the defeat of the Contras, Daniel concluded, especially through pressures on the United States and Honduras.

And then in 1989, as Dillon has noted, "the Sandinistas launched a political offensive on a dozen domestic and international levels," ranging from intensive pressures upon the U.S. Congress to efforts to split the Contras. On the first day of the Sapoa talks between the Sandinistas and the Contras on Nicaraguan territory—a meeting the former had steadfastly proclaimed would never take place—Humberto Ortega announced a unilateral cease-fire. Although some encounters continued, in the broader sense the war was over.

The hidden agenda of the Sandinistas was evident, however, in the National Directorate's approval of the Soviet-initiated armament program discussed above. When this plan for military expansion was put to and accepted by the Directorate, there wasn't the slightest concern that it violated absolutely the spirit of the Esquipulas II accord Daniel Ortega had just signed on behalf of the nation in Guatemala. Part VII of the Esquipulas agreement clearly implied the signatories' intention to reduce armaments in the region when it said the five states, in cooperation with the Contadora Group, would continue negotiations with respect to security, verification and control according to the draft Contadora Act. Costa Rican president Arias affirmed this in an interview with the *New York Times* on 20 December, shortly after Roger Miranda had made the planned buildup public. Arias said: "When we met in Guatemala City on the 7th of August in our minds and in our hearts, our aim was to limit and reduce the size of the armies—and never for any reason to increase the sizes."

And the letter of the Esquipulas II agreement was immediately violated as well, in a variety of ways. Two important examples: after the signing of the accord, the Cubans sent 500 rifles and 1.5 million bullets to the FMLN guerrillas through Nicaragua and the Sandinistas took fifteen FMLN guerrillas to Nicaragua for training in the use of "Red Eye" and Soviet C2M and C3M land-to-air missiles. Missiles were sent to them later.

Clearly the Sandinista leaders considered the Guatemala peace plan nothing more than a device for ending the Contra War—that kind of peace—even as they were planning a military that virtually guaranteed greater conflict with the United States and in the region. If anything was clear in Nicaragua in October 1987, it was that the people wanted peace. Yet the Sandinistas, far from grasping at the chance provided by the Esquipulas II agreement, had instead decided to drag the country deeper into militarism than ever before. But things were changing in the Soviet Union and the arms were never delivered. And the 1990 election took the Sandinistas out of formal power, though they began to operate as a sort of co-government during the early 1990s.

Notes

1. Bernard Nietschmann, *The Unknown War: The Miskito Nation, Nicaragua and the United States* (New York: Freedom House, 1989), 67.
2. Ibid., 62–63; and Stedman Fagot, *La Moskitia: autonomía regional* (S.1: s.n., 1986?), 143.

3. Nietschmann, *The Unknown War*, 63.

4. Ibid., 64–5.

5. Ibid., 67–68, 87. For a more detailed description of the negotiations, see Ibid., 68–89.

6. See the account of Frank McNeil, former U.S. ambassador to Costa Rica and member of the U.S. delegation headed by Enders, in *War and Peace in Central America*, 167–69, emphasis in original.

7. McNeil, *War and Peace*, 168.

8. The committee consisted of Humberto Ortega; Tomás Borge; Vice President Sergio Ramírez; Foreign Minister Miguel D'Escoto; Julio López, the chief of the Department of International Relations; Julio Ramos, the chief of military intelligence; and Renán Montero, a Cuban who had become a Nicaraguan citizen several years earlier and was chief of intelligence in the Ministry of the Interior.

9. The United States had anticipated this ploy. In late 1981, when the Sandinistas denied knowledge of a Salvadoran guerrilla command and control center in Managua, Enders said Americans would be glad to guide Sandinista leaders to it. Ratliff interview with Fontaine, 6 May 1992.

10. *New York Times*, 22 February 1985; *Washington Post*, 25 February 1985. Actually, the first top U.S. official to focus on the need for a democratic or pluralistic Nicaragua was Thomas Enders in an August 1982 speech at the Commonwealth Club of San Francisco.

11. See Douglas Payne, "How the Sandinistas Turned the Tide: A Chronicle of the 'Peace Process,'" *Strategic Review*, Fall 1987: 19.

PART VI

The Collapse of Sandinismo?

19

Sandinismo:
From Government to Opposition

Between 1988 and 1992, the Contra War ended through a negotiated settlement and popular will turned increasingly against the FSLN, as was demonstrated most conclusively by the landslide victory for the opposition candidates in the March 1990 presidential and congressional elections. After the inauguration of the new government of President Violeta Chamorro and her National Opposition Union (UNO) coalition, some freedoms that had been partially restored during the election campaign were extended, many of the hundreds of thousands of Nicaraguans who had fled abroad returned home, and faltering efforts were launched to rescue the plummeting economy. In short, Nicaragua turned several corners, but even after several years of the new regime it remains to be seen if those turns will put Nicaragua on the road to a better future or simply leave the people and nation going in circles, spiraling down, perhaps to a new era of Somocismo without Somoza.

War and the "Peace" in Nicaragua

By the time President Arias launched his peace initiative in early 1987, the Contras had been around years longer than the Sandinistas expected and had put up a fight that drained the spirit and coffers of a nation expiring under across-the-board economic burdens. The Contras had not only persisted, they had been revived by the $100 million in military and other aid the U.S. Congress voted to give them after mid-1986. But even as U.S. aid was arriving and being used to expand Contra activities in rural regions two things happened that almost assured the Contras' demise. The first was the Iran-Contra scandal, which by associating Contra aid with the then widely hated Iran substantially decreased the prospects for any significant new support for the resistance from the U.S. Congress, barring some particularly outrageous new Sandinista action like an invasion of Costa Rica. The second was the Arias peace initiative and the signing of Esquipulas II. As Daniel Ortega said in the wake of the August 1987 agreement, under the circumstances the Sandinistas decided they would be ahead to make some at least temporary political concessions, even some democratization, if it meant getting rid of the Contras for good.

But while signing the Esquipulas II accord did indeed contribute substantially to the demise of the Contras, the political concessions proved to be greater than Sandinista leaders had expected and in a sense constituted a Contra victory—at least in the short and medium term. The first concession, direct talks with the Contras, beginning in 1988, implicitly recognized that the guerrillas represented a segment of opposition within the country that could no longer be denied. The second and more important was allowing greater political freedom, culminating in the elections of March 1990. What the Sandinistas did, in effect, was ask the people to give them an electoral vote of confidence. That is to say, they asked the Nicaraguan people to affirm their confidence in a regime that had devastated the national livelihood with sterile, repressive domestic policies directed primarily toward building a war economy to fight the United States, most neighboring countries and, increasingly, most of its own people. They didn't get the vote of confidence.

Signing the Esquipulas II accord did not mean the nine comandantes had suddenly become—much less always had been—democrats, as some of their supporters and many outside observers claimed; their extensive violations of human and civil rights at Nandaime in July 1988 and elsewhere, the conduct of much of the campaign itself, and then their reaction to their electoral loss, demonstrated conclusively that they would tolerate opposing views only when they had no alternative to doing so or had a way to recoup apparent losses. From the mid-1980s on, domestic and international economic pressures had become so intense that simply changing mistaken domestic economic policies was not enough. The Sandinistas began to understand that if they were to have any chance of getting the economy moving, they would have to ingratiate themselves in some degree to international critics who had the money and markets Nicaragua needed. But by the late-1980s Nicaraguans and foreigners, including the countries of the Soviet bloc, had totally lost confidence in the Sandinista government and the country's future under FSLN rule. This is where the monumental political miscalculation came in and showed how much FSLN leaders had lost contact with the Nicaraguan people. Like their foreign supporters, whose blindness could at least be blamed on their residence most of the time abroad, the Sandinistas actually thought they had solid majority support in the country or could manipulate the elections so as to guarantee their victory and the continuation of their dominant role in the nation. A secret report to the National Directorate in September 1989 by Carlos Carrión, the mayor of Managua and a former chief of army intelligence, gave the comandantes an alternate—and more accurate—reading of the situation, for it indicated substantial popular disillusionment with the government.[1] But the Sandinistas seem to have been content to draw only secondary lessons from the report. For example, the transformation of Daniel Ortega through an American-style political campaign. The previously dour and aloof Ortega suddenly became a hip man of the people, accompanied by loud, swinging music and beautiful girls. They concluded that cosmetic changes—and a bit of strong-arming—would give them the day. American pollsters and their pro-Sandinista Nicaraguan employees found the Sandinistas were winning during the campaign and informed the world. But pollsters from Costa Rica, Venezuela, and Chile, among other countries, which placed sound methodology above partisan politics, accurately predicted a Chamorro victory, but got no attention in the United States or Europe.

So the Sandinistas remained convinced of the rightness of their mission and took it on faith that the majority of the people both supported what they were doing and blamed the United States and the Nicaraguan opposition (armed and unarmed) for the country's woes. To the extent that there was significant opposition, the Sandinistas thought they could control or overwhelm it in several ways. One way was the manipulation of state resources controlled by the Sandinistas, from the media to transportation to state funds. Another was simple intimidation. The Sandinistas spread their own rumors that no matter what was said publicly, the vote would *not* be secret and Sandinista intelligence would know who voted for whom and settle scores later.

Predictably, the Sandinistas tried to keep all their options open. One of the FSLN's most serious failures prior to the election had been its inability to defeat and/or disarm the Contras. But FSLN leaders decided they could use the continued presence of the Contras to their advantage and in November 1989 suddenly ended the cease-fire agreement that had been in effect since March 1988. Ortega said this was in response to a surge in Contra activity, which he alleged was directly linked to the campaign and candidacy of Violeta Chamorro; both of these allegations were lies. In fact, the Sandinistas blamed the Contras for breaking the cease-fire for two reasons: in order to provide a pretext for stationing troops around the country who would silently intimidate the population, and as a step toward cancelling the elections "due to the rising Contra threat" if the Sandinistas concluded they might lose. As the election approached, even some in UNO doubted they would be allowed to win and began striking deals to get what they could for themselves.

The 1990 Elections: The Second Revolution

But the election was held and the Sandinistas lost to a coalition of fourteen parties consisting of organizations ranging from the right to the Marxist-Leninist left. Violeta Chamorro walked off with the presidency taking 54.7 percent to Daniel Ortega's 40.8 percent of the vote. The Sandinistas won only thirty-eight of ninety seats in the National Assembly and they lost in rural, urban, and even some military communities. But even this landslide doesn't adequately convey the popular rejection of the Sandinistas. One must consider that almost 15 percent of registered voters didn't bother to vote, and thus obviously were not devoted supporters of the Sandinistas. Also, most of the hundreds of thousands of Nicaraguans who were living abroad did not vote because of FSLN-imposed electoral restrictions and the vast majority of these people opposed the Sandinistas. And finally, in the judgment of one of the other presidential candidates, Moisés Hassan, and others, many Nicaraguans were intimidated enough by the Sandinistas to vote for Ortega even when they didn't want him. Hassan suggests that probably only about 20 percent of voting age Nicaraguans, or fewer, actually wanted the Sandinistas back in office.[2]

When the vote came in for the opposition, the Sandinistas had two obvious choices, with variations: accept the verdict of the people, or reject it. Some Sandinistas militants and many resident foreign internationalists shouted, "Don't give up power. We've got the guns," and some of the comandantes indeed wanted to toss out the election and stomp on the opposition, just as Manuel Antonio Noriega had done in 1989 in Panama. Luis Sánchez Sancho, a top leader of Nicaragua's oldest communist party, the PSN, and a member of the UNO coalition, has explained that he was willing to sign the much-criticized transition protocol because after the FSLN lost the election "the country was on the brink of national disaster. Part of the Sandinista high command ... was ready to put down the entire UNO leadership and willing to drown any possible reaction on the part of the people in bloodshed. This gloomy prospect," Sánchez concluded, led to negotiations, supported by international observers, and to the protocol which in effect made Humberto Ortega co-ruler of the new government with Violeta Chamorro.[3] The Sandinista decision to accept the electoral results also was influenced strongly by the bright international spotlight then on Nicaragua, deriving in large part from the presence of thousands of preelection and election day observers, including delegations led by former U.S. president Jimmy Carter and one under the auspices of the Organization of American States.

So the Sandinistas accepted the vote on the negotiated terms and tried to make the most of it by securing for themselves, while they were still in office, an enormous chunk of property and power for the years ahead.

First, as described earlier, with the piñata, they gave themselves title to almost all of the private and state property owned by the state or enemies in the private sector. Second, they secured FSLN political and military power through decrees passed while they still ruled, deals with the incoming government during the transition period—particularly the transition protocol—and pressures on the new government in the streets after it took office. The "Law of Military Organization of the EPS," a decree dated 27 December 1989, was printed in the official *Gazette* on 23 February 1990 but not distributed until mid-September 1990, almost six months after Chamorro's inauguration. The decree made the military virtually autonomous and set the stage for the deal struck with the new government whereby Humberto Ortega retained his position as commander in chief of the army. Thus, the Chamorro government, in an effort to promote reconciliation and avoid confrontation with the Sandinistas, authorized the establishment of a parallel, and in an important sense dominant, co-government.[4]

At the beginning of 1992 the main sources of institutional and extra-legal firepower remained under the control of the Sandinistas, usually

Humberto Ortega. These were: (1) the military, reduced from eighty thousand regular forces to just over twenty thousand; (2) the security forces under Lenín Cerna, who was transferred with the DGSE from MINT to the EPS; (3) the police, still in the hands of René Vivas, a confirmed Sandinista who was nominally under the command of the minister of government; (4) the Re-compas, an informal force consisting of "fired" members of the EPS who were organized, armed and to some degree supplied by Humberto Ortega in order to resist reemerging Re-contras who could not be attacked openly by the EPS; (5) tens of thousands of Sandinista supporters who were given weapons before or after the election of Violeta Chamorro. In March 1992 Minister of Government Carlos Hurtado, who resigned shortly thereafter, said the government still needed to collect some eighty thousand rifles from "unorganized" civilians, most of whom were Sandinistas. By early 1992 many Re-compas had concluded that Humberto Ortega had abandoned them just as the Re-contras believed Violeta Chamorro had reneged on her agreements. Increasingly the two joined forces to protest government policies, at times with armed actions. They were then called the revueltos, the forces that were "all mixed up" or "scrambled," like eggs.

Governing from Below and from Behind

Domestically, after April 1990 the Sandinistas began trying to "govern from below," in Daniel Ortega's phrase. Governing from below came through violent occupations of buildings and businesses, and other forms of intimidation, designed to block the major economic and institutional reforms UNO promised the people in its campaign. The stated objective was "to preserve the accomplishments of the revolution." The Sandinistas also, in the words of Moisés Hassan, began to "govern from behind," in the form of Humberto Ortega's extraordinary influence as a power parallel to—or behind—the president and her son-in-law and chief aide, Antonio Lacayo, the dominant figure in the new government. Reportedly, Lacayo was responsible for convincing the incoming president that she should not go ahead with her original plan to fire Humberto Ortega before taking office, while the international spotlight was still on Nicaragua. It is widely believed that Lacayo—who was never elected to any position by anyone but immediately seized power from other UNO leaders—had private agreements with Ortega even before the election.

It is also widely believed that with the advent of the new government Lacayo and Ortega became political and business partners, with Ortega the stronger of the two. Lacayo is simply the most important of many instances of nepotism in the Chamorro government.

In early 1992, enormous issues remained for the nation, to an overwhelming degree inherited from, or directly and/or indirectly caused by, the Sandinista government, its greedy exit and the obstacles it has placed in the way of UNO reforms. In broad terms, as stated by UNO at the end of November 1991, the issues included: the property law (or "piñata"), constitutional amendments, implementation of effective civilian disarmament, democratization and modernization of the judicial branch, state preservation of public order, state corruption, depoliticizing the army and police, privatization, economic revival, and verification and follow-up of dialogue agreements. On 24 November 1991 the Nicaraguan Episcopal Council issued a long pastoral letter which charged that the executive branch of government had failed to enforce national laws and that the government seemed incapable of meting out justice. "This situation appears even more deplorable when there is an attempt to disguise it as a desire for reconciliation and peace." The letter, which was signed by Cardinal Obando y Bravo and others, called for a cut in military expenditures.[5]

Because of the wide variety of organizations within the opposition, political rivalries, and other matters, UNO has usually failed to act as a unit. One important example of the disunity within UNO occurred in December 1991 when a few UNO representatives split off to vote with the Sandinistas to pass a government budget which included military funding most UNO delegates had wanted to cut. Thus not only did the military continue to receive substantial funding, the state still had a foreign debt of about $10 billion, a bloated bureaucratic structure the FSLN has done everything it can to keep in place, and a rapidly rising crime rate and general incidents of violence.

At the same time, some positive changes have occurred: the military has been reduced dramatically, though the remaining members are those most loyal to Humberto Ortega; many workers are showing strong support for non-Sandinista unions; and the FSLN has verbally agreed to accept some planks of the UNO program, including privatization of banks, foreign trade, and profitable state companies, under the right conditions.

Foreign investors and governments have been slow to come to Nicaragua's aid for a variety of reasons: the investment climate is uncertain, in large part because the rule of law has not been established in the country, and international attention has shifted to other regions of the world and other problems. For example, the United States pledged $537 million in aid to Nicaragua during the 1990–91 fiscal years, but delivered only a bit over $200 million by mid-1991, mainly on the grounds that the Managua government had failed to reform the banking system and privatize the economy. In September 1991, however, the United States wrote off Nicaragua's debt to Washington, amounting to just under $300 million. Most parties praised the action, while *Barricada* on 27 September said it was nothing more than "charity given by the empire" since in fact, according to the World Court ruling, the United States owed Nicaragua many times that amount for damages inflicted during the war. In early 1992 a government delegation, including Daniel Ortega, went to the United States to talk with negotiators of several nations and left with promises of aid amounting to $600 million annually during 1992 and 1993.

The reality, as a large headline on the front page of *La Prensa* put it on 23 October 1990, is that "Central America has lost the attention of the United States." This was demonstrated when only about one hundred congressmen showed up to hear Violeta Chamorro address a joint session of Congress in May 1991. The government's hiring of Paul Reichler, who for so many years had represented the Sandinistas in the United States, did not increase U.S. enthusiasm for Chamorro's government, and the American consultant was soon released.

In June 1991 the Nicaraguan legislature, led by Assembly head Alfredo César, began seriously looking into ways to recover the major properties taken by the Sandinistas before and just after the 1990 election. But two groups opposed the move: (1) the Sandinistas and (2) the Chamorro government and a minority of UNO legislators, on the grounds that it threatened the government's policy of "reconciliation." The FSLN legislators walked out of the Assembly and, under the leadership of former foreign minister Miguel D'Escoto, seized the mayoral offices in Managua and several other cities. Sandinista thugs also bombed the homes and offices of UNO leaders. Daniel Ortega warned that conditions were more tense than at any time since the 1990 election and that war might be just around the corner. Similar confrontations occurred during the last half of the year and again Ortega insisted on "the people's" need to use violence in response to violence to defend their rights against the step by step reimposition of Somocismo in Nicaragua. Ortega's main targets have been Assembly president César, Vice President Virgilio Godoy and Managua mayor Arnoldo Alemán.[6]

Whither Sandinismo?

The Sandinistas held their first congress in July 1991 amidst much agitation and skepticism among many party members regarding the prospects for serious reforms. A commentator in *El Nuevo Diario*, long an unflinching pro-Sandinista daily, warned that "the main problem facing the next congress" [is] "the enormous distrust felt by most Sandinist members and supporters concerning the sincerity of party leaders about changes which—and on this the majority agree—are needed in order to try to win back the government."[7] The FSLN was having particular trouble winning the support of women, youth, and peasants. Among those calling for major reforms, including the individual election of members of the National Directorate, were former Sandinista Assembly deputy speaker Rafael Solís Cerda and former FSLN ambassador in Washington Carlos Tünnermann.

At the congress, however, the old Directorate was reelected as a group, with a few new appointments made before the vote by the old Directorate. Despite a strong campaign on behalf of a woman member for the Directorate, conducted by some women and portions of the Sandinista youth—the preferred candidate was Dora Maria Téllez—men still hold all the positions. Thus the Directorate refused to admit its innumerable errors during the past decade, or pay more than a token price for what it has caused, but rather persisted in frustrating its reform-minded and more imaginative members. Individual voting was allowed for deputies for the 120-member Sandinista Assembly, however, and only about one-third of the old members were reelected; the losers included the most outspoken reformers, but many others as well, including Daniel Ortega's unpopular wife, Rosario Murillo. From his position as FSLN secretary general, a new position in the party, Daniel Ortega announced that at the next congress, in 1995, voting for individual members of the Directorate will be allowed.

Discussion, disputes and rivalries persisted and grew after the congress. Most Sandinistas claimed they wanted unity in the party, but on
what terms? In early 1992 the breakdowns were generally as follows.
One analyst argued in *La Prensa* that the main divisions were not
ideological, but interests: the haves vs. the have-nots among Sandinista
members, essentially those who filled their pockets and bank accounts
during the piñata and those who didn't. Certainly the vast majority of
FSLN members were angry about the way the nine comandantes and
other top officials had enriched themselves; in February 1992 the
Sandinista Youth called on the FSLN to "review party property abuse
cases decisively and punish those who have violated the policy and
morals of the FSLN." Father D'Escoto, who has one of the largest of the
seized mansions, called César, who was leading the attack against the
piñata, a "mercenary" in the service of the U.S. government.[8]

But there were other divisions as well. Aldo Diaz Lacayo presented
one in *El Nuevo Diario* in late-February and early-March 1992. He
argued that there are three organic sections to the FSLN. They are led by
Humberto Ortega, and are part of the coalition government; those led by
Sergio Ramírez, who are working in the official structures of the state;
and those led by Daniel Ortega, based in the party's labor sector, claiming
to defend the social conquests of the revolution. Daniel Ortega had more
rank and file support than the others, but Humberto Ortega and then
Ramírez, had greater institutional, extra-party clout. Just the same, the
vast majority of Sandinista members and supporters were dispersed and
atomized; they had little use for any of the factions. In particular, Díaz
agreed, the property grabbing of the piñata had "opened up vast and
insurmountable distances between [the cadres who had helped them-
selves] and the vast majority of party members, something that is totally
contrary to the Sandinist ethic." The new reality of the party is

> the breakdown of the consensus in the National Directorate, the insistent demand for
> the de-ideologization of Tercerismo, the organic dispersion and the atomization of
> the rank and file, the differing interpretations of the transition protocol, the fictional-
> ization of the party, the socioeconomic shift of the leadership cadres, and the
> obsolescence of the structures. . . .[9]

In March Daniel Ortega stated that the FSLN and the National Workers
Front (FNT), who after the 1990 inauguration of President Chamorro
often worked together with him to disrupt the economy, are "enemies of
chaos and instability." After a ten hour meeting on 14 March 1992

between the National Directorate and the government's economic cabinet, Daniel Ortega stated that the FSLN would cooperate with the government in finding civic and peaceful solutions to problems. Ortega accompanied a government delegation to Washington a week later.

Since the late 1970s, Humberto Ortega has been the most important single Sandinista leader, though his predominance was not always recognized abroad. After the 1990 election he became openly more powerful than any other member of the party, though as head of the military he claimed to have no active party affiliation. Then in late January 1992, many Sandinista leaders and rank and file concluded that Humberto himself had sold out to the imperialists when he suddenly gave the Camilo Ortega award to the U.S. military attaché in Managua, Lieutenant Colonel Dennis Quinn, the Nicaraguan representative of the "imperialist army" the Sandinistas have always claimed waged an unholy war against Nicaraguans throughout the century, and not least during the 1980s. Humberto explained his action:

> From that day in 1989 [when Quinn arrived] until he completed his tour of duty, he maintained relations that helped bring Nicaraguans, in this case, the armed forces, together with the armed forces of a country that has historically been our enemy. . . Any effort that brings us closer to that power with which we have historically been at odds is constructive. . . if we proceed conservatively, trying to make everyone understand totally, then we will not be able to keep up with the speed of the process which events dictate. . . If electroshock treatment is administered by . . . a person with a proven revolutionary background, it would be very biased to think that he would hurt a cause to which he has devoted his entire life. . . Thanks to improved relations with the United States. . . another 50,000 will not have to die.[10]

Indeed, this action marked the most fundamental of all possible changes for a top Sandinista leader, for it constituted a renunciation of the anti-Americanism that had set the direction of Sandinista policies—including the alliances with Cuba and the Soviet Union, the militarization of the country, the aid for the Salvadoran guerrillas and the civil war—from Fonseca on. Indeed, ironically and tragically, the first fifty thousand Nicaraguans referred to by Ortega needn't have died either if the comandantes had said and actually believed this in July 1979.

Notes

1. The Carrión report is cited in Douglas Payne, "How the Sandinistas Lost Nicaragua's Second Revolution," *Freedom at Issue* (1990 supp.): 13-14. A coalition of three hundred pro-Sandinista groups in the United States, which called itself

the Nicaragua Network, was so sure of a Sandinista victory that it bought a large "Congratulations Nicaragua!" advertisement in the *New York Times* on 26 February, the day after the election. President Ortega and other Nicaraguans, whose voices were "usually muted in the U.S. media," were scheduled to tell how in the election Nicaraguans had once again stood up to the relentless pressures and interference of the United States.

2. Ratliff interview with Hassan, Stanford, CA, 2 May 1991.
3. Luis Sáncho Sanchez, *La Prensa*, 5 March 1992, in *FBIS* (Latin America), 6 April 1992.
4. See Douglas Payne, *Democracy vs. Dynasty: The Battle for Post-Election Nicaragua*, a Freedom House Special Report, 1990.
5. Pastoral Letter published in *La Prensa*, 24 November 1991, summarized in *FBIS* (Latin America), 27 November, 11-12; UNO criticism broadcast on Radio Corporation on 29 November, in *FBIS*, 2 December.
6. William Ratliff, "Out of Power, Sandinistas Still Act Like Kings," *The Wall Street Journal*, 26 July 1991.
7. Francisco X. Chamorro G, *El Nuevo Diario*, 14 February 1991, in FBIS, 21 March 1992.
8. José M. Alvarado, *La Prensa*, 13 February 1992, in *FBIS*, 20 March 1992; 19 July National Committee of Sandinista Youth, in *Barricada*, 20 February 1992, in *FBIS*, 25 March 1992; and Miguel D'Escoto, quoted on Managua Radio Sandino, 18 June 1991, in *FBIS*, 19 June 1991.
9. Aldo Diaz Lacayo, *El Nuevo Diario*, 28, 29 February and 1 March 1992, in *FBIS*, 7 April 1992.
10. Humberto Ortega interview in *El Semanario*, 30 January-5 February 1992, in *FBIS*, 6 March 1992.

Conclusions

*The Sandinista Front should be considered re-
sponsible for whatever happens in this country...
for the good and for the bad, for omissions and
for excesses.*

—Bayardo Arce, interview in
Barricada, 14 August 1982

Nicaragua's prospects were never brighter than in July 1979 when the
Sandinistas, with the strong support of the vast majority of Nicaraguans,
overthrew the decades-old Somoza dynasty. The Nicaraguan people
rejoiced and foreign governments, led by the United States, looked
forward to new and more profitable bilateral and multilateral relations.
Edén Pastora recounts a meeting of top Sandinista leaders in Tomás
Borge's house shortly after Somoza's fall which touched on this subject.
Pastora correctly said that no other revolution in history had had such
universal support as theirs and that none had such an ideal opportunity
for true independence and non-alignment. But Henry Ruiz interrupted,
saying that Pastora didn't understand imperialism, that in the contemporary world you were either with Washington or with Moscow and
freedom from Washington was what the revolution had been all about.[1]
And it was this historically and ideologically generated hostility and
mind-set, shared then by all the Sandinista leaders—who made themselves the sole decision makers for the country—as well as personal
ambitions, that quickly turned unprecedented opportunity into bitter
tragedy. This is the critical point of the Nicaraguan revolution that has
been hidden, ignored, or missed or played down by all manner of
observer, from simple toadies to serious analysts.[2]

A number of often closely related conclusions can be drawn from the
experiences of the Sandinista period—its origins, years in open and
partial power. These will help explain what happened in Nicaragua, how
such a small nation became a significant but minor actor in the Soviet-
bloc cast of a show—the Cold War—that was about to be hooted from
the world stage, and what the future might have in store for Nicaraguans
and North Americans. Some more generic conclusions can be drawn
from the study of messianic ruling elites who seize all power for themselves and who purport to act in the name of the people.

The Civil War in Nicaragua

- The vast majority of the Nicaraguan people fervently supported the Sandinistas in the war that brought Somoza down, but they did not subscribe to most of the militant domestic and international policies pursued by the nine comandantes who took the future of the country into their own hands.

- The Sandinista comandantes governed Nicaragua through the most tumultuous years in the country's existence. They forced wrenching changes on many levels of the nation's traditional society, though in some fundamental respects the patterns of leadership were the same as under the deposed Somozas. More than ever before, Managua's policies had a major impact on neighboring countries, making the 1980s one of the most unstable decades in the history of Central America and in the history of U.S. relations with Central American countries.

- From late 1977 through July 1979 the public statements of the comandantes were generally moderate and expressed the interests and aspirations of the vast majority of the Nicaraguan people. Thus when the FSLN took power, hopes were very high in Nicaragua and abroad that a new era had arrived. And a new era *had* arrived, but not what the majority expected, for the Sandinista leaders had a hidden agenda that they intended to pursue without consulting anyone but themselves and their few foreign allies. Like their mentor, Fidel Castro, the Sandinistas were masters of deception, disguising their true intentions while overthrowing Somoza and to a remarkable degree continuing to deceive many people for years after taking power. They lined up sympathetic followers at home and abroad, some of whom agreed with their use of deceit in pursuit of broad strategic objectives, and others of whom were no doubt well-meaning but naive and/or ignorant.

- The great myths the comandantes and their followers cultivated at home and especially abroad were that the Sandinistas were creating a new society notable for its domestic political pluralism, mixed economy, and nonaligned foreign policy. The only obstacles to their success, they said, were Nicaraguan counterrevolutionaries created and backed by the American imperialists and their lackeys. In reality, the comandantes cultivated a political system in which a clique of nine had all the power to make decisions, a state directed and dominated economic system which was even worse than many other such statist systems, and an international tilt that was aggressively anti-American and deliberately aligned to the Soviet bloc in the East-West conflict.

• The overriding FSLN belief was that a confrontation with the United States was inevitable, with all other international ties, and most domestic and foreign policies, flowing directly or indirectly therefrom. Their aggressively anti-American position was prompted by conclusions drawn from their reading of modern history: that the United States as a political and economic system—not just individual leaders—was responsible for the underdevelopment and repression Nicaragua and the Third World generally had experienced during the twentieth century. They believed that Nicaragua would never escape from its bleak past until it broke from the political and economic orbit of the United States. They were convinced that the Soviet bloc offered: a more productive economic model; a Leninist leadership model that suited their taste for absolute power both to carry out socialist reforms and to enrich themselves personally; and international ties that would sustain them economically and help them defend themselves militarily during the dangerous transition period from American colony to supposedly free nation.

• Among the most persistent and influential myths promoted on the international level was one holding that the Sandinista revolution was nonaligned. Its supporting corollaries were that the conflict with the United States was the fault of the Reagan administration and that the FSLN was not aligned to the Soviet bloc or supplying tangible support to the Salvadoran guerrillas. In truth, Sandinista ties to Fidel Castro long preceded the July 1979 victory, while alliances with Soviet bloc countries, the development of the Sandinista People's Army into the largest army in Central American history and aid to the Salvadoran guerrillas, all began immediately after the FSLN took power, during the Carter administration. For almost a year—in some respects longer—even the Reagan administration, despite its anti-communism, actively sought a nonviolent resolution of the differences between Washington and Managua, even if not always in the most subtle of terms. But the Sandinistas, in the flower of their revolutionary enthusiasm, were not then remotely interested in a political settlement that would have seriously influenced either their domestic or international policies.

• The Sandinistas were influenced above all by Fidel Castro and through him made contacts with the international allies of the Cuban Revolution. Castro had blazed the trail in ultranationalistic anti-Americanism and the Sandinistas, like many others in Latin America, were swept up by his cheeky defiance of the "gringo imperialists." But Castro was a model for the Sandinistas in other ways as well. He insisted on having all significant power in the country in his own hands and used whatever means necessary to keep that power, from sweet-talking to repression and violence. The Sandinistas took power through violence, which had a long tradition in Nicaragua, and once in power tended to see both domestic and international affairs through the same glasses as Fidel. The role of violence fitted in with the Sandinista belief in the inevitability of a military confrontation with the United States as the latter sought to maintain its position in Central America. Castro also offered political and economic models and aid that during much of the 1980s still seemed to give hope to Nicaragua and other underdeveloped countries. Finally, like Fidel, they sought to obtain from the Soviet Union both economic support and a military shield against the Americans.

• Many Americans failed to appreciate, however, that there were important points of tension between the Sandinista leaders and their allies. This was particularly true of relations with Cuba since over the years it became clear to the comandantes that Castro's agenda did not necessarily complement their own and that Fidel would overlook the FSLN's interests when he considered it in his interest to do so.

• The benefits of the alliance with Cuba and the Soviet bloc, which were very substantial for some years, included economic and military aid, guidance in forming a Leninist-type power structure, and a level of international fame and involvement they could never have dreamed of otherwise. But in the longer term, the relationship was a tragic one for the same reason it was tragic for Cubans and many others. For several decades many in the Third World and in certain intellectual ghettos of the developed world considered Marxism of a Leninist variety synonymous with breaking the bonds of repression and underdevelopment. The Sandinistas, among others, climbed aboard this bandwagon to a presumably historically predestined future of freedom and development just as the world was about to learn that in its theoretical and institutional aspects Leninist Stalinism brought just the opposite of what it promised. Only a few years after the Sandinistas made their commitment to this ideology, and to those countries around the world that practiced it, the whole international structure of the system was exposed for the fraud it always had been, and in most countries it crumbled, at least in its 20th century forms, into the dustbin of history. Thus the Sandinistas became a last-minute example of the fruits of petty totalitarian leadership and government.

• For a short time the Sandinistas themselves seemed to be the wave of the revolutionary future. In July 1979 many radical Latin Americans thought the Sandinista guerrilla movement, working with broad sectors of the Nicaraguan people, offered a new model for political liberation and transformation in the region under the tight control of a revolutionary vanguard. Indeed, this model became a feature in Cuban propaganda aimed toward the hemisphere during the early 1980s. In the early 1990s, over a decade later, that road is, at least for a while, totally discredited. During the 1980s generally, a trend toward democratic transformations became the norm in Latin America, though not necessarily a permanent one. And, at the end of the decade, in the wake of collapse of the Soviet bloc, free market economic reforms came into vogue. This is the road Violeta Chamorro said she wanted to take during her 1990 electoral campaign, though in power she has been prevented in many ways from implementing appropriate policies. Recent developments do not preclude a return to Leninist-Stalinist systems in Nicaragua, or other countries, in the future.

• The combination of self-righteous perseverance and ill-conceived ideas and alliances, together with the temptations of raw power, proved too much for most of the top Sandinista leaders, who quickly became new Somozas dependent on a different superpower. Once again in Nicaragua an elite ruled the poverty-stricken majority, the former enjoying the perks familiar throughout history to dictators and their cliques of the right or of the left. It was as if the ghosts of the Somozas had taken over the minds and bodies of the comandantes, causing them to maintain and even perfect many of the worst traits of the dictatorship they had overthrown. Their final act of contempt for the Nicaraguan people, the fleecing of the destitute nation in what was called the "piñata," turned many Sandinistas against their own top leaders. Even some of the Sandinistas' most devoted foreign admirers found this evidence that the comandantes themselves represented "Somocism without Somoza" humiliating and hard to stomach.

• Whether one judges by freedom or food on the table, most Nicaraguans lived worse under the Sandinistas than they had under the Somozas. The primary responsibility for this falls on the comandantes, as Bayardo Arce said responsibilities for what happened during the 1980s should, since it was their decisions that precipitated most of the domestic and international developments that most affected them during the 1980s. The war alone, which need never have been fought, was enormously costly in human, economic, and other terms. And the personal and group hostilities and resentments of the decade, despite efforts at reconciliation, will not be soon overcome.

• During the early 1990s the Sandinista movement was again experiencing internal tensions and conflict, but not primarily between various strains of Marxism as in the 1970s. During the 1990s the conflict was primarily over whether a small clique should continue to control the movement and what FSLN relations should be to other groups and institutions in Nicaragua as well as to a very changed world beyond its borders. The Sandinistas held their first congress in July 1991 and the nine comandantes absolutely failed to accept responsibility for their actions: for what they had given themselves and what they had brought upon the country, a very heavy burden to bear. They maintained the institutional—but certainly not the intellectual or moral—integrity of the National Directorate. But the Sandinista movement as a whole broke into factions, the most important tied to Daniel Ortega and the militant labor movement, calling for actions to maintain the accomplishments of the revolution, on the one hand, and Humberto Ortega, as an independent arm of the Chamorro government and seeker after personal power, on the other.

• The Chamorro government, if it is not subverted by the Sandinistas and/or its own ambivalence or incompetence, now has the chance the Sandinistas threw away in 1979, to make Nicaragua an economically viable democracy. Sandinista efforts to "govern from below" through labor activism, violent attacks, and demonstrations aimed at the opposition, and to "govern from behind" through continuing control of the army and police, have severely limited the reform options available to the Chamorro government, seriously slowed potential development, and sometimes soured relations with the United States. As of this writing, the Chamorro government did not have the power—military, police, judicial—or perhaps the will to produce and enforce the laws of the nation or the policies of a viable government.

• The example of Costa Rica to the south is rich in lessons on economic "dos" and "don'ts" and other matters, perhaps most importantly in the question of abolishing the standing army. By 1990

Central American leaders had started discussing the desirability of eliminating armies in all the region's countries: Chamorro has spoken favorably of the concept and after her term in power began former Costa Rican
president Oscar Arias visited Nicaragua to promote the idea. In 1991
Panama followed Costa Rica's lead and the substantial reduction of the
size of the Nicaraguan military may (or may not) be a step in the same
direction. But the military budget for 1992 was not reduced as much as
most UNO representatives wanted because the Sandinistas, the government and UNO renegades supported maintaining it at a higher level.

• If eliminating the army is not possible, and during the early 1990s
armies in several countries—including Argentina, Haiti, Peru and Venezuela—reasserted themselves in varying ways, while others retained
strong influence on national policy, then at the very least it must be
drastically reformed. Nicaragua's democracy will never become secure
until the military's loyalty is turned away from both ideology and loyalty
to an individual or family, the dominating characteristic of Somoza's
National Guard. While during the early 1990s the size of the Nicaraguan
army was substantially reduced, an examination of the officers removed
and the weeding out of draftees who didn't want to be in the military
anyway, suggests that it is not more professional now than it was despite
the watering down of Sandinista ideology. On the contrary, Humberto
Ortega clearly is trying to turn it into a personal guard of the Ortega
family, a streamlined reincarnation of Somoza's guard. Yet even today
there are good officers and soldiers in the army—only Humberto Ortega
among the top officers has no family ties to the current government—
who could lead it in the direction of professionalism and social democracy, the foremost among them being Major General Joaquín Cuadra.

• Humberto Ortega has been the pivotal leader of the Sandinista
movement since the late-1970s. After the Sandinista defeat in the 1990
elections, he became the only comandante to work alongside the Chamorro government, in some respects guiding the hand of Antonio Lacayo.
He often has proven adept at taking advantage of circumstances, or even
making circumstances, to benefit himself. In January 1992 he stood the
fundamental anti-American tenet of Sandinismo on its head when he
gave the Camilo Ortega Award to a military attaché in the U.S. embassy
in Managua. He argued that times have changed, that any move to
improve relations with Washington will reduce the likelihood of another
war, and that a dramatic demonstration of changing times was needed to

bring the new reality to members of the party. Many Sandinista leaders strongly opposed Ortega's move. Most Nicaraguans and some foreigners are convinced that Ortega is trying to play the role of a new Somoza in Nicaragua and cultivate appropriate relations with the United States. It remains to be seen if Doña Violeta and Washington will accept him in this new role.

• Nicaragua is a long way from establishing a true and lasting democratic system. If it is to do so, it must have the following:

1. a non-political judicial system and the rule of law;

2. a professionalized military and police subordinated to civil authority, and a professionalized public sector that works for the nation as a whole;

3. less personalism in politics generally, ranging from the elimination of nepotism to a constitutional amendment forbidding a president to succeed her/himself in office;

4. clearly defined and enforced property rights;

5. the cultivation of civil society, with its stabilizing web of organizations and relationships;

6. economic reforms to encourage creativity and productivity so as to meet the basic needs of the population.

• American policy-makers, from the White House to Congress, and all those who apply pressures on them from outside, for a variety of reasons worked at cross purposes during the 1980s. This made it impossible for the United States to develop and carry out a consistent, long-term policy and resulted instead in a painful tragedy for much of Central America, particularly Nicaragua, and in its way for the United States. In his book-length analysis of U.S. policy toward Nicaragua during Somoza's final years, Anthony Lake gives Washington "outsiders" a sense of the enormous and often destructive personal and systemic problems that affect U.S. leaders who try, or should try, to conduct a constructive and consistent foreign policy. The complications and contradictions were even more intense during the 1980s, and though there were significant additional factors, the underlying problems Lake discusses continued during the next decade.[3]

• U.S. responsibility for the Nicaraguan situation during the 1980s is substantial, but it must be seen in a long-term perspective, a point the American left makes and the right tends to ignore. It is no coincidence that the two Latin American countries that were seized and governed for years by intensely anti-American Leninist-Stalinist revolutionary individuals and groups were Cuba and Nicaragua. These two countries—the first quite well off by Latin American standards when its revolution occurred in 1959, and the second quite poor in 1979—had extensive histories of U.S. military intervention during the twentieth century. U.S. actions, however justified they may have seemed to Americans and some Nicaraguans at the time, had the cumulative effect in both countries of intensifying suspicion, resentment, and dependence toward the United States, which are found in lesser degrees in most small countries within the U.S. sphere of strategic and economic influence. Thus U.S. policies over many decades laid the emotional and historical foundations for the anti-Americanism of both Fidel Castro and the Sandinista comandantes even though their extreme positions did not reflect the feelings of the vast majority of Cubans or Nicaraguans.

• Carter administration policies and non-policies contributed substantially to the downfall of Somoza, in a way that unintentionally strengthened the FSLN as against the country's more moderate and democratic forces. When the Carter administration left office in January 1981, it bequeathed a foreign policy nightmare in Central America to the Reagan administration: an aggressively interventionist Castroite regime in Managua and an explosive civil war in neighboring El Salvador. The Reagan administration's handling of these conflicts was uneven, in part because of its own mistakes but even more so because of the kinds of personal and systemic problems Lake discusses with respect to the late 1970s. And the policies were often unpopular in the United States and abroad, because they were inconsistent, inadequately explained and contrary to the preferences of those around the world who for varying reasons supported the Sandinistas or just opposed everything the United States tried to do.

• The experiences of the 1980s in Central America highlight the need for the United States to do better in the future, to conduct more long-term, constructive policies toward individual Latin American countries and the region as a whole. Prospects have never been better for such a change with respect to Latin America than they are in the early 1990s. Never before have dictatorial political systems and statist economic systems been in such low repute. There are more democracies in Latin America today than ever before, though to be sure they are not all equally representative or stable. And almost every government in the hemisphere is striving in varying ways and degrees to develop a market economy and free international trade, though some or many may not make it. The Bush administration has proposed an economic plan, the Enterprise of the Americas, that aims to promote free trade throughout the hemisphere, and that has been received well by government leaders in most countries. But the United States must back up this rhetoric with action, which it often has not done in the past. The danger is that De Tocqueville will be proven right once again, that U.S. democracy will not be able to conduct a rational foreign policy in its own and others' long-term interests.

Better long-term relations throughout the hemisphere will not come about easily, both because of the enormous obstacles to successful reform in Latin America and because the United States traditionally does not take the region seriously, does not conduct forward-looking policies, and does not do what it says it will. But more than ever before, the well-being of the United States as well as that of Nicaragua and other Latin American countries depends on finding common ground and a common bond that will serve everyone's interest within the Hemisphere.

Notes

1. Ratliff interview with Pastora, 24 March 1992.
2. Among the serious analysts who miss this point is Dennis Gilbert, *Sandinistas: The Party and the Revolution* (Cambridge, Mass: Basil Blackwell, 1988).
3. Anthony Lake, *Somoza Falling* (Boston: Houghton Mifflin, 1989).

Index

Agüero, Carlos, 46
Alejandro: car shot up, 62; Soviet military adviser, 121
Alemán, Arnoldo, 279
Allen, Richard, 163n7
Amaya Montes, Melida (Ana Maria): guerrilla leader murdered by comrades, 144–47
Amnesty International: reporting on human rights, 92, 171–72, 173n7
America Department (DA) in Cuba, 39, 98, 107, 112, 146; early contacts with FSLN, 97, 102; aid to Central American guerrillas, 137, 149
Andropov, Yuri: no "umbrella" for Cuba, 224, 225
Anti-Sandinista Popular Militias, 234
Anti-Somoza Popular Militias, 234
Arafat, Yassir: visits Nicaragua, 211
Aráuz, José del Carmen (the Segovian), 227
Arce, Bayardo, 5n, 13, 20, 21, 23, 24, 35, 47, 55, 62, 109, 123, 226; on Contras and Contra war, 28, 231, 239; on control of EPS, 27; and deception, 81, 84, 87, 111, 136; Directorate radical, 82; Directorate, ranking, 30; Directorate, voting, 29; disputes with H. Ortega, 30, 40–41, 42; on elections, 87; FSLN responsibility for whatever happens in Nicaragua, 283, 287–88; and Guatemalan guerrillas, 32; heads FSLN guerrilla-support program, 33, 40–41, 136, 137, 140; nicknamed "the growler," 51; on power, 87, 189; and Thomas Enders, 31, 155–56, 157
ARDE. See Contras
Arias, Oscar, 289; on U.S. view of FSLN, 153
Arias peace plan. See Esquipulas II
Armed Forces of National Resistance (FARN), 136
Armed Forces of the People (FAP), 149

Armed People's Organization (ORPA), 149
Aronson, Bernard: on importance of Contras, 250

Baldivia, Encarnación (Tigrillo), 231
Baldizón, Alvaro: on Cuban advisers in Nicaragua, 100–01; on deception techniques, 91, 172–73; poisoned in Los Angeles, 174n8
Baltodano, Alvaro, 223
Batista, Fulgencio, 9
Bendaña, Alejandro: challenges U.S. policymakers, 89; on Sandinista failures, 176, 231, 234
Bergold, Harry, 20; talks with H. Ortega, 161
Bermúdez, Enrique: assassinated, 251n19; Contra military leader, 235; critical role of Contras, 250–51; propaganda against, 231, 249; setbacks caused by U.S. 240, 241
Bernardo de Cuapa. See Martínez, Bernardo
Bilbonick, Ricardo: Noriega introduced FSLN to Medellín Cartel, 161
BLI. See Irregular Warfare Battalions
Bolaños, Enrique: critic has property confiscated, 187
Bolaños, Lourdes, 214
Bolívar, Simón, 75
Borge, Tomás, 3, 9, 23, 24, 109, 117, 131, 139, 161, 257, 283; asylum plans, 41; and Cayetano Carpio murder, 145–47; on murder of Tropas Pablo Ubeda, 33–35; Cuban advisers, 100; Cuban inspiration for revolution, 10; deception and propaganda, 90–92, 136; Directorate radical, 82; Directorate ranking, 30; goals of revolution, 4, 73; government positions, including Interior Minister, 20–21, 189–201; high living, 59–60, 62; and human rights, 172–73, 190–91, 192, 195,

COSEP. *See* Higher Council of Private Enterprise

Creole. *See* Miskito

Cross, Richard, 245

Cruz, Arturo, 4, 198, 231

Cuadra Chamorro, Joaquín, 215

Cuadra Lacayo, Joaquín, 20, 28, 35-36, 49, 50, 216; biographical sketch, 214-15; differs with Soviet adviser, 121, 122; explains Diriangen to Directorate, 119-20; meets with Salvadoran guerrillas, 140; nicknamed "Achilles" because H. Ortega doesn't trust, 52, 215; ran EPS and war, 206; social democrat and professional officer, 20, 289

Cuadra, Pablo Antonio; on deception, 94n2

Cuba, ix, xii, 4, 37, 49-50, 54, 62, 71, 97-113, 121, 128-33, 159, 168, 176, 215, 221, 237; aid delivered, 100-01; aid not delivered, 101-02; anti-Americanism, 71; 291; and Borge, 90-92, 136; Carrión on, 86-87; and Cayetano Carpio incident, 146-47, 148-50; and EPS, 204, 205, 222-30; FSLN link to Soviet Union, 115-17, 118, 128-33; influence on non-military institutions, 169, 189, 190, 191, 193, 286; inspires Sandinista revolution, 9-10, 75, 222-30, 233, 285-86; medicine and doctors, 55, 213-14; military support from, 32, 82, 88, 89, 116-17, 124-25, 205, 206, 207-10, 239, 262, 266, 286; and "people's property," 59; promotes Sandinista revolutionary model, 112-13, 287; relations with Sandinistas, 5, 70, 77, 97-113, 115-17, 118, 124-25, 128-33, 157, 168, 256, 281; representatives in Managua, 102-04; role in MiG affair, 104, 128-33; Rolexes and symbols of the elite, 39, 105; and Sandinista drug activities, 160-61, 163n16; Sandinista leaders in, 35, 46-47, 52, 60, 97-99, 105-06, 108, 119; and Sandinista military strategy, 32, 129, 209-10, 222-30; similarities to Nicaragua, 110-14; supports regional guerrillas through FSLN, 137-

38, 141-42, 143-44; tensions with Sandinistas, 104-08, 128-33; ties to FSLN, 97-113

Deception, x-xi, xii, 58, 81-95, 94n10, 111, 169, 189, 284; Arce on, 81, 84, 87, 111, 136; called manipulation, 81; in Contra war, 92-94, 172-73, 194, 245-47, 265-66; in deaths of journalists Torgerson and Cross, 245-46; and D'Escoto, 88, 142; D. Ortega acknowledges use of on public, 147-48, 155-56; during FSLN government, 84-94; during war against Somoza, 82-84; and economy, 86, 87; elements of, 82; examples of 87-89, 147-48; focus on Americans, 89-92; fooling foreigners generally, 86-89; in human rights, 171-73; internationalist shot by EPS blamed on Contras, 246-47; Miranda involved, 84-85, 86, 89, 247; political pilgrims and, 90-92; prime themes and successes of, 186, 284; problems maintaining, 84-85; sabotage own facilities to discredit Contras, 246

Democratic centralism, 70

Dalton, Roque: assassination of, 144, 150n8

Debayle, Luis Manuel, 59

Department of Organization and Masses (DORMA), 21

Department of Propaganda and Political Education (DEPEP), 21

D'Escoto, Miguel, 51, 141; among "new rich," 60, 280; and Alexander Haig, 157-58; deception, 88, 142; directs seizures of government property, 278; foreign minister, 21; lived in U.S., 38; and Thomas Enders, 155, 156; on U.S. policy, 156, 157-58, 246

Dessers, Paul: Belgian volunteer and deception, 246-47

Diamond, Steve: on state control of economy, 177

Dickey, Christopher, 92; describes Borge, 189

Dictatorship of the proletariat: H. Ortega on, 83; Arce on, 87

Mining of harbors: consequences of, 158, 162, 240, 244, 255; catastrophic covert action, 240, 250

Ministry of the Interior (MINT), 21, 117, 121, 189-201; accountability, 200; Borge conflict with H. Ortega, 25, 36; Borge, minister of, 25-26; Borge's pool for officers from, 60; bureaucracy, 179; Carrión made vice-minister of, 31; and Cayetano Carpio incident, 147; and censorship of media, 85; and Chamorro government, 276; Contra war and EPS, responsibility for running, 205-06, 227, 241; Cuban advisors, 100-01; derringers from Soviet Union for, 116-17; divine mobs, 196-98; divisions of 189-90; El Chipote, 191; and Executive Commission, 21; exemplary punishments, 192-96; foreign guerrillas supported, with EPS, 137; Guzmán, Luis Armando, 137, 150n3; and human rights, 172, 190; justice twisted, 198-200; Lenín Cerna, chief of DGSE, 190-91; medical treatment for chiefs of, 214; "Ministry of the People's Happiness," 189-201; and Miskitos, 255; Montero, Renán, Cuban who was chief of intelligence, 267n8; Pastora as vice-minister, 100; propaganda shows for visitors, 91; state security (DGSE), 190; structure of control, 169, 189-90; torture by, 191; and TPU, 33-35

Miranda, Roger, xi, 35, 213; on aid from Libya, 132, 211; biography, 215-16; on "Black Bird" incident, 37; on Czech L-39 planes, 131; on Comandantes' escape plans, 41; and deception, 84-85, 86, 89, 247; fixes draft dodging for D. Ortega, 205; and Grenada invasion, 230n3; and H. Ortega bank account, 64; H. Ortega quoted, 26, 30, 50, 52; on H. Ortega, 49-50; on rural inspection tour in 1987, 243; on Institute for Study of Sandinismo, 41; and National Directorate, 22; meeting with Castro, 105; on peasant insurrection, 243; on Rosario Murillo, 54; on Sandinista

indoctrination, 10-11; on shipping arms to FMLN, 140-41; on Soviet military advisers, 121; Soviet military aid plans revealed, 35-6, 43n4, 119-20, 266; trip to Soviet Union and Korea, 132; on U.S. relations, 161; visit to Castro, 239

Miskito Indians, 198; deception on, 92-93; EPS used against, 92, 206, 238, 253-56; H. Ortega's guard executes group, 53; near genocide against, 193-94; "peace negotiations," 253-56

MISURA. See Contras

Molina, Father Uriel, 214

Mondragón, José Efrén, 195

Monge, Luis Alberto: sponsors first regional peace conference, 257

Monsanto, Pablo, 149

Montero, Renán: Cuban, chief of Sandinista intelligence, 267n8

Moran, Rolando, 149

Montealegre, Augusto, 142; revealed as informer, 11

Mora Valverde, Manuel, 149

Mora Valverde, Manuelito: received arms from FSLN, 149-50

Morazán, Francisco, 75

Moreno, Gustavo: second head of Buro Ernesto, 140

Movement of the Revolutionary Left (MIR), of Chile, 216

Muravchik, Joshua: on media and FSLN, 94n10

Murillo, Rosario: cultural activities, 48, 54; Humberto critical of, 53, 54; style, 53-4; tensions with E. Cardenal, 48, 54; voted out of Sandinista Assembly in 1991, 55, 279

National Guard (Somoza), 1, 2, 4, 15, 69, 178, 196, 213, 221, 236, 238, 241, 249, 289; arms go to FMLN, 138; and Contras, 92, 231, 235, 237, 243; demolished by war, 203-04, 223; factor in Sandinista defensive strategy, 222; FSLN vengeance toward, 198-99; intelligence of, 11; members tried, jailed, executed, or killed by "mobs," 192, 197, 199; killed Miranda's